Reviews:

"This is a book of grand scope. It is a treasure trove of information for the dedicated Bible student. Samuel Abraham is a man of great integrity, and a lifelong student of the Word of God. But more than that he is a gifted teacher. Pastor Abraham has made it possible for novices in the Bible to learn tremendous amounts of information in very little time. That is a truly remarkable accomplishment. I will be proud to have this book in my library and I will refer to it often. It is my pleasure to enthusiastically recommend this book to all!"

Thomas M. Hughes, MA
Ohio conference pastor and biker evangelist, author, recording artist, friend, and mentor.

"In this book, Pastor Samuel Abraham elucidates the deep truths and seminal teachings revealed in the Holy Bible. Reading this book will certainly direct the reader to the knees and inspire them to read God's Word. Consequently, our shared journey with Christ will be a meaningful, joyous, and fulfilling experience. This book should be read by every sincere seeker of truth."

Melchizedek M. Ponniah, Ph.D.
Retired Professor, Andrews University

"I am delighted to write about this book called 'Amazing Truth.' I can call it as a great guide to the believers and non-believers and all the clergies in every part of the world. This book can also be called a contextualization book for the whole of humanity, seen equally without any discrimination of color, creed, caste and languages. The specialty of this book is that it is an eye-opener to the whole world. Mrs. E. G. White's writings are called the 'lesser light' leading to the greater light. But this book has revealed seventeen great secrets that are not written even by Mrs. White. This contains the authors of the Bible, types of prophecy such as single prophecy, twin prophecy, consecutive prophecy, and numerological prophecy. Chronology, archaeology, astronomy, anthropology, doctrines, evolution, and science, etc. It also talks about types of Salvation, sins, seven holy ordinances, 105 specifications in the Ten Commandments, reformation, and reformers all through the ages, and a clear picture about Triune God. Moreover, it is talking about the sixteen periods in the Bible and these sixteen periods still come under three periods in the Bible. Such as compelled period, grace period and probation period. Also, this book is talking about 66 books, the authors, and their periods. Even the revelation of all the secrets till today. So, in a nutshell this book is not ordinary, but extraordinary, by which people of the entire world would be led to a greater light, the only light Jesus Christ. At last this book is talking about everlasting to everlasting for those who are living in the end time of the end time."

Pr. Jacob Samuel BLA, MA, MA.
(BM Conference Evangelist)

AMAZING TRUTH!

The Revelation of Jesus Christ to the Remnant

By Samuel Abraham

TEACH Services, Inc.
P U B L I S H I N G
www.TEACHServices.com • (800) 367-1844

World rights reserved. This book or any portion thereof may not be copied or reproduced in any form or manner whatever, except as provided by law, without the written permission of the publisher, except by a reviewer who may quote brief passages in a review.

The author assumes full responsibility for the accuracy of all facts and quotations as cited in this book. The opinions expressed in this book are the author's personal views and interpretations, and do not necessarily reflect those of the publisher.

This book is provided with the understanding that the publisher is not engaged in giving spiritual, legal, medical, or other professional advice. If authoritative advice is needed, the reader should seek the counsel of a competent professional.

Unless otherwise indicated, all Scripture quotations are from the *New King James Version®* (NKJV), copyright © 1982 by Thomas Nelson. Used by permission. All rights reserved. Italics indicate words added in the translation that are not in the original text.

Other versions used are *The Revised Standard Version of the Bible* (RSV), copyright © 1946, 1952, and 1971, the Division of Christian Education of the National Council of the Churches of Christ in the United States of America. Used by permission. All rights reserved. *The Original Aramaic New Testament in Plain English, with Psalms and Proverbs*. Copyright © 2007; 8th edition Copyright © 2013. All rights reserved. Used by Permission. *The Christian Standard Bible*. Copyright © 2017 by Holman Bible Publishers. Used by permission. Christian Standard Bible®, and CSB® are federally registered trademarks of Holman Bible Publishers, all rights reserved.

Copyright © 2020 Samuel Abraham

Copyright © 2020 TEACH Services, Inc.

ISBN-13: 978-1-4796-1232-1 (Paperback)

ISBN-13: 978-1-4796-1233-8 (ePub)

Library of Congress Control Number: 2020908812

Introduction

People are impressed by different things. It was in 1995 that I first came to know about the debate between Ahmed Hoosen Deedat, a South African writer and public speaker of Indian descent, best known as a Muslim missionary, and Jimmy Swaggart, the charismatic preacher of the United States, that took place in 1986. Deedat's point was that the Bible is not the word of God, but a fabrication by human beings. As I grew up in India, I had witnessed more than eighteen living religions practiced, and I questioned to myself, "Why do I need to follow Christianity?" That guided me to study comparative religion in my BLA degree.

After meeting my mentor and watching the debate, I wanted a deeper understanding in my Bible and I wanted to know myself, "Can the Bible be proved right? Or is the Bible the fabrication of human beings.?" That diligent study and the guidance of my mentor led me to put this book into your hands.

What has impressed me is hearing the beauty of the Word of God as given to me through my mentor. Doing so has inspired me to put into writing the truths that impressed my mind, and it is why I am pleading with God to follow His word every day of my life. At the same time, I would also like to share the truth I have learned with others.

It was in the God's providence that I should learn that the Word of God, together with genuine science, reveals Jesus Christ—the real living God. It is through Him that we have eternal salvation. The Bible says, "In Him was life, and the life was the light of men" (John 1:4). Without Jesus Christ, the life that we see and hear in the world would not have existed. Neither would it have existed anywhere else in the universe. The main reason for writing this book is that, in the 21st century, we have been challenged by academics to disprove the modern materialistic way of understanding life in light of the life that comes from Christ and God alone. As spiritualism and atheistic socialism continue to increase in our world, doubts and questions about God and about the Holy Bible have also increased.

Scholars have many questions regarding God's creation of the universe, the origin of the languages of the world, the authenticity of the Holy Bible, whether God's holy law is objective and unchanging, whether the prophecies of the Bible are true, the possibility of the existence of a true church, the present and future rule of God's kingdom, and, above all, whether there is eternal life through Jesus Christ. Through careful and diligent study of the Word of God and the inspired testimonies of God, I have discovered the real meaning of life in Jesus Christ and eternal salvation through Him alone. I have also found satisfying answers to the false science that dogmatically declares that life on this planet arose through evolutionary material causes without God. In this book, I have compiled what the Lord has revealed to me so that others, who have the same desire and concerns, can come to know the importance of eternal salvation through Jesus Christ. The source material is here. The challenge for the reader is to devote the time to reading it. May God richly bless you as you jump into the Word of God.

Though all truth originates with the Lord Jesus Christ—may His name be praised and glorified—the main human contributor for this book has been my mentor, Mr. Nelson David, who helped me understand God's Word. I would like to thank him and thank God for the passion that He gave him.

Samuel Abraham

Table of Contents

Chapter 1 The Holy Bible

Chapter 2 The Bible's Chronology of Human History

Chapter 3 The Concept of the Triune God

Chapter 4 Creation vs. Evolution

Chapter 5 God's Church During the Former and Latter Rain

Chapter 6 Seven Holy Ordinances

Chapter 7 God's Unchangeable Law and Its 105 Specifications

Chapter 8 180 Prophecies Concerning Our Eternal Salvation

Chapter 9 Church History

Chapter 10 Validating the Creation Story from World Population and Morality

Chapter 11 God's Last Church Starts in the Wilderness of America

Chapter 12 The 144,000, a Special Group of People

Chapter 13 Armageddon and the Seven Last Plagues

Chapter 1
The Holy Bible

In our postmodern world, people tend to believe that the Bible is an old book that is irrelevant for present society. They also question its authorship, its authenticity, its importance, its language, and many other things about it. In this first chapter, we will study the importance of the Bible as the Word of God, given by divine inspiration through God's holy people as "moved by the Holy Spirit" (2 Peter 1:21). The infallibility of God's revelation in the Bible is not dependent on anyone's understanding. The Bible proclaims God's will and is the standard for character, and it is the only authoritative revelation of human history.

The Nature of the Thirty-nine Bible Writers

As the Bible was being written, the early writers did not have all the facts that would eventually be included in Scripture. They received visions from God, did careful research of the facts, were inspired in gathering words of wisdom, and wrote according to the scientific knowledge of their day. God knew that their limited grasp of truth would be expanded by other Bible writers, for, in the days to come, knowledge would increase.

The Holy Bible is a compilation of the writings of some thirty-nine writers, yet the author behind the book is the God of heaven. As Paul wrote, "All Scripture is given by inspiration of God" (1 Tim. 3:16). The Bible writers received God's messages at different periods in history and wrote for the people then living, though its principles apply to us today. According to Isaiah 8:20–31, God's written guidance has two parts—"The Law and the Testimony." The "Law" is the fifteen verses of the Holy Ten Commandments written by the finger of Jesus Christ (see Exod. 25:21; 31:18; Isa. 33:22; James 4:12). The other 31,158 verses are called "Testimony," to explain the Moral law of the Ten Commandments. The Ten Commandments are the Constitution of the Kingdom of Heaven. Because of the Ten Commandments, the Bible is Holy not of the other 31,158 verses. The Bible is centered on the main author Jesus Christ and His Ten Commandments, the other authors had to be inspired by Him and the Holy Spirit to have the whole Bible.Understanding the law of God's Ten Commandments, by which we know what sin is (Rom. 3:20), enables us to understand the importance of the death of Jesus Christ. God included many things in the Bible to make known to humankind the early history of the world, including the good and the bad, the pure and the profane.

The Importance of the Bible

Among all the books in the world today, the Bible alone provides the real history of mankind—from the Creation to the return of Christ and the fulfilling of the kingdom of God on earth one thousand years later. (In this book, I assume 4159 BC to be the year of the Creation.) Of the 180 prophecies in the Bible, all but a few have already been fulfilled. The Bible provides the foundation and inspiration for the study of all areas of knowledge. These include physical science, geology, history, medicine, and astronomy, among others. The true story of the creation of humankind and of our early history, thinking, and lifestyles, as well as the future of humankind after death, is found in this wonderful book. Also, we learn that the knowledge of human morality in the Ten Commandments is the "seventh sense" that God communicated to humankind through the Bible.

Only through the Bible can we understand God, His providence in dealing with His creatures, and His nature and character.

Only through the Bible do we understand the cruelty of sin and the greatness of God's love. Only through the Bible can we claim God's forgiveness of our sins through Christ's death, as symbolized by the sacrificial system. Only through the Bible, do we learn about the resurrection that will come at the Second Advent of Jesus Christ when God fulfills His promise of eternal life as we enter heaven and then return to earth after the millennium. These are the wonderful themes found in the Holy Bible. There are eighteen world religions, but none but that which comes from the Bible tells us that the God of Heaven came down to this earth, lived among men, and died for humankind to redeem us from the clutches of sin. This redemption came through the ministry of Jesus Christ, who is revealed in God's holy book, the Bible. He is the only means of eternal salvation for humankind.

Writing What God Revealed

According to 1 Samuel 3:21, God revealed Himself to Samuel in Shiloh. God did not dictate what the thirty-nine writers of the Holy Bible were to put down. Rather, He gave them visions and asked them to write what they saw and understood. After God gave them a vision, they needed to remember what they saw and heard (see Rev. 1:11). Then, according to their own vocabulary and knowledge, they wrote the verses that appear in their particular book of the Bible. If God Himself had dictated to these thirty-nine Bible writers, there would be no room for error. The text would have been written perfectly from the start. But God only gave the prophets visions from which to write. That is why many people have misconceptions about the Bible.

When the Holy Spirit came on people and they received a vision, they entered into an altered mental state. Either standing or sitting, their eyes were open, but their eyelids would not move. The person would not breathe through either the nose or mouth, yet his or her heart would function as usual. One could check the person's pulse by hand. However, even if a burning candle were placed near the person's nose or mouth, the flame would not flicker as a result of the person's respiration. Following the vision, the person would return to normal consciousness after taking a long breath. This process is what is involved in a vision from God.

From 4159 BC to AD 100, God gave visions to various Bible writers of various cultures and levels of knowledge. What they wrote about included, as we have noted, even people's bad character traits.

God inspired the writers of the Bible to include, for example, ten cases of incest among the acts of the patriarchs so that people could understand their failures and not repeat them. Understanding this, no one should question why God would have all these bad examples included in the Bible. He has given as a mirror the holy Ten Commandments, the constitution of the Kingdom of God, that we might all practice them through the grace that is in Jesus Christ. From Adam until today, no one has been either holy or a perfect saint.

How Long Did It Take to Write the Bible

The Bible was written between 1531 BC and AD 97, a span of 1627 years. Genesis was the first book written.

According to present literary standards, without the author's name and the year of publication, a book may be considered a fictitious storybook. History and the pen of inspiration give evidence for the year of writing of each book and the name of the likely author. The Bible is not a counterfeit book; it is God's book. The books of the Bible, with the name of the probable author(s), are listed below in the order in which they were likely written.[1]

Chart 1.1. The Chronological Order of the Books of the Old and New Testaments

Bible order	Book	When written	Author(s)
1	Genesis	1531–1491 BC	[1] Moses
18	Job	1520 BC	Moses
2	Exodus	1491–1451 BC	Moses
3	Leviticus	1491–1451 BC	Moses
4	Numbers	1491–1451 BC	Moses
5	Deuteronomy	1491–1451 BC	Moses (Joshua likely recorded Moses' death)
6	Joshua	1491–1425 BC	[2] Joshua[1] (Samuel likely recorded Joshua's death)

---

1 Source: "Who wrote the Bible?" available at http://www.bibleinfo.com/en/questions/who-wrote-the-bible#codewordOT, accessed 4/12/17.

Chart 1.1. The Chronological Order of the Books of the Old and New Testaments

Bible order	Book	When written	Author(s)
7	Judges	1425–1312 BC	[3] Samuel (see 1 Sam. 3:21)
8	Ruth	1322–1312 BC	Samuel
9	1 Samuel	1141–1050 BC	Samuel
10	2 Samuel	1060–1017 BC	Samuel[2]
19	Psalms	1440-1400 BC, 1063 BC	[4] David, Moses, [5] Asaph, [6] sons of Korah, [7] Heman, [8] Solomon, [9] Ethan[3]
11	1 Kings	1015–897 BC	[10] Jeremiah[4]
13	1 Chronicles	1056–972 BC	[11] Ezra[5]
12	2 Kings	1056–957 BC	[12] Jeremiah[6]
13	2 Chronicles	1015–588 BC	Ezra[7]
22	Song of Solomon	1014 BC	Solomon
20	Proverbs	980 BC	Solomon, [13] Agur, and [14] Lemuel
21	Ecclesiastes	977 BC	Solomon
32	Jonah	862 BC	[15] Jonah
29	Joel	800 BC	[16] Joel
30	Amos	787 BC	[17] Amos
28	Hosea	785 BC	[18] Hosea
23	Isaiah	765–698 BC	[19] Isaiah
33	Micah	790–710 BC	[20] Micah
34	Nahum	713 BC	[21] Nahum
24	Jeremiah	629–562 BC	Jeremiah

12 *Amazing Truth!*

Chart 1.1. The Chronological Order of the Books of the Old and New Testaments

Bible order	Book	When written	Author(s)
36	Zephaniah	630 BC	[22] Zephaniah
35	Habakkuk	626 BC	[23] Habakkuk
27	Daniel	607–537 BC	[24] Daniel
26	Ezekiel	595–574 BC	[25] Ezekiel
25	Lamentations	588 BC	Jeremiah
31	Obadiah	587 BC	[26] Obadiah
12	Ezra	536–495 BC	Ezra
17	Esther	521–495 BC	[27] Mordecai
37	Haggai	520 BC	[28] Haggai
38	Zechariah	520 BC	[29] Zechariah
16	Nehemiah	476–437 BC	[30] Nehemiah
39	Malachi	397 BC	[31] Malachi

Bible order	Book	When written	Author(s)
40	Matthew	AD 31–33	[1(32)] Matthew
41	Mark	AD 31–33	[2(33)] Mark
42	Luke	AD 31–33	[3(34)] Luke
43	John	AD 31–33	[4(35)] John
44	The Acts	AD 31–66	Luke
52	1 Thessalonians	AD 54	[5(36)] Paul
53	2 Thessalonians	AD 54	Paul
48	Galatians	AD 58	Paul
46	1 Corinthians	AD 59	Paul
47	2 Corinthians	AD 60	Paul
45	Romans	AD 60	Paul
59	James	AD 60	[6(37)] James
60	1 Peter	AD 60	[7(38)] Peter
49	Ephesians	AD 64	Paul

Bible order	Book	When written	Author(s)
50	Philippians	AD 64	Paul
51	Colossians	AD 64	Paul
57	Philemon	AD 64	Paul
58	Hebrews	AD 64	Paul
56	Titus	AD 65	Paul
54	1 Timothy	AD 65	Paul
55	2 Timothy	AD 65	Paul
61	2 Peter	AD 66	Peter
65	Jude	AD 66	[8(39)] Jude
62	1 John	AD 90	John
63	2 John	AD 90	John
64	3 John	AD 90	John
66	Revelation	AD 97	John

Moses wrote the largest number of the thirty-nine books of the Old Testament. Of the twenty-seven books of the New Testament, Paul wrote the largest number, followed by John. Of these books, five were written by disciples of Jesus and three by "junior apostles." Thirty-one Old Testament authors plus eight New Testament authors equals thirty-nine authors. Thus, thirty-nine writers composed the Holy Bible over a period of 1628 Years. Here are some notable facts about the Bible:

1. The biggest book of the Bible is the Psalms with 150 chapters.

2. The smallest book of the Bible is Second John with one chapter of thirteen verses.

3. The biggest chapter in the Bible is Psalm 119 with 176 verses.

4. The smallest chapter in the Bible is Psalm 117 with only two verses.

5. Paul wrote fourteen books of the Bible, while Second Chronicles contains material from six prophets—Isaiah, Jeremiah, Nathan, Iddo, Ahijah, and Shemaiah.

14 *Amazing Truth!*

Some verses in the Bible contain colloquial usages, discrepancies, or terms with a hidden meaning. Because God wants to meet people where they are, He did not dictate the words that the Bible writers were to use but had them use language that people would understand, and He expanded the knowledge of truth over time through other writers. As Isaiah 28:10, says: "For precept *must be* upon precept, precept upon precept, line upon line, line upon line, here a little, there a little." Later in the chapter we will consider several verses with colloquial usages, discrepancies, or hidden meanings.

Since the Bible was originally written in Hebrew, Aramaic, and Greek, copyists and translators have tried their best to put God's message in the right words, and communicating the exact meaning has frequently escaped them. Yet, it is in the providence of God that we now come to properly understand the Bible's message within our postmodern world.

Bible Translation

After the dispersion of the apostles from AD 34 onward, the Bible was not at first translated into many languages. However, from the 14th century onward, God raised up people to translate His Holy Word into the languages of the people so that the reformation of His church might be realized. In 1400, John Wycliffe, who was known as "the Morning Star of the Reformation," started translating the Latin translation into English. Later, William Tyndale, William Carey, and other scholars translated the Bible into many languages from the original Greek, Hebrew, and Aramaic. In 1435, Johannes Gutenberg of Germany invented the printing press and printed the Bible in German. From that time until this, millions of Bibles have been printed and distributed all over the world. In 1611, King James of Great Britain authorized a new English translation of the Bible—"The King James Version." There is an amazing story behind each translation of the Word of God that "stands forever" (Isa. 40:8).

The History of the Bible From AD 100 to 1611

God declared through Jeremiah, "Behold, I will send for many fishermen," says the LORD, "and they shall fish them; and afterward I will send for many hunters, and they shall hunt them from every mountain and every hill, and out of the holes of the rocks" (Jer. 16:16). From AD 34 onward, unbelieving Jews killed believers in the Messiah, and they stoned Stephen, the first martyr, as Saul (later to become Paul) witnessed the event. Then the successors of Julius Caesar killed millions of Christians by throwing them to hungry lions in the amphitheater and putting them to death in other horrible ways from AD 44 to 70. Later Christians died by the hundreds and thousands because of the Holy Bible.

Some of the persecuting dictators of the Roman Empire were:

1. Hadrian, (compared to Hercules) (AD 117–138)
2. Marcus Aurelius (AD 161–180)
3. Decius (AD 249–251)
4. Valerian (AD 253–260) and
5. Diocletian (AD 284–305) and his successors Galerius and Galerius Valerius Maximinus fulfilled the prophetic "ten days" (a literal ten years) of Revelation 2:10 through the ten years of persecution lasting from AD 303 to AD 313.

During these ten years, more than a million Christians were killed to suppress Christianity. Then, from AD 320–508, under the Emperor Constantine and his successors, hundreds and thousands more died for the sake of the truth.

During the Dark Ages, from AD 508–1798, the Roman Empire and the mighty popes persecuted the Christian world. When the Bible was translated, faithful Christians were not allowed to keep even small portions of the Bible. If any Scriptures were found in their possession, their houses were burned to the ground.

Memorization of the Holy Bible

God protected His faithful people, like the Waldenses, the Albigenses, and the Huguenots. The faithful were ready to meet any challenge to be able to preserve God's Word. They stood against the Roman Catholic forces. When they could not distribute Scripture openly, they memorized the Bible word for word and secretly shared pieces of Scripture as traveling merchants, sharing the gospel of Jesus Christ with hundreds and thousands of people. Parents lost children; babies were dipped in boiling oil, dying in front of their persecuted parents. In some places, their young virgin girls, who were ready to witness for the name of Jesus Christ (Acts 4:12), were buried alive because of their faith in Jesus Christ. (See *The Great Controversy*, p. 239.)

God Raised Up Martin Luther the Reformer

In 1517, Martin Luther, at the time a Roman Catholic priest and university professor, protested against the use of indulgences by the Roman Catholic Church. He stood by the Word of God and proclaimed, "The Bible and the Bible alone." Ultimately, he left the Roman Catholic Church and started the first Protestant Christian denomination in the world—the Lutheran church.

The Uniqueness of the Indian Tamil Translation

Through the guidance of the Holy Spirit, the Tamil translation of the Bible from Hebrew and Greek was commenced in 1844 and completed in 1864 by Mr. Segan from Germany and Mr. Falgaun. They came to South India; both learned the Tamil language with the help of Mr. Duraisamy of Palayamkottai in Tamil Nadu. The first Tamil Bible was printed in Tharangampadi of Karaikal, as well as in Pondicherry, once this state was under the control of France.

The importance of the Tamil Bible is, by my reckoning, that it has fewer translation mistakes than the regular English translation. I have located only three translation mistakes as compared to one hundred sixty-one in the King James Version.

Ten Principles for Studying Our Holy Bible

To understand and properly handle the Bible, consider the following ten principles:

1. "Let your 'Yes' be 'Yes,' and *your* 'No,' 'No' " (James 5:12). James' statement reminds us that God's revelations in Scripture are definite and simple.

2. "God *is* not a man, that He should lie" (Num. 23:19); nor is He "a man that He should repent" (1 Sam. 15:29). Balaam and Samuel declared that God's word always tells the truth.

3. "My covenant I will not break, nor alter the word that has gone out of My lips" (Ps. 89:34). God does not go back on His promises. "God speaketh once, and repeateth not the selfsame thing the second time" (Job 33:14 DRA). God speaks once and does things once, He will not repeat the same thing again and again since He is almighty God.

4. "The blessing of the LORD makes *one* rich, and He adds no sorrow with it" (Prov. 10:22). God says, "those who honor Me I will honor, and those who despise Me shall be lightly esteemed" (1 Sam. 2:30). Our blessings either come from God or from Satan. However, God's blessings are permanent.

5. As with the terms "heart" and "soul" (Matt. 12:34; Ps. 103:1), we need to understand that many verses have colloquial usages and hidden meanings.

6. Daniel 8:14 is a prophecy that was to be fulfilled but once. If there is another fulfillment, it will be the work of Satan.

7. Light on the "testimony" comes from the 31,158 verses of Scripture outside the "testimony" (Isa. 8:20). Any creed should be weighed in the balances of the holy Ten Commandments (Matt. 5:18). Not only that, but all answers to questions on a particular subject should come from the Bible.

8. God has given a timely message regarding the commandments in the Bible (Matt. 5:19; Rom. 2:22–24). The commandments made by men should not be followed in the place of God's commandments (Col. 2:22; Matt. 15:9). To say that the Ten Commandments were nailed to the cross is to take God's name in vain (Rom. 3:31; Mark 7:7).

9. The record of the various incidents in the Bible was written for those who first received it. All of the promises were for the people at that time. When the thief on the cross was given eternal salvation through Jesus Christ, that did not automatically mean that every thief will go to heaven unless he repents as did the one hanging beside Jesus. Also Jesus forgave Mary Magdalene, the harlot. Yet, that does not mean that every prostitute automatically will go to heaven unless she repents, as did Mary Magdalene. Christ's dealing with these individuals speaks to us. We should not beat around the bush but should deliver the straight testimony to them.

10. When people understand the law of God and the love of Christ, they can have eternal life. As the standard of human behavior, the law points out our sin (Rom. 3:20; 7:7; 1 John 3:4). The love of Christ provides for our forgiveness and moves us to live holy lives (Rom. 8:35–39; Eph. 3:18–20; 2 Cor. 5:14).

With the above-mentioned principles revealed to us, we should be very careful to handle the Bible properly to grasp the timely messages sent by God. The following are examples of verses containing discrepancies, colloquial usages, or hidden meanings. These examples confronted me when I began studying the Scriptures.

1. **The thinking of the heart.** "For out of the abundance of the heart the mouth speaks" (Matt. 12:34). Colloquial usage.

    Modern science verifies that the brain, and not the heart, is where thinking takes place. The heart pumps the blood 12,000 miles through the blood vessels. However, any thinking that does not trigger emotions and stimulate the heart will not change human behavior. It is right for the Bible writers to connect the heart and mind for behavior modification. (876 verses in the Bible use "heart" or "hearts" in this sense)

2. **The actions of the soul.** "Bless the LORD, O my soul" (Ps. 103:1). Colloquial usage.

    No literal part of the body is called a "soul." However, the functions of the "soul" can be associated with what we refer to as "consciousness." (501 verses in the Bible use the words "soul" or "souls.")

3. **The relation of the Father, the Son, and the Spirit.** "Go therefore and make disciples of all the nations, baptizing them in the name of the Father and of the Son and of the Holy Spirit" (Matt. 28:19). Hidden meaning.

    This statement describes the unity of the Godhead. First John, chapter 5, verse 7, which does not appear in any Greek manuscript before 1500 AD, says, "For there are three that bear witness in heaven: the Father, the Word, and the Holy Spirit; and these three are one." Jesus came to this world having "all the fullness of the Godhead bodily" (Col. 2:9). Yet, he "emptied himself, taking the form of a servant, being born in the likeness of men" (Phil. 2:7, RSV). (221 verses)

4. **Human beings are not by nature holy.** "By that will we have been sanctified through the offering of the body of Jesus Christ once *for all*" (Heb. 10:10). Hidden meaning.

    Paul described the believers in various churches as "saints" (Rom. 16:15; 2 Cor. 1:1; Eph. 1:1; Phil. 1:1; Col. 1:12). Peter quoted Proverbs 11:31 to say: " *'If the righteous one is scarcely saved, where will the ungodly and the sinner appear?'* " (1 Peter 4:18). How is it possible that these believers were "saints," or "holy ones," when Paul quoted Psalm 14 as saying: "As it is written: *'There is none righteous, no, not one"* (Rom. 3:10). The statement contains a hidden meaning about how the unrighteous become saints. (96 verses in the Bible use "saint(s)" in this sense)

5. **Seventy-six generations from Adam to Jesus (Luke 3:22–38; Matt. 1:2–17).** Discrepancy.

    Matthew lists only forty-one generations from Abraham to Jesus while Luke has fifty-six generations from Abraham to Jesus and seventy-seven generations from Adam to Jesus (Luke 3:22–38).[2] The *Original Aramaic New Testament in Plain English* provides an explanation in its version of Matthew 1:16: "Yaqob begot Yoseph the guardian of Maryam, her from whom was begotten Yeshua, who is called The Messiah." Thus, Matthew is talking about the Joseph who was Mary's guardian and not the Joseph who was her husband. The Joseph who was Mary's husband is in Luke 3. (This accounts for the difference in the lineages of the different Josephs.) It was her guardian who was connected to King David in this case and not Joseph her husband.[3] Another discrepancy is that Luke follows the Septuagint, which has the extra generation of Cainan after Arphaxad instead of going directly from Arphaxad to Salah, as in the Hebrew text (Luke 3:36; cf. Gen. 10:22, 24). (16 verses)

6. **Lucifer was called the "son of the morning."** "How you are fallen from heaven, O Lucifer, son of the morning! *How* you are cut down to the ground, you who weakened the nations!" (Isa. 14:12). Hidden meaning.

    Conceited with his beauty, Lucifer's thinking fell out of harmony with God, and sin entered heaven. Lucifer misunderstood God's triune nature, His power, and His actions because of his own egotism. (14 verses)

7. **The Holy Spirit descending as a dove.** "When He had been baptized, Jesus came up immediately from the water; and

---

[2] David is counted twice in the statement, "So all the generations from Abraham to **David** *are* fourteen generations, from **David** until the captivity in Babylon *are* fourteen generations, and from the captivity in Babylon until the Christ *are* fourteen generations." (Matt. 1:17).

[3] Her husband Joseph was a descendent of David (see Matt. 1:20).

behold, the heavens were opened to Him, and He saw the Spirit of God descending like a dove and alighting upon Him" (Matt. 3:16; cf. Mark 1:10; John 1:32). Hidden meaning.

Matthew described the motion of the Holy Spirit in descending upon Jesus. Luke described the appearance of the Holy Spirit in the form of a dove (Luke 3:22). While Jesus came in the likeness of Adam, with human blood, flesh and bone (Luke 3:22), Jesus was also full of the Spirit. Thus, God can take the form of either spirit or flesh. "Take careful heed to yourselves, for you saw no form when the LORD spoke to you at Horeb out of the midst of the fire, lest you act corruptly and make for yourselves a carved image in the form of any figure: the likeness of male or female, the likeness of any animal that *is* on the earth or the likeness of any winged bird that flies in the air, the likeness of anything that creeps on the ground or the likeness of any fish that *is* in the water beneath the earth" (Deut. 4:15–18). The Holy Spirit descended from heaven as a dove does. He did not descend from heaven as an actual dove. The motion was something like a helicopter coming down to land on earth. (10 verses)

8. **The sun rises and goes down.** "The sun also rises, and the sun goes down, and hastens to the place where it arose" (Eccles. 1:5; see also Psalms 19:6.) Colloquial usage.

    The description is from the perspective of observers on earth. In reality, the sun neither rises nor goes down. It is the earth that rotates at 18.5 miles per second. The earth orbits around the sun. In making the sun "stand still" (Joshua 10:12, 13), God performed a miracle for Joshua by slowing the earth's rotation. (16 verses)

9. **Spiritual blessings.** "Blessed *be* the God and Father of our Lord Jesus Christ, who has blessed us with every spiritual blessing in the heavenly *places* in Christ" (Eph. 1:3; see also Col. 1:9; 2 Cor. 3:6–8; Gal. 6:1; 1 Cor. 2:13; 14:2, 15; 3:1; 15:44; Rom. 8:1). Hidden meaning.

    God reveals His spiritual blessings during the time of the latter rain, and He asks us to hold onto what He reveals (Zech. 10:1). We are to ask the Lord for rain in the time of the latter rain, and He will make the clouds flash with lightning and give us showers of rain that will produce grain in the fields for everyone.

There is no single, widely agreed upon definition of spirituality in the postmodern world. Surveys of the definition of the term, as used in scholarly research, show a broad range of definitions, with limited similarity.[4]

According to Kees Waaijman, the traditional meaning of spirituality is reformation that "is aimed at the recovery of the original form of man, the image of God. To that end it orients itself to a form which makes present the original figure: the torah in Judaism, Christ in Christianity, Buddha in Buddhism, Mohammad in Islam ..." (*Spirituality: Forms, Foundations, Methods*, p. 463). (10 verses)

10. **The Father is greater than Jesus.** "You have heard Me say to you, "I am going away and coming back to you.' If you loved Me, you would rejoice because I said, 'I am going to the Father,' for My Father is greater than I" (John 14:28). Hidden meaning.

The Father is superior to Jesus Christ, as many verses in the Bible confirm. Additionally, it was the Holy Spirit who resurrected Jesus Christ (John 14:28; Heb. 2:9; 1 Cor. 1:3; 3:23; 15:15; Gal. 1:1; 1 Peter 3:18).

Either the Father (the first Person of the triune God) or the Holy Spirit (the third Person of the triune God) is greater than Jesus Christ or He is not. Since all possess the fullness of the Godhead, they should be equal in all respects. Yet, when the great controversy between Christ and Satan began in heaven and Christ humbled Himself (John 10:17) to come to this world to redeem fallen man, He used the phrase "Father and Son." Nonetheless, Jesus is addressed as "Everlasting Father" (Isa. 9:6); "O God" (Heb. 1:8, 9); and "Teacher and Lord" (John 13:13). (9 verses)

11. **Man was made a little lower than the angels.** "For You have made him a little lower than the angels, and You have crowned him with glory and honor. You have made him to have dominion over the works of Your hands; You have put all *things* under his feet" (Ps. 8:5, 6; cf. Heb. 2:9). Hidden meaning.

---

4 See "Spirituality," available at https://en.wikipedia.org/wiki/Spirituality, accessed 4/11/17.

God created Adam above the angels in his reflection of God's likeness and in his ability to think like God. However, the angels were created with wings of power, while man was not. And angels are "ministering spirits sent forth to minister for those who will inherit salvation" (Heb. 1:14). (9 verses)

12. **Is salvation present or future?** "For we were saved in this hope" (Rom. 8:24; see also Eph. 2:5, 8) "And you will be hated of all for My name's sake. But he who endures to the end will be saved" (Matt 10:22; cf. Matt. 24:13; Mark 13:13). "For if when we were enemies we were reconciled to God through the death of His Son, much more, having been reconciled, we shall be saved by his life" (Rom. 5:10).

    Nobody can prejudge our eternal salvation. Since we are living in the time of judgment (Rev. 14:7) and only God knows whether our names have been called or not, let us simply do what God has asked us to do and trust our salvation to Him. (6 verses)

13. **The "spirit" will return to God.** "And the spirit will return to God who gave it" (Eccles. 12:7). Hidden meaning.

    The return of the spirit of man to heaven does not refer to the carbon dioxide that all humans breathe out or that the leaves of trees and plants breathe in. The statement in Ecclesiastes refers to the breath of God, with which God will resurrect His children at the second coming of Jesus Christ. That spirit is the power and mystery of God's creation (1 Cor. 15). (6 verses)

14. **The birth of Jesus Christ.** "Now the birth of Jesus Christ was as follows: After His mother Mary was betrothed to Joseph, before they came together, she was found with child of the Holy Spirit" (Matt. 1:18; see also Luke 1:35). Hidden meaning.

    Since Jesus Christ is the Lord, He emptied Himself and changed His divine form into a fertilized zygote in the womb of the Virgin Mary and was born a human baby in a manger (Phil. 2:7). (5 verses)

15. **Jesus Christ's moving star.** "Where is He who has been born King of the Jews? For we have seen His star in the East and have come to worship Him" (Matt. 2:2). Hidden meaning.

A bright shining group of angels appeared in the sky like a star. It was certainly not a real star, or it could not have traveled in the sky (Matt. 2:9). Luke described the angels' appearance (Luke 2:9–13). The Spirit of Prophecy identified the star as a group of angels. "The wise men had seen a mysterious light in the heavens upon that night when the glory of God flooded the hills of Bethlehem. As the light faded, a luminous star appeared, and lingered in the sky. It was neither a fixed star nor a planet, and the phenomenon excited the keenest interest. That star was a distant company of shining angels, but of this the wise men were ignorant" (*The Desire of Ages*, p. 60).

Of the origin of heavenly luminaries, Genesis says: "Then God said, 'Let there be lights in the firmament of the heavens to divide the day from the night; and let them be for signs and seasons, and for days and years; and let them be for lights in the firmament of the heavens to give light on the earth'; and it was so. Then God made two great lights: the greater light to rule the day, and the lesser light to rule the night. *He made* the stars also. God set them in the firmament of the heavens to give light on the earth, and to rule over the day and over the night, and to divide the light from the darkness. And God saw that *it was* good. So the evening and the morning were the fourth day" (Gen. 1:14–19).

Scientific evidence points to the creation of the sun, moon and millions of stars 4.5 billion years ago, which is before the triune God's six days of creation (Job 38:6–7, Heb. 1:1–2). Yet, in the six-day Creation, the Lord Jesus Christ lined up the earth, which was far away from the sun and covered with water and ice, bringing it closer to the sun. After three days of warmth, the water molecules dispersed as a hollow watery sphere above the earth's atmosphere, creating something like a glass that would enable humans, once we were created, to see the sun, moon and stars with our naked eyes (Gen. 1:1, 2, 6). (4 verses)

16. **There was war in heaven.** "And war broke out in heaven: Michael and his angels fought with the dragon; and the dragon and his angels fought" (Rev. 12:7). Hidden meaning.

   Prophecy is generally given in symbols. The description of Revelation 12 concerns Lucifer's sin against God. Once

Lucifer and a third of the angels had rebelled, they could not remain in their Creator's immediate presence, which would have destroyed them instantly. Therefore, they were cast down to earth from heaven (Luke 10:18). (4 verses)

17. **Forgiveness comes from God.** "If you forgive the sins of any, they are forgiven them; if you retain the *sins* of any, they are retained" (John 20:23). Discrepancy.

    According to Matthew 6:14, 15, we can forgive others their debts and their indiscretions against us, yet, ultimately, we cannot forgive their sins, for sins are the direct violation of one or more of God's Ten Commandments. Only God can forgive that. Jesus' point is that we forgive others to prepare us to receive God's forgiveness. (1 verse)

18. **Spirit of God dwelling in a human body.** "Or do you not know that your body is the temple of the Holy Spirit *who is* in you, whom you have from God, and you are not your own?" (1 Cor. 6:19). Hidden meaning.

    This verse teaches the spiritual reality that God's Spirit can live in the body, and, therefore, we are not to mistreat God's property. (1 verse)

19. **Little ones have a guardian angel.** "Take heed that you do not despise one of these little ones, for I say to you that in heaven their angels always see the face of My Father who is in heaven" (Matt. 18:10). Hidden meaning.

    From birth, every man, woman, and child has his or her own guardian angel. Through these holy guardian angels, God watches over every person living on this earth. (1 verse)

20. **The mother of Hiram (or Huram), builder of Solomon's temple, was either from the tribe of Naphtali or from the tribe of Dan.** "He *was* the son of a widow from the tribe of Naphtali, and his father *was* a man of Tyre, a bronze worker; he was filled with wisdom and understanding and skill in working with all kinds of bronze work. So he came to King Solomon and did all his work" (1 Kings 7:14). Discrepancy.

    Hiram was not from the tribe of Naphtali. He was of the tribe of Dan, as we learn from 2 Chronicles—"(the son of a woman of the daughters of Dan, and his father was a man of Tyre)" (2 Chron. 2:14). The tribe of Dan also furnished the artisans of the Ark of the Covenant in 1491 BC, Bezaleel and Aholiab. "And I, indeed I, have appointed with him Aholiab the son of Ahisamach, of the tribe of Dan; and I have put wisdom in the hearts of all the gifted artisans, that they may make all that I have commanded you" (Exod. 31:6). A solution to this discrepancy might be that Hiram's mother was from the tribe of Naphtali by her father but from the tribe of Dan by her mother. (1 verse)

21. **The height of the columns in Solomon's temple.** "And he cast two pillars of bronze, each one eighteen cubits high, and a line of twelve cubits measured the circumference of each" (1 Kings 7:15). Discrepancy.

    According to 1 Kings 7, these two pillars of brass, which Solomon named Jachin and Boaz, were twenty-three cubits tall (18 + 5 = 23). However, 2 Chronicles says: "Also he made in front of the temple two pillars thirty-five cubits high, and the capital that *was* on the top of each of *them* was five cubits" (2 Chron. 3:15). This would mean that the two pillars of brass were 40 cubits tall (35 + 5 = 40). These pillars obviously did support Solomon's temple, which was 120 cubits tall (2 Chron. 3:4). Thus, they were freestanding. There are three possible solutions to the discrepancy as can be found at http://www.thywordistrue.com/contradictions/119-two-pillars-of-brass and http://apologeticspress.org/apcontent.aspx?category=6&article=714. (1 verse)

22. **The price for the site of the Jerusalem temple.** "So David bought the threshing floor and the oxen for fifty shekels of silver" (2 Sam. 24:24; 1 Chron. 21:18; 2 Chron. 3:1; 5:5). Discrepancy.

    Second Samuel gives fifty shekels of silver as the price for Ornan's threshing floor. First Chronicles says that he gave much more. "So David gave Ornan six hundred shekels of gold by weight for the place" (1 Chron. 21:25). The explanation of the discrepancy is that the larger figure is a purchase of a larger amount of land upon which to build the temple, though David was prohibited from doing the construction. Solomon, the son of David, built the great golden temple, and it cost him much more than both of these amounts. (1 verse)

23. **Prostitution of the daughters of Moab (Num.** 25:1; 2 Kings 23:13). Discrepancy. (1 verse)

    1 Corinthians 10:8 "Nor let us commit sexual immorality, as some of them did, and in one day twenty-three thousand fell."

    Numbers 25:9 "And those who died in the plague were twenty-four thousand."

24. **The number of people who fell at Baal-Peor.** "Nor let us commit sexual immorality, as some of them did, and in one day twenty-three thousand fell" (1 Cor. 10:8). Discrepancy.

    Number 25:9 And those who died in the plague were twenty-four thousand. If twenty-four thousand died, then certainly twenty-three thousand died, and it is quite possible that the twenty-three thousand did die in a single day, while twenty-four thousand died over all. (1 verse)

25. **How the Lord is a Spirit.** "Now the Lord is the Spirit; and where the Spirit of the Lord *is*, there *is* liberty" (2 Cor. 3:17). Hidden meaning.

    "Lord," in this passage, refers to Jesus Christ, who was not the Spirit. Yet, the Holy Spirit of God is indeed Spirit, and by His power the early rain was given to apostles and they performed many miracles. Jesus Christ came in the flesh and ascended to heaven in the flesh. Yet, the Lord Jesus can be present with us in the form of the Spirit. (1 verse)

26. **Moses did not write the Ten Commandments.** "And He wrote on the tablets the words of the covenant, the Ten Commandments" (Exod. 34:28; 31:18; Deut. 4:13; 9:10; 10:4). Discrepancy.

    When the text says 'He wrote' that is not Moses, but "the LORD"—the Lord Jesus Christ Himself, who wrote the Ten Commandments the second time, as well as the first, and gave it to Moses on Mt. Sinai. (1 verse)

27. **Second man.** "The first man *was* of the earth, *made* of dust; the second Man *is* the Lord from heaven" (1 Cor. 15:47). Discrepancy.

    One might think that Jesus Christ is no longer a human but has been re-united in form with the triune God of heaven. However, as we pointed out above, Jesus ascended to heaven in the flesh. It is through His flesh that we have access to the grace of heaven (Heb. 10:20). He is identified in heaven as "the son of man," a Hebraic expression that means a "human being" (Acts 7:56; Rev. 1:13). "In taking our nature, the Saviour has bound Himself to humanity by a tie that is never to be broken" (*The Desire of Ages*, p. 25). (1 verse)

28. **Holy man.** "So Judah acknowledged *them* and said, 'She [Tamar] has been more righteous than I, because I did not give her to Shelah my son' " (Gen. 38:26). Discrepancy.

    "As it is written: *'There is none righteous, no, not one'* " (Rom. 3:10). Judah was saying Tamar, his daughter-in-law, was more *correct* than he was, for he deprived her the right to bear a son by refusing to give her a younger son to replace his son who had died. (152 verses)

29. **Jesus is our friend.** "These things He said, and after that He said to them, 'Our friend Lazarus sleeps, but I go that I may wake him up' " (John 11:11; cf. John 15:14). Discrepancy.

    Jesus Christ is our Savior and our Creator. Yet, He calls us His friends and invites us to call Him ours. Nonetheless, we must always respect Him as our Creator, Redeemer, and Sustainer. (7 verses)

30. **The names of the twelve disciples of Jesus.** "Now the names of the twelve apostles are these: first, Simon, who is called Peter, and Andrew his brother; James the *son* of Zebedee, and John his brother; Philip and Bartholomew; Thomas and Matthew the tax collector; James the *son* of Alphaeus, and Lebbaeus, whose surname was Thaddaeus; Simon the Canaanite, and Judas Iscariot, who also betrayed Him" (Matt. 10:2–4). Discrepancy.

    In another list, the place of Lebbaeus (surnamed Thaddaeus) is filled by Judas the son of James. "Simon whom He also named Peter, and Andrew his brother; James and John; Philip and Bartholomew; Matthew and Thomas; James the *son* of Alphaeus, and Simon called the Zealot; Judas *the son* of James, and Judas Iscariot who also became a traitor" (Luke 6:14–16). I prefer this list. Perhaps Matthew used a different name to distance Judas, son of James, from Judas Iscariot. Jerome called him the "Three-named." (1 verse)

31. Jesus Christ did not baptize. "After these things Jesus and His disciples came into the land of Judea, and there He remained with them and baptized" (John 3:22). Discrepancy.

John 4:2 clarifies who did the baptizing: "(though Jesus Himself did not baptize, but His disciples)." (1 verse)

The list that I have presented here contains a total of 1,975 verses in our Holy Bible that contain discrepancies, colloquial usages, and hidden meanings. With assistance, the new student of the Bible can find explanations to understand them.

Chapter 2
The Bible's Chronology of Human History (From 4159 BC to the Present)

In this chapter, we are going to see how the Bible explains the chronology of the human race. No other book on the face of the earth provides such a simple and direct account of the origin of the earth and of human civilization. Historians divide the history of the human race into "ages"—the Stone Age, the Bronze Age, and the Iron Age. According to the Bible, no such ages existed, because brass and ironwork existed very early in human history (Gen. 4:22). Moreover, Christ was in charge of human history from the beginning until the present. Historians may say that human beings first used stone to create knives and spears for hunting and then used the striking of stone to spark a fire to cook their food, but human beings throughout history have used stone tools whenever other tools were unavailable. It was Christ and His holy angels who taught humans the basic skills for survival.

God is very particular in all that He does. He preserved human genealogy and chronology so that we could understand who and what we are, where we are going, how long ago the earth and life on this earth were created, and to know when we will attain God's everlasting kingdom. In the history of the human race, the greatest of stories is Christ's loving mission to save humankind. Is it possible to follow the chronology of the human race from the six days of the Creation until the present? Can we trace out history and discover how the loving and living God preserved the human race?

Seventy-six Generations in the Chronology of the Gospel of Luke

From the sin of Adam and Eve to the birth of Jesus Christ, there are seventy-six recorded generations of individuals. Of the hundreds and thousands of books in the world that detail the billions of people who have been born on the face of the earth, there is only one genealogy of the Lord Jesus Christ that goes back to Adam. Here is that genealogy, taken from the Gospel of Luke:

(1) Jesus, (2) Joseph (Mary's guardian), (3) Heli, (4) Matthat, (5) Levi, (6) Melchi, (7) Janna, (8) Joseph, (9) Mattathiah, (10) Amos, (11) Nahum, (12) Esli, (13) Naggai, (14) Maath, (15) Mattathaiah, (16) Semei, (17) Joseph, (18) Judah, (19) Joannas, (20) Rhesa, (21) Zerubbabel, (22) Shealtiel, (23) Neri, (24) Melchi, (25) Addi, (26) Cosam, (27) Elmodam, (28) Er, (29) Jose, (30) Eliezer, (31) Jorim, (32) Matthat, (33) Levi, (34) Simeon, (35) Judah, (36) Joseph, (37) Jonan, (38) Eliakim, (39) Melea, (40) Menan, (41) Mattathah, (42) Nathan, (43) David, (44) Jesse, (45) Obed, (46) Boaz, (47) Salmon, (48) Nahshon, (49) Amminadab, (50) Ram, (51) Hezron, (52) Perez, (53) Judah, (54) Jacob, (55) Isaac, (56) Abraham, (57) Terah, (58) Nahor, (59) Serug, (60) Reu, (61) Peleg, (62) Eber, (63) Shelah, (64) Cainan, (65) Arphaxad, (66) Shem, (67) Noah, (68) Lamech, (69) Methuselah, (70) Enoch, (71) Jared, (72) Mahalalel, (73) Cainan, (74) Enosh, (75) Seth, (76) and Adam (Luke 3:23–38).

From Jesus Christ back to Adam, there are seventy-six generations of names that have been faithfully recorded. These names draw a direct line from AD 4 back to 4159 BC—from the birth of the Savior in the manger back to the sin of Adam.

The Detailed Chronology of Scripture

Beginning in 4159 BC, the Son of God and the Holy Spirit joined together during the six days of Creation to create life on the earth with the beautiful Garden of Eden. From the first day to the fifth, they created the environment for the present animal kingdom. On the sixth day, God created land animals and Adam and Eve, the crown of the Creation. They were much taller than humans and most animals are today. According to the pen of inspiration, Adam was "more than twice as tall as men now living upon the earth," and Eve was "not quite as tall as Adam. Her head reached a little above his shoulders" (*Signs of the Times*, Jan. 9, 1879). If Adam were fourteen feet tall, that would mean that Eve would have been about thirteen feet tall. Both were made of miry clay and given life by the power of God. God made beautiful rivers that flowed around the Garden of Eden—the Pishon, the Gihon, the Hiddekel, and the Euphrates (Gen. 2:11–14). These caused the garden to flourish and to bring forth living riches upon the earth. During the Flood, in 2503 BC, these rivers were washed away, though a river by the name of the Euphrates still flows in the Middle East in Iraq and Iran. The name is a reminder of God's creation of the Garden of Eden.

God's Plan of Salvation Revealed to Adam and Eve

In 4159 BC, Adam and Eve sinned against God. Immediately after sinning, they felt naked, and God came in search of them and found that they had covered themselves with fig leaves—not a very warm or durable form of clothing. God offered a sacrifice and clothed them with the skin of a slain animal (Gen. 3:21). By this, God taught Adam and Eve how to offer sacrifices as a way of pointing forward to the Messiah who would come to redeem them from their sins. In sacrificing the animal, Adam had to lay his hand on the head of the lamb and confess his sins. Then God would send fire down from heaven and consume the sacrifice. Hebrews 9:22 says, "And according to the law almost all things are purified with blood, and without shedding of blood there is no remission."

Adam and Eve failed the main task assigned them—that of obeying God. After they sinned, Eve gave birth to two sons whom she named Cain and Abel. Eve also gave birth to many daughters. Cain was a gardener, and Abel was a shepherd. God guided them in understanding the importance of shedding blood for the remission of sin.

However, Cain followed Satan and brought vegetables as an offering, while Abel brought an animal from his flocks to sacrifice to God. God accepted Abel's sacrifice, but He rejected Cain's. Angry with God and jealous of his brother, Cain killed Abel and ran away from the presence of God.

The First Period of Civilization

After instructing the human family on the new system of animal sacrifice, God instructed them about appropriate dress. These were the first aspects of civilization that God taught the human race. Besides these, they learned how to cook food and build homes, and they established villages and cities. Initially, they married their own sisters since their genetics were not then contaminated and no other mates were available. Adam, the first man, had so much life that, even after he sinned, the cells of his body did not quickly degenerate, and he lived until he was nine hundred and thirty years old (Gen. 5:5). The chronology of the human race began the day Adam sinned in 4159 BC.

Chart 2.1. Biblical Chronology of the Human Race

4159 BC	Adam was created (Gen. 1:26).
	Adam was **130** years old when his son Seth was born (Gen. 5:3), and he lived a total of 930 years (Gen. 5:5).
4029 BC	Seth was born.
	Seth was **105** years old when his son Enosh was born, and he lived a total of 912 years (Gen. 5:6–8).
3924 BC	Enosh was born.
	Enosh was **90** years old when his son Cainan was born; and he lived a total of 905 years (Gen. 5:9–11).
3834 BC	Cainan was born.
	Cainan was **70** years old when his son Mahalalel was born, and he lived a total of 910 years (Gen. 5:12–14).

Chapter 2 The Bible's Chronology of Human History   33

Chart 2.1. Biblical Chronology of the Human Race

3764 BC	Mahalalel was born.
	Mahalalel was **65** years old when his son Jared was born, and he lived a total of 895 years (Gen. 5:15–17).
3699 BC	Jared was born.
	Jared was **162** years old when his son Enoch was born, and he lived a total of 962 years (Gen. 5:18–20).
3537 BC	Enoch was born.
	Enoch was **65** years old when his son Methuselah was born, and he was taken to heaven at 365 years of age (Gen. 5:21–24).
3472 BC	Methuselah—the longest living human in history—was born.
	Methuselah was **187** years old when his son Lamech was born, and he lived a total of 969 years (Gen. 5:25–27).

3285 BC	Lamech was born.
	    Adam died when Lamech was 56 (Gen. 5:5).
	    Enoch left for heaven when Lamech was 113 (Gen. 5:24).
	    Seth died when Lamech was 168 (Gen. 5:8).

	Lamech was **182** years old when his son Noah was born, and he lived a total of 777 years (Gen. 5:28–31).

3103 BC	Noah was born.
	    Enosh died when Noah was 84 (Gen. 5:11).
	    Cainan died when Noah was 179 (Gen. 5:14).
	    Mahalalel died when Noah was 234 (Gen. 5:17).
	    Jared died when Noah was 366 (Gen. 5:20).

Chart 2.1. Biblical Chronology of the Human Race

2623 BC	When Noah was **480** years old, God called him to build an ark (Gen. 6:3, 14–12; see also *Patriarchs and Prophets*, p. 92). God gave him instructions for building a watercraft that would be 600 feet long, 100 feet wide, and 60 feet high. It was the very first ship to be built. At this time, God put a further restriction on the marriage system, from the marrying of a sibling to the next level of the marrying of a cousin. Yet, the people violated God's instructions and did wickedness in His sight. Rebelling against God, they started killing animals and one another, as well as committing adultery (Gen. 6:11, 2). God also called upon Noah to preach to the people a warning about the judgment of the Flood (2 Peter 2:5). When Noah began to build the ark, the people mocked him and did not repent of their sins.
2603 BC	Noah passed his **500th** year when his son Shem was born (Gen. 5:32; see especially Gen. 11:10), and he lived a total of 950 years (Gen. 5:32).
2601 BC	Shem, Ham and Japheth were born after Noah's 500th year (Gen. 5:32)
	From 4159 BC until 2503 BC there was neither rain nor rainbows. This was **the first period of human civilization**.
2503 BC	The Flood came upon the earth in Noah's **600**th year, and it lasted a year (Gen. 7:6, 11; 8:14).
2502 BC	After the Flood, God promised Noah that He would never again destroy the earth with a flood, and He placed the rainbow in the sky and He established the seasons (Gen. 9:16; 8:22) when He changed the tilt of the earth from 90º to 23½º. At this time, there were sixty-nine gases in the earth's atmosphere.
2502 BC	The second period of human civilization began.

Chart 2.1. Biblical Chronology of the Human Race

2501 BC	Shem was **100** years old when his son Arphaxad was born (two years after the flood), and Shem lived a total of 403 years (Gen. 11:10, 11).
	After the flood and the birth of Ham's son Canaan, Noah drank wine and lay naked. His son Ham discovered his father and laughed at him. When Noah's sons Shem and Japheth heard about it, they walked into the room backwards and covered their father's nakedness. Because he violated God's law by disrespecting his father, Ham's children were cursed. As the people divided and spread over the earth, Ham became the father of the Negro peoples.
2466 BC	Arphaxad was **35** years old when his son Salah was born, and he lived a total of 403 years (Gen. 11:12, 13).
2466 BC	Salah was born.
	Salah was **30** years old when his son Eber was born, and he lived a total of 403 years (Gen. 11:14).
2436 BC	Eber was born.
	Eber was **34** years old when his son Peleg was born, and he lived a total of 430 years (Gen. 11:16, 17).
2402 BC	Peleg was born.
2372 BC	Peleg was **30** years old when Rue was born, and he lived a total of 209 years (Gen. 11:16–19).
2372 BC	Reu was born.
2340 BC	Reu was **32** years old when Serug was born, and he lived a total of 207 years (Gen. 11:20, 21).
2340 BC	Serug was born (Gen. 11:22).

Chart 2.1. Biblical Chronology of the Human Race

	Reu introduced the system of the dividing of land (it is possible that the phrase, "was the earth divided," refers to the dividing of the continents through plate tectonics, Gen. 10:25), and Reu became the first of the world's many kings to rule different nations. In Reu's time, **the third period of human civilization began.** More than fifty-nine tribes joined together against God and started building the tower of Babel in the land of Shinar (this today is located in Iraq, whose capital city of Baghdad lies at 150 feet above sea level). There has been an attempt to link all languages as having a common origin, yet the evidence points to diverse families of languages. Otherwise, there are only a few superficial similarities between the languages besides "loanwords." The Bible tells how God came down and confused human language. This means that God encoded more than two thousand languages in their brains to disperse them throughout the earth (Gen. 11:7–9). God introduced many other languages besides what may be considered the original language, Hebrew. This act of God was the origin of the various language families. Since the people at the tower could not understand each other's language, they called the place "Babel," which means "confusion." It was built on the site of later "Babylon" (which is the Greek name for "Babel"). After the dispersion, God destroyed the tower with lightning. The dispersion from Babel is the origin of the many ethnic families of the earth.
2310 BC	Serug was **30** years old when his son Nahor was born, and he lived a total of 200 years (Gen. 11:22, 23).
2310 BC	Nahor was born.

Chart 2.1. Biblical Chronology of the Human Race

2281 BC	Nahor was **29** years old when his son Terah was born, and he lived a total of 119 years (Gen. 11:24, 25).
2211 BC	Terah was **70** years old when his son Abram was born, and he lived a total of 205 years (Gen. 11:26). Interestingly, Noah died when Abram was 40 (Gen. 9:28).
2136 BC	God called Abram to a land of promise—Canaan (Gen. 12:1–4).
2136 BC	Abram left Ur of the Chaldeans without questioning God and traveled with Sarai and Lot his brother's son to the Promised Land of Canaan. Abram was the nineteenth generation from Adam and the tenth generation from Noah. After the Flood, the world turned to idol worship. God called Abram to come out from among the idol worshipers (Joshua 24:2). Abram traveled to the land of Canaan (present-day Syria, Lebanon, Jordan, Israel, the northwestern corner of Saudi Arabia, all the way east to Iraq and south to the northeastern tip of Egypt). More than ten years later, God's promise of a son was not fulfilled. During this time, Sarai doubted God's word and gave Abraham permission to take Hagar as his wife. Hagar gave birth to Ishmael, the father of the Muslim nations, among whom the Islamic religion originated.
	After the birth of Ishmael, God changed Abram's name to Abraham and Sarai's name to Sarah (Gen. 17:5, 15).
2125 BC	Ishmael was born, son of Abraham and Sarah's handmaid (Gen. 16:16).
2111 BC	Sixteen years later, when Abraham was **100** years old, Isaac was born (Gen. 21:5).
2036 BC	Abraham lived 175 years (Gen. 25:7).
2051 BC	When Isaac was **60** years old, Jacob was born (Gen. 25:26).

Chart 2.1. Biblical Chronology of the Human Race	
1988 BC	Ishmael lived a total of 137 years (Gen. 25:17).
1951 BC	**When Jacob was 100** years old, Joseph was born (Gen. 41:46; 47:9).
1921 BC	Joseph was 30 years old when he stood before Pharaoh king of Egypt and became prime minister of Egypt (Gen. 41:46).
1921 BC	During this time, Jacob left Canaan because of the famine in the land and went to Egypt at 130 years of age (Gen. 47:9).
	Joseph settled Jacob and seventy other residents of Canaan, which was the Promised Land, into the land of Goshen, and they lived there seventeen years before Jacob died (Gen. 47:28).
1900 BC	Joseph introduced and invented the script for the Egyptian language.
1880 BC	**The fourth period of human civilization began.** By the power of Jesus Christ, Joseph introduced, in Egypt, letters for the very first language, that of Hebrew. This system of written language was introduced in the fourth period of civilization, as different systems of writing were developed in the different countries with the different languages.
1841 BC	Joseph ruled over Egypt 80 years and died in Egypt, living a total of 110 years (Gen. 50:26)
	After the death of Joseph, the descendants of Jacob, who were called "the children of Israel," multiplied into the millions, and their strength increased. Such strength threatened the new Pharaoh, and he enslaved the Israelites and put them to work in Egypt (Exod. 12:40, 41). During this time, they built the two big store cities of "Pithom and Raamses" (Exod. 1:11), and they also built one of the large pyramids, which is one of the seven wonders of the world today.

Chart 2.1. Biblical Chronology of the Human Race

1796 BC	God prophesied to Abraham that his posterity would sojourn four hundred years in a foreign land with slavery (Gen. 15:13; see also Exod. 12:40). The Samaritan Pentateuch clarifies that the 430 years of Exodus 12:40, 41 refers to the sojourn of Abraham and his posterity in both "Canaan and Egypt," for it fits that period of time precisely. From Abraham's entrance into the promised land, when he was 75 years old (**2136 BC**), until the birth of Isaac was **25** years; Isaac was **60** when Jacob was born; Jacob was **130** when he went into Egypt; then he and his children continued there an additional **215** years. The total of these is **430** years. (For evidence for this earlier time period, see the 2014 documentary video, "Patterns of Evidence: Exodus.") When the 430 years were fulfilled, God used Moses to bring their slavery to an end (Exod. 12:40, 41). Moses was then 80 years old (Exod. 7:7).
	Who was the very first prophet of God? (Gen. 20:7; Exod. 7:1).
1571 BC	1491 + 80 years means that Moses was born in Egypt in 1571 BC, being of the family of Levi.
	According to God's plan, Pharaoh's family adopted Moses, and he lived as a prince in Egypt and received an Egyptian education to prepare him to be the wise ruler of the nation. However, at the age of forty, he killed an Egyptian with his own hand and ran for his life to the wilderness. He ended up in Midian at the home of Jethro, the father of Zipporah, who became his wife. In Midian, he worked as a shepherd, learning patience and developing character in the university of the living God so he could lead his stiff-necked people out of bondage.

Chart 2.1. Biblical Chronology of the Human Race	
1531–1491 BC	While Moses was in the wilderness, God instructed him to write the book of Genesis (as well as the book of Job) under the guidance of the Holy Spirit (Gen. 15:13).
1491 BC	God set them free from their bondage (1531 BC – 430 = 1491 BC).

God called Moses and Aaron to be messengers to the pharaoh, using the ten plagues to punish the land and bring Egypt to its knees by His mighty power that God's people might enter the Promised Land. More than six hundred thousand people left Egypt to reach Sinai on the first day of the third month. God asked them to purify themselves before He gave them His eternal and everlasting covenant of Ten Commandments. It was the Son of God Himself who had appeared to Moses in the bush, and it was He who wrote the Ten Commandments with His own finger (Exod. 3:14; 19:1, 2; 24:12; 31:18; Deut. 9:10; notice that God's name "LORD," which is Yahweh, comes from "I AM" and that Jesus identified Himself, in John 8:58, as the "I am" who preceded Abraham).

The Ten Commandments

Jesus Christ descended from heaven to Mount Sinai, where He first spoke the Ten Commandments to the children of Israel and then wrote the Ten Commandments with His finger, giving them to Moses (1 Cor. 10:1–4; Exod. 20:1-17; Exod. 31:18). These are the only fifteen verses in the Bible that God wrote directly Himself.

The Seventh Sense

It is a scientific fact that human beings have five senses (plus speech, which I have labeled a sixth sense) that enable us to talk and rule over the world. With the Ten Commandments, God added an additional sense—a seventh sense—that links us to the foundation of His kingdom, that is, God's Ten Commandments. That they are the foundation of His kingdom needs to be taught to men, women, and children in as many ways as possible. God instructed the children of Israel to teach their children the holy law both day and night (Deut. 6:7; Joshua 1:8). Through the moral law, God instructed them to love

God and their fellow human beings. Along with the moral law, God also asked Moses to write and teach the ceremonial, physical, and civil laws, comprised of almost 1,532 verses in the Old Testament. Christ, as the sacrifice for the human race, is the focus of the ceremonial law. Besides the moral law, the other laws pertain to daily life. The Ten Commandments were placed in the Ark of the Covenant. The other laws that made up the Mosaic law were kept beside the ark.

The Sanctuary Services

God instructed Moses to build a sanctuary "according to the pattern" he had received from heaven and to establish an ecclesiastical system that would symbolize Christ's first coming and the remission of sin (Acts 7:44). The children of Israel followed the instructions that Moses had received and built the sanctuary, launching a new civilization in the wilderness and **the fifth period of human civilization**.

Through Moses, the people learned how to cut diamonds and precious stones. God introduced the new ecclesiastical system with its sacrificial offerings that were officiated by the priest in the tabernacle. Jesus Christ Himself was responsible for giving the pattern for the holy tabernacle to Moses. The presence of both Christ and the Holy Spirit are represented in the Most Holy Place above the mercy seat upon the ark of the covenant. They officiated the sacrificial offering through the high priest and forgave sins apart from the Ten Commandments. The 70 elders and the congregation would stone to death those who committed the unpardonable sins of violating the Ten Commandments as open sinners. Others, who sought mercy, received mercy by the blood sprinkled upon the mercy seat above God's holy law.

God taught the people how to carve wood and stone and make utensils for cutting diamonds, for shaping the Urim and Thummim in the breastplate of the high priest and carving the two gold-covered cherubim. Theocracy was the basis of their government; He loved them and took care of their needs in the wilderness. However, the children of Israel did not understand the love of God, and they rebelled against the loving God. What would have been a forty day's journey turned into forty years of travel. All but two of the six hundred thousand men who left Egypt perished in the wilderness because of their unbelief and disobedience. Only Caleb and Joshua reached the Promised Land.

Chart 2.2. Biblical Chronology of the Human Race—continued

1491 BC	Six hundred thousand people left Egypt.
	At the end of the forty years of wilderness wandering, Moses died and was buried in an unmarked grave in a valley in the land of Moab, next to Bethpeor and near Mt. Nebo (Deut. 32:49; 34:5, 6). According to evidence from the book of Jude, God later took him to heaven (Jude 9).
	Joshua and Caleb entered with the next generation into the Promised Land of Canaan.
	Joshua defeated thirty-six kings around there, and they possessed the Promised Land by God's help.
	Joshua lived 110 years and then died (Josh. 24:29).
	After the death of Joshua, Jesus Christ raised fourteen judges to rule the children of Israel.
	For **40** years of this period, others ruled over Israel (Judges 3:9–11).
1386 BC	During this period, the king of Mesopotamia troubled them for eight years.
	For **8** years of the period, "Ehud" led Israel (Judges 3:15–30).
1306 BC	The king of Moab was disturbed for 18 years.
	For **40** years, "Deborah" judged Israel (Judges 5:31).
1226 BC	Midian was disturbed for 7 years (Judges 6:1).
	For **23** years, "Tola" judged Israel (Judges 10:1, 2).
1203 BC	For **22** years, "Jair" judged Israel (Judges 10:3).
1181 BC	For **6** years, "Jephthah" judged Israel (Judges 12:4–7).
1175 BC	For **7** years, "Ibzan" judged Israel (Judges 12:8, 9).
1168 BC	For **10** years, "Elon" judged Israel (Judges 12:11).
1158 BC	For **8** years, "Abdon" judged Israel (Judges 12:13–15).
1150 BC	For **20** years, "Samson" judged Israel (Judges 15:20).
1130 BC	For **40** years, "Eli" the high priest judged Israel (1 Sam. 4:18).

Chart 2.2. Biblical Chronology of the Human Race—continued

1090 BC	**Samuel judged Israel** with his sons who took bribes and perverted judgment with the people.
	The 70 elders of Israel joined together and came to Samuel to ask him for a king. They wished for a king to rule over them because Samuel's sons were not true to God. Conceding their wish, God instructed Samuel to ordain a king for them.
1057 BC	Saul was ordained the first king of Israel. Yet, he did not rule as king over Israel according to God's will for 2 + 7 = 9 years.
1048 BC	When God rejected King Saul, Samuel ordained David to be the second king (1 Sam. 13:1; 16:13).
	David ruled over Israel for **33** years and then died (1 Sam. 16:13; 1 Kings 2:10). With the monarchy, there was no more theocracy.
1015 BC	Nathan the prophet ordained King Solomon. According to 1 Kings 6:1, 3, it was 480 years from the Exodus to the fourth year of King Solomon's reign, when he began to build the temple. Using one set of dates, that would be 1491 − 480 = 1011 BC.

Chart 2.2. Biblical Chronology of the Human Race—continued

1011 BC	King Solomon, who laid the foundation stone for the first golden temple in Jerusalem, which was very famous in the world's **sixth period of civilization.** Jesus Christ instructed them to build the 240-foot tower of the golden temple, and He had earlier given wisdom to Bezalel to do all types of art works with gold, silver, brass, stone, and iron (Exod. 37:1; 2 Chron. 1:5). They cut very large stones from the mountain, brought them to Jerusalem, and built the temple without the sound of a hammer or chisel. It was exquisitely designed by Jesus Christ, and the Holy Spirit was the crown of civilization in this world. The construction of God's holy temple used 3,750 tons of gold, 37,500 tons of silver, 675 tons of brass, and 3,750 tons of iron (1 Chron. 22:14; 29:4–7). King Solomon's construction of this golden temple took seven years. There was no stone or bronze age.
1004 BC	King Solomon dedicated the golden temple in Jerusalem.
	For the second time in Israel's history, Jesus Christ and the Holy Spirit continued to dwell in the golden temple from 1004 BC to 607 BC as they had done in the time of Moses from 1491–1451 BC. There they officiated over the sacrificial ordinances.

Chart 2.2. Biblical Chronology of the Human Race—continued

	For 40 years (from 1015 to 975 BC), Solomon ruled as the world's wisest and richest king. According to 1 Kings 9:7–9, God exhorted him to keep God's word that the temple might remain longer for God's glory and honor. Yet, Solomon chose to take 700 wives and 300 concubines (1 Kings 11:3). Since the theocracy had been transformed to a monarchy, Solomon went against God in building temples to Moloch and worshiping with his idol-worshipping queens. God's blessing was withdrawn from Solomon, and God gave ten parts of his nation to his servant Jeroboam. Only one other tribe—the tribe of Benjamin—remained with Judah in making up the kingdom of Judah (1 Kings 11:13; 12:21). In the end, Solomon, the wisest and richest king of Israel, wrote three books of the Bible and went against God as a result of his foreign and unbelieving wives. When King Solomon died, eighteen of his descendants ruled the nation as king until 607 BC.

Chart 2.3. The List of the Kings of Judah and Israel

#	DATE	KINGS OF JUDAH	TEXT	#	KINGS OF ISRAEL	TEXT	DATE
1	975 BC	Rehoboam	1 Kings 11:43; 14:21 (17 years)	1	Jeroboam	1 Kings 11:28	973 BC
2	956 BC	Abijam	1 Kings 15:1–2 (3 years)	2	Nadab	1 Kings 15:25	954 BC
3	951 BC	Asa	1 Kings 15:9, 10 (41 years)	3	Baasha	1 Kings 16:8	953 BC

Chart 2.3. The List of the Kings of Judah and Israel

#	DATE	KINGS OF JUDAH	TEXT	#	KINGS OF ISRAEL	TEXT	DATE
4	914 BC	Jehoshaphat	1 Kings 22:41, 42 (25 years)	4	Elah	1 Kings 16:13	900 BC
5	896 BC	Jehoram	2 Kings 8:16, 17 (8 years)	5	Zimri	1 Kings 16:10, 15	925 BC
6	872 BC	Jehoash (Athaliah 6 years)	2 Kings 12:1 (40 years)	6	Omri	1 Kings 16:22	915 BC
7	839 BC	Amaziah	2 Kings 12:21 (25 years)	7	Ahab	1 Kings 16:29	918 BC
8	810 BC	Azariah	2 Kings 15:1, 2 (52 years)	8	Ahaziah	1 Kings 22:40	896 BC
9	758 BC	Jotham	2 Kings 15:32, 33 (16 years)	9	Jehu	2 Kings 13:1 (2 Kings 9:2)	884 BC
10	742 BC	Ahaz	2 Kings 16:1–2 (16 years)	10	Jehoahaz	2 Kings 13:1	856 BC
11	726 BC	Hezekiah	2 Kings 18:1, 2 (29 years)	11	Jehoash	2 Kings 13:10	841 BC
12	698 BC	Manasseh	2 Kings 21:1 (55 years)	12	Jeroboam	2 Kings 14:16	794 BC

Chart 2.3. The List of the Kings of Judah and Israel

#	DATE	KINGS OF JUDAH	TEXT	#	KINGS OF ISRAEL	TEXT	DATE
13	643 BC	Amon	2 Kings 21:18, 19 (2 years)	13	Zachariah	2 Kings 14:29	773 BC
14	641 BC	Josiah	2 Kings 22:1 (31 years)	14	Shallum	2 Kings 15:10	772 BC
15	610 BC	Jehoahaz	2 Kings 23:31 (3 months)	15	Menahem	2 Kings 15:14	771 BC
16	610 BC	Jehoiakim	2 Kings 23:34–36 (11 years)	16	Pekahiah	2 Kings 15:22	761 BC
17	599 BC	Jehoiachin	2 Kings 24:6 (3 months)	17	Remaliah	2 Kings 15:24	759 BC
18	590 BC	Zedekiah	2 Kings 24:17, 18 (11 years)	18	Pekah Hoshea	2 Kings 16:1 2 Kings 15:30	739 BC

Chart 2.4. Biblical Chronology of the Human Race—continued	
800 BC	Joel prophesied the former and latter rain (Joel 2:23–31).
765 BC	Isaiah prophesied the first coming of Jesus Christ to this world (Isa. 7:14; 9:6).
720 BC	Assyria conquered the ten tribes of Israel.
609 BC	Jeremiah prophesied about the destruction of Jerusalem as a result of Sabbath violation (Jer. 17:27).
607 BC	Jesus Christ instructed the prophet Jeremiah to remove the ark (2 Maccabees 2:4, 5).

Before the king of Babylon invaded Jerusalem, God asked Jeremiah to remove the holy articles from the Most Holy Place in the golden temple and take them to an undisclosed cave and seal them up. These articles included the Ten Commandments, with the covenant box and its two cherubim on top, and the breastplate with the Urim and Thummim. It is thought that this cave is in Mt. Nebo of Jordan, where Moses once saw the Promised Land of Canaan (in 1451 BC). Jeremiah obeyed God's instructions, in 607 BC, taking the holy articles to this place of hiding. *Prophets and Kings*, p. 453, says, "With mourning and sadness they secreted the ark in a cave, where it was to be hidden from the people of Israel and Judah because of their sins, and was to be no more restored to them. That sacred ark is yet hidden. It has never been disturbed since it was secreted."

Chart 2.5. Biblical Chronology of the Human Race—continued	
607 BC	God handed over Judea to Nebuchadnezzar, the king of Babylon, who invaded Jerusalem in 607 BC and destroyed it by fire (2 Kings 24:1; 25:9–11).

In 1981, four Americans found the sacred ark. Yet, they did not dare touch it or approach it.

World History After King Solomon

King Nebuchadnezzar of Babylon had a dream regarding world history. We find it recorded in Daniel 2. His dream is paralleled by the two great prophecies in Daniel 7 and 8, which cover the whole of world history until Christ's kingdom comes. Daniel is the most comprehensive world history, from the reign of Babylon in 606 BC to the reign of Great Britain in AD 1840.

In Daniel 2:31–45, God revealed through a great image made of gold, silver, bronze and then iron mixed with clay the following kingdoms.

Chart 2.6. Biblical Chronology of the Human Race—Continued	
603–538 BC	The head of the image was of gold and represented the mighty and wealthy kingdom of **Babylon**, which ruled as an empire over all the world.

Chart 2.6. Biblical Chronology of the Human Race—Continued	
538–331 BC	The breast of silver represented the kingdom of **Medo-Persia**, which ruled as a world empire, from India to Ethiopia, over 127 provinces (Esther 1:1).
331–168 BC	The brass belly of the image represented the **Greek** Empire of Alexander, from 331 BC to 168 BC. After his death, it was divided between his four generals. Cassander took the west; Lysimachus took the north; Seleucus took the east; and Ptolemy took the south, including Egypt and Ethiopia in Africa. The record is in the history books.
168 BC–AD 476	The legs of iron represented the mighty **Roman** Empire, which came to power under Julius Caesar's leadership as he systematically conquered the western world. Since iron was first worked, it has been one of the strongest metals in the world. Though not mentioned in the passage, the two legs may represent the two divisions of the Roman Empire.
476 AD–the present	Lastly, the feet of iron mixed with clay (which likely had ten toes) represented the ten kingdoms into which the Roman empire divided from AD 476 to AD 1840. The mighty British Empire was one of the "strong" (and not "fragile") parts of the feet in the prophecy (Dan. 2:42).
4 BC	The birth of Jesus Christ in this world
AD 27	The baptism of Jesus Christ in the River Jordan
AD 31	The death and resurrection of Jesus Christ
AD 31–100	The former rain (Joel 2:23) was given to the disciples through the Holy Spirit.
AD 31–100	**The New Testament** was written by eight followers of Jesus Christ and added as Scripture to the Old Testament, making a volume of 66 books.

Chart 2.6. Biblical Chronology of the Human Race—Continued	
AD 34	Stephen was stoned to death and the prophecy of the great multitude started in fulfillment of Jeremiah 16:16.
AD 70	The temple in Jerusalem that had been enhanced by Herod the King was completely destroyed by Titus the Roman general, fulfilling Jesus' prophecy—"Assuredly, I say to you, not *one* stone shall be left here upon another, that shall not be thrown down" (Matt. 24:2).
AD 34 to AD 100	The twelve apostles were persecuted and killed by Jewish and Roman authorities. No apostle escaped the persecution predicted in prophecy (Jer. 16:16; Rev. 2:27; and Dan. 7:24, 25; 9:24–26). The people had declared, "His blood *be* on us and on our children" (Matt. 27:25). The curse was fulfilled in dreadful completeness in AD 70 when Titus the Roman general attacked Jerusalem. The city of Jerusalem was decimated, the temple was completely destroyed, and a great majority of the Jewish people, including women and children, were killed. The Jews could not escape the perils of the biblical prophecy of Matthew 24:19, 25, which was fulfilled to the letter. They brought the curse upon themselves, and the posterity of those who could flee for their lives to forty-six other countries remained exiles from their homeland for 1879 years.

5,005 Verses Against the Jewish People

There are 5,005 verses written against the Jewish people that have been fulfilled through the centuries. From AD 70 onward, the Jewish people scattered to many countries. From AD 70 to 1949, there were more than 1820 years that there was no land for the Jewish people as a nation. The Jews were exiled from their homeland and often lived under deplorable conditions. The Jews must reap the consequence of their deeds, and these judgments will be meted out until the end of the world under the curse of God. No one can stand before God.

The Rise of the Modern Nation of Israel

Is the modern nation of Israel a fulfillment of biblical prophecy? Before World War I, almost all the countries in the Middle East were under the control of the Islamic religion. After the two great Islamic wars, in giving these countries independence France fulfilled biblical prophecy. These included: Syria in 1946, Lebanon in 1943, Djibouti in 1925, Algeria in 1962, Turkey in 1956, Morocco in 1956, Central Africa in 1960. At the same time, Great Britain also gave independence to the following Islamic countries: Saudi Arabia, the Islamic religious holy land, was given as a gift to the king of Saudi Arabia in 1902; the United Arab Emirates gained its independence in AD 1961; Somalia in 1920; Kuwait in 1922; Egypt in 1922; Iran in 1905; Libya in 1942; Chad in 1960; Bahrain in 1961; Uganda in 1963; Sudan in 1965; Afghanistan in 1965; South Yemen in 1967; Jordan in 1946; Qatar in 1971; North Yemen in 1967. The independence of these nations was possible because of the fall of the Ottoman Empire in 1840. It can be said in all fairness that the above-mentioned twenty-five Islamic nations began from AD 537 onward and not before the birth of Christ. These nations came into being by war and the gift of the living Christ. They would help fulfill prophecy regarding Israel as land would be designated for the establishment of a Jewish nation so that the nation of Israel could stand as a witness to Christ's crucifixion and His second coming (Matt. 26:64). Alongside the twenty-five Middle Eastern Islamic countries mentioned above, a twenty-sixth country, the Jewish nation of Israel, was also formed. This Jewish nation belongs to Abraham's descendants through the son of his wife Sarah, whose son Isaac had a son named Jacob, who was given the name "Israel." At the same time, the above-mentioned twenty-five Islamic countries came through the son of Abraham's second (and unlawful) wife Hagar's son Ishmael. They are the tribes of Islam. The first twenty-three Islamic countries were captured by Great Britain and France during World War I. In 1917, the land of Israel also fell into the hands of Great Britain from Islamic people. At the time, very few Jewish people lived in Israel, for the majority of the land's inhabitants were of the Islamic faith. During the period of 1854 to 1917, after a second Islamic war, only the Jewish people were restricted in entering their own country because of the agitations of the existing inhabitants of the Islamic religion who called themselves Palestinians, as though their occupancy of the land went back to Palestine named after the Philistines of Canaan.

Chapter 3
The Concept of the Triune God

Dear friends and believers, now we are going to enter into a very important subject. It is about God the Creator. Many are confused about this subject. Many have questions such as: Who is the real God? Where did He come from? Where does He live? What is His function? What was His reason for creating this earth and human beings? Hundreds of questions remain unanswered. Let us go directly to Scripture and see what it says about the triune God.

An Explanation from the Word of God

Then God said, "Let Us make man in Our image, according to Our likeness; let them have dominion over the fish of the sea, over the birds of the air, and over the cattle, over all the earth and over every creeping thing that creeps on the earth" (Gen 1:26).

The words, "Let Us make man in Our image, according to Our likeness" means that Adam is a copy of Jesus Christ in bodily shape. If Adam could stand with Christ, they would look very much alike. At the same time, we should be careful about comparing them with the modern height of human beings, because the pen of inspiration says that Adam was created taller than modern man. "As Adam came forth from the hand of his Creator, he was of noble height, and of beautiful symmetry. He was more than twice as tall as men now living upon the earth, and was well proportioned. . . . Eve was not quite as tall as Adam. Her head reached a little above his shoulders. She, too, was noble—perfect in symmetry, and very beautiful" (*The Spirit of Prophecy*, vol. 1, p. 25). This means that Adam was about fourteen feet tall, and Eve was up to his shoulder.

The Mirror Explanation

The following mirror explanation should be understandable to anyone. With three big mirrors in front of Adam's large form, there will be three reflections:
1. The first mirror will reflect the first Person of the triune God, the Father.
2. The second mirror will reflect the second Person of the triune God, Jesus Christ.
3. The third mirror will reflect the third Person of the triune God, the Holy Spirit.

Like Adam, who had blood, flesh, and bone, Christ took on all of the same, though He had to change into the form of a spirit in the instant that he was becoming a human being. Still, the bodily shape that He took on in coming to earth will remain like that of Adam. Understanding this fact, even children will have a clear concept of the triune God.

The Image and Likeness of God

The simple way to understand the image and likeness of God is to recognize the four dimensions of the image of Jesus Christ, that likeness means that Jesus Christ is a photo replica of the Father.

The Nature of the Triune God of the Bible

1. God is holy (Rev. 4:8; 1 Peter 1:16).
2. He is great in power, and His understanding is infinite (Ps. 147:5).
3. "He looks on the earth, and it trembles; He touches the hills,

and they smoke" (Ps. 104:32). God has the power to control things on earth.
4. "For our God *is* a consuming fire" (Heb. 12:29).
5. He "*is* a jealous God" (Exod. 34:14; Josh. 24:19).
6. "All things *are* naked and open to the eyes" of God (Heb. 4:13).
7. "God *is* Spirit" (John 4:24).
8. God dwells in light, therefore His garment is light. (1 John 1:5; Ps 104:2).
9. God is "dwelling in unapproachable light" (1 Tim. 6:16).
10. Once God has spoken twice man will hear (Ps. 62:11).

The Character of God

1. "God is love" (1 John 4:8).
2. God is "merciful and gracious, long-suffering and abounding in goodness" (Exod. 34:6; see also Ps. 86:15).
3. God is righteous and merciful (Ps. 116:5).
4. God will "abundantly pardon" even the wicked if they repent (Isa. 55:7).
5. God does not tempt any man (James 1:13).
6. "God is not a man, that He should lie" (Num. 23:19).
7. He is a "jealous God, visiting the iniquity of the fathers upon the children to the third and fourth *generations*," while, at the same time, "showing mercy" to those who keep His commandments unto a thousand generations (Exod. 20:5, 6).

God is the Creator

1 Corinthians 8:6 says, "yet for us *there* is one God, the Father, of whom *are* all things, and we for Him; and one Lord Jesus Christ, through whom *are* all things, and through whom we *live*." God is the Creator.

The first chapter of the book of Genesis talks about only six days of active creation, with the seventh day being the Sabbath, or a day of rest. The first and second chapters of the book of Job talk about other created beings—angels and other sons of God. Thus, it is easy to understand, before 6000 to 7000 BC, that God created from nothing without even an atom or any matter, in the twinkling of an eye, the numberless holy angels who have the shape of humans with heads, legs, faces, and multiple wings to fly swiftly to earth and other planets. He has the power to perform miracles like bringing fire down from the sky. Though they appear on earth as humans, He created them as spirits and not with flesh and bone like a man. Conversely, Adam cannot change his flesh-and-blood into the form of a spirit like the angels.

God is the Triune God

1 John 5:7 says, "For there are three that bear witness in heaven: the Father, the Word, and the Holy Spirit; and these three are one." There are other writers who provide evidence to help us understand about the triune God (for example, see Matt. 28:19; Luke 3:22).

What is the Meaning of the "Trinity"?

"Trinity" is a common term for God within Christianity. Some interpret "Trinity" as meaning that the first Person of the triune God (the Father) acted as Jesus Christ on earth and as the Holy Spirit. Such a teaching does not go along with the teachings of the Word of God. We should rather follow the Scriptures regarding the triune God.

Jesus said, "He who has seen Me has seen the Father" (John 14:9). Paul, in the Epistle to the Hebrews, points out how God personally revealed Himself: "God, who at various times and in various ways spoke in time past to the fathers by the prophets, has in these last days spoken to us by *His* Son, whom He has appointed heir of all things, through whom also He made the worlds; who being the brightness of *His* glory and the express image of His person . . ." (Heb. 1:1–3).

God Himself gives witness about Jesus Christ, showing their equality. Throughout the Bible, the three persons of the triune God have the same power and character, and they all have roles in saving human beings. So, the three members of the three-person Godhead join together as one God. It is like the mathematical dimensions of one cubic inch. It is one inch by one inch by one inch. There is one God who is equal in all respects. The first Person of the triune God and the second Person of the triune God, who is Jesus Christ, and the third Person of the triune God, the Holy Ghost, remain equal in all respects. All the members of the triune God possess the fullness of the Godhead. None is less or more God than the others, though they each play a different role with regard to the universe and with regard to humankind.

Monotheism vs. Polytheism

After such an analysis, some people may point to Deuteronomy 6:4, which says, "Hear, O Israel: The LORD our God, the LORD *is* one!" The statement is a response to the idea that there are multiple gods, as the children of Israel left Egypt had been taught while living with the Egyptians. At the time, Jesus did not reveal everything to Moses that He would later reveal to John the Apostle and the other writers of the New Testament. Yet, there is a sense of plurality in Genesis that continues throughout the rest of the Bible. (Besides saying "Let Us make man in Our image," the name for God in Genesis 1 is consistently *Elohim*, the plural form of *El*, which means "god.") So, though we worship the triune God, we still believe in monotheism (that there is one God) and not polytheism (that there are many gods).

The Unique Ability of the Triune God to Synchronize Minds

When Christ walked on earth, He read the minds of the people. God knows our thoughts and actions. He knows what will take place—even hundreds and thousands of years in advance. This demonstrates that He is God (Acts 4:24). God does not need to communicate through the mouth and ears when He can communicate through the mind.

The Equality and Passion of God

Someone may question whether all three personalities are the same. Concerning the Father and the Son, how is it possible that the Father and Son are equal? It is a good question, and God's word has a good answer. Paul wrote about "the mystery of godliness," and he described Christ as being "over all, *the* eternally blessed God" (1 Tim. 3:16; Rom. 9:5). The main reason that God chose the designations "Father" and "Son" is to connect with humanity, whom, in His love, He desires to save. That is the hidden meaning of the terms "Father" and "Son." There are many scriptures that talk about the Father and the Son. Ironically, Isaiah 9:6, which foretells Christ's birth, calls the "Son" who "is given," "Everlasting Father."

When the Bible shares in the Ten Commandments, "You shall have no other gods before Me" (Exod. 20:3), it is talking about the equality of the Godhead. When people think that God the Father is higher than Christ and that the Holy Spirit is lower than Jesus Christ, it is good for them to go back to the Bible and study again about the oneness of God.

Sin in Heaven

People wonder how sin originated in heaven, the very holy place that it is. Satan failed to understand the synchronization of the mind of God and considered Christ to be lower than the first Person of the triune God. The book of Job addresses this point. Job 1:6 says, "Now there was a day when the sons of God came to present themselves before the LORD, and Satan also came among them."

When Christ walked on the earth and Satan came to tempt Him, Satan used the word "if" in his statement to interject doubt in Christ's mind concerning Christ's divine authority and power. Since Satan could not understand the synchronization of the mind and power of God, he gambled that he could overcome his own Creator, and he lost. This oversight is the main reason the great controversy began in heaven.

The Birth of Jesus Christ

Some people believe that Christ must have needed help in coming to this world, but these people overlook the many ways that the triune God has been at work to save human beings and accomplish the plan of salvation. In creation and in redemption, yes, even in glorification it is easy to see the members of the triune God working together. At the same time, each member of the triune God has sufficient power to work individually. One can readily see that Matthew and Luke's view of the birth of Jesus Christ was different than that of Paul. Paul's view emphasized the uniqueness of Christ while He faithfully played His own unique role in meeting the great controversy.

Matthew wrote: "Now the birth of Jesus Christ was as follows: ... Mary ... was found with the child of the Holy Spirit" (Matt. 1:18). Luke wrote: "*The* Holy Spirit will come upon you, and the power of the Highest will overshadow you" (Luke 1:35). I would assert that

Christ did not inherently need any help from the Father or the Spirit in coming to this world to save us and combat the devil in the great controversy. Paul describes the power that Jesus Christ, as Creator, Redeemer, and Sustainer, gave up in coming to earth (Phil. 2:5–7), and John tells us: "In Him was life, and the life was the light of men" (John 1:4).

Philippians 2:7 (RSV and Tamil translation) says: "He emptied Himself taking the form of the born servant and coming in the likeness of men." It is a fact of Scripture that, when Christ came to this world, He came on His own (Gal. 1:4; 2:20; Eph. 5:25; 1 Tim. 6:6; Titus 2:14; Heb. 9:14), and, when He came, it was much like a test tube baby. That means that, when Jesus came in "the fullness of the time" (Gal. 4:4), He emptied Himself from a fourteen feet tall spiritual body and became a very tiny male zygote, implanted into the uterus of the Virgin Mary with her permission, just as test tube babies are now artificially implanted in the uterus of hopeful mothers. After nine months, He was born in a manger.

But if Christ came through the help of the Holy Spirit, as Matthew describes, then it could be said that He is the Son of the Holy Spirit. By this same thinking, would it not require the help of the Most High for Him to be the Son of the Most High? If either of these is the case, would it not disqualify Him to be Christ the Savior? The Bible plainly says, "The Word became flesh and dwelt among us" (John 1:14). Since the Jews could not comprehend God in heaven, Christ had to explain their relation in terms of Father and Son. Since Christ has revealed so much to the present world, it is good to understand the uniqueness of Jesus Christ. Today, Muslim scholars argue about Matthew 1:18 and Luke 1:35 concerning Jesus Christ's birth, but they do not seem to realize that God's word has its own way of explaining this truth. Philippians 2:7 nullifies their argument.

Chapter 4
Creation vs. Evolution

Many questions remain about the origins of the earth, of life itself, and of how long ago it was that these origins took place. While scientific knowledge has increased exponentially, people of this postmodern age prefer judging everything by their own knowledge and experience. Scientists rely on carbon dating and other methods of dating based on radioactive decay to determine the age of the earth rather than accepting the Bible's account of God's creation of the natural world within the last several thousand years. I would assert that, discarding the Word of God, no one can understand the real truth about the Creation. True science does not contradict the Bible. So, let us jump into the word of God and see what it reveals about the beauty of the Creation.

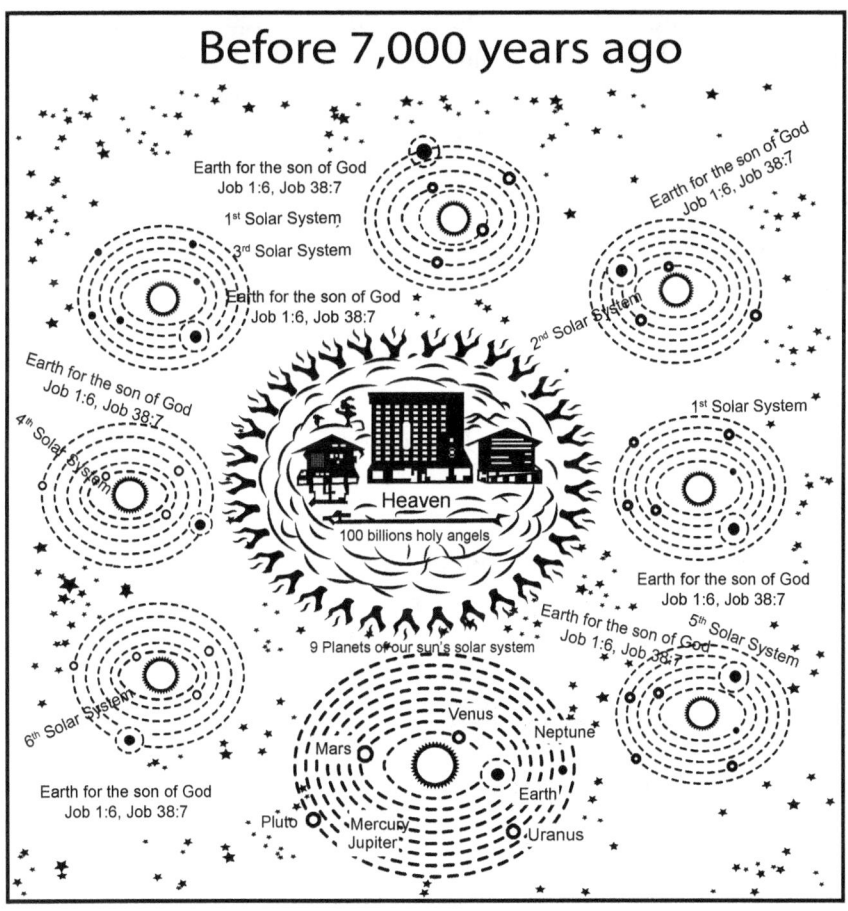

The Bible and the Creation

The very first thing to understand the book of Genesis (and the Bible itself) is the account of the six days of the Creation and the seventh-day rest. This account tells how the earth and the things on earth as well as human beings, who are the crown of the Creation, were all created. Yet, it does not describe the creation of the angels. They must have been created prior to this event, indicating that there has been more than one creation.

Now let us consider the ten words that begin the account: "In the beginning God created the heavens and the earth" (Gen. 1:1).

The implication is that God's throne is at the center of all the galaxies, one of which is our Milky Way, which has many solar systems. A proper model of the universe will have God's throne at the middle of His creation (1 Kings 8:30; 2 Chron. 30:27; Ps. 11:4; 123:1).

Hebrews says that Jesus "made the worlds" (Heb. 1:2). For each of these worlds, He also must have created thousands of solar systems to support them. The solar system in which we live has eight planets including the Earth on which we live.

In the beginning, God spoke the heavens and the earth into existence. Yet, we have no idea how many years passed, because the next verse in Genesis 1 says, "The earth was without form, and void; and darkness *was* on the face of the deep. And the Spirit of God was hovering over the face of the waters" (Gen. 1:2). No one but God knows what that form was. Yet, when God said, "Let there be light," that was the beginning of the six days of the Creation that took place six thousand years ago, since only the Bible and real science, which backs the Bible, can tell us the real story.

The Sons of God Witnessed the Creation of the Earth

After Job had gone through his trial of faith, God asked him, "Where were you when I laid the foundations of the earth? Tell *Me*, if you have understanding. Who determined its measurements? Surely you know! Or who stretched the line upon it? To what were its foundations fastened? Or who laid its cornerstone, when the morning stars sang together. And all the sons of God shouted for joy?" (Job 38:4–7). This text points out that, since the sons of God beheld the six days of the Creation, God must have created them before the six days of the Creation and the seventh-day rest, so there must have been a prior creation or prior creations.

The book of Psalms describes God's mighty act of creating: "By the word of the LORD the heavens were made, and all the host of them by the breath of His mouth.... For He spoke, and it was *done*; He commanded, and it stood fast" (Ps. 33:6, 9). The evidence from Scripture would seem to indicate that God created the galaxies before the six days of Creation. Since no one knows how many creations there were, we assume that the sons of God were made in a creation prior to the six-day Creation and seventh-day rest.

The First Creation of the Triune God: the Holy Angels

In the prior creation, God created sons of God, which included hundreds and thousands of angels. We estimate from the book of Revelation (and other passages of Scripture) that there are approximately a hundred billion angels. Revelation 5:11 says, "Then I looked, and

I heard the voice of many angels around the throne, the living creatures, and the elders; and the number of them was ten thousand times ten thousand, and thousands of thousands."

In the prior creation, when God declared, *Let there be angels*, thousands and thousands of angels came into being. Since this took place before the record of the six days of the Creation, we have no record of how God formed any of these celestial "sons of God."

The galaxy must have many solar systems like ours and many planets like ours, which was made to be inhabited (Isa. 45:18). With so many planets in the billions of solar systems in the universe, there must have been numerous sons of God created by the Creator God before the six-day Creation.

Sons of God

Job 1, verse 6, and Job 2, verse 1, say: "Now there was a day when the sons of God came to present themselves before the Lord, and Satan also came among them. ... Again there was a day when the sons of God came to present themselves before the Lord, and Satan came also among them to present himself before the Lord." These verses imply that, after the Fall, Satan represented this planet in the presence of God. Adding further evidence that the sons of God were created before the six days of the Creation.

The Creation of Lucifer

Many have weird ideas about Satan. Yet, the Bible indicates that God did not create Satan (which means "Adversary"). Rather, God created Lucifer (which means "Light Bearer"), and he was a leader of all the angels. The books of Isaiah and Ezekiel describe his fall from perfection. Ezekiel 28:12 declares: "You *were* the seal of perfection, full of wisdom and perfect in beauty." Isaiah exclaims: "How you are fallen from heaven, O Lucifer, son of the morning! ... For you have said in your heart: 'I will ascend into heaven ... on the farthest sides of the north; ... I will be like the Most High,' yet you shall be brought down to Sheol, to the lowest depths of the Pit" (Isa. 14:12–15). No, God did not create Satan, an evil angel. He created Lucifer, a beautiful angel who stood in the presence of God. Yet, Lucifer became Satan, who fell from heaven after he failed to properly understand God.

The Fall of Lucifer

Many recognize that sin entered heaven through Satan's pride about his beauty, but the way one understands this fact is different after researching the Bible and the Spirit of Prophecy on the subject. Why do people become proud? Why do they refuse to humble themselves like Jesus Christ who washed the feet of the disciples? When people do not understand themselves and do not understand that there is a power higher than themselves, their hearts are filled with pride and haughtiness. In heaven, Lucifer did not understand how the mind of the creature could synchronize with the mind of God. Jesus can talk to the first Person of the triune God through brain synchronization as well as to the third person of the triune God, the Holy Spirit. The Bible does not give any evidence that there was any mother to teach the sons of God about their father in heaven or how they came to be. Lucifer assumed that only the first Person of the triune God is the Creator. Lucifer mistakenly thought that he could be equal with Jesus Christ. This mistaken notion was what gave rise to the great controversy between Christ and Satan. Revelation the twelfth chapter gives greater detail about the war between Christ and Lucifer who became Satan because he did not want to obey the authority of Christ.

The Angels of Heaven Divided into Thirds

Revelation 12 says of Satan, who was symbolized by a dragon, "His tail drew a third of the stars of heaven" (Rev. 12:4). The Bible explains how Satan deceived one-third of the angels of heaven while two-thirds of the angels remained loyal to Jesus Christ. The book *Early Writings* gives a vivid picture of the fall of Satan and the beginning of the great controversy in heaven. "They rebelled against the authority of the Son. All the heavenly host were summoned to appear before the Father to have each case decided" (*Early Writings*, p. 146). The question is: Could God still love His creatures once rebellion had entered the universe? Yes, He loved them still and revealed His loving care and creative power by taking six days to create the earth, a tiny speck among the galaxies. So, two-thirds of the angels believed that both Jesus Christ and the Holy Spirit are God while one-third of rebellious angels believed only that the first Person of the Godhead is God. This is how sin entered heaven. When someone does not understand the Creator, he or she will go against the Creator's plan.

The First Plan of Salvation

The triune God, whom we worship, is a loving God. The Bible says plainly: "He who does not love does not know God, for God is love" (1 John 4:8). It is my understanding that the loving God formed a plan for Satan and the fallen angels. It would have gone into effect when the LORD, who created the heavens in the twinkling of an eye, took six days to create this tiny earth. He created birds with wings to teach that the angels, who also have wings, that Jesus Christ was also their Creator, for, as John declared: "All things were made through Him, and without Him nothing was made that was made" (John 1:3). Because Satan warred against Christ, the six days of the Creation were accomplished by Christ and the Holy Spirit.

When God created Adam and Eve, He gave them a crucial command concerning the tree of knowledge of good and evil, "You shall not eat it, nor shall you touch it, lest you die" (Gen. 3:3). In obeying God's word, Adam and Eve were to demonstrate, before Satan and the angels who fell from heaven with him, their acceptance of the authority of God (*Early Writings*, p. 147). Witnessing Adam and Eve's obedience, Lucifer and the fallen angels should have asked forgiveness from Jesus Christ, and they would have re-entered heaven. This is what I am calling the first plan of salvation.

The Second Plan of Salvation Was for Humanity

However, since Adam and Eve failed to obey God, the first plan of salvation was set aside as God gave Adam and Eve the first prophecy regarding the plan for the redemption of humankind. We find it immediately after the story of their fall: "And I will put enmity between you and the woman, and between your seed and her Seed; He [Jesus] shall bruise your [Satan's] head, and you shall bruise His [Jesus'] heel " (Gen. 3:15). The plan of salvation was offered to Adam and Eve through God's love and mercy. The plan of salvation for the human race was fulfilled at the cross, as Jesus bruised the head of Satan, at the very time Satan was walking "like a roaring lion" (1 Peter 5:8), seeking to destroy God's people who are under God's plan of salvation. Satan will ultimately be destroyed at the third coming of Jesus Christ.

The Six-Day Creation Only by Jesus Christ and the Holy Spirit

Since the great controversy took place between Christ and Satan, only Christ and the Holy Spirit were involved in carrying out the six-day Creation. The Bible says, "Not that anyone has seen the Father, except he who is from God; He has seen the Father" (John 6:46; cf. John 1:18; 1 John 4:12). Of all humans, Enoch, Moses, and Elijah are the exceptions, since they alone have been taken to heaven. No one else has seen the first Person of the triune God. This validates the assertion that the great controversy is between Christ and Satan. The first creation was the work of the triune God. The six-day creation of the earth was the work of Christ and the Holy Spirit (Gen. 1:1, John 1:1).

Angels Are Ministering Spirits

The purpose of God's angels is to minister to the inheritors of salvation. The book of Hebrews 1:14 says, "Are they not all ministering spirits sent forth to minister for those who will inherit salvation?" Today people are tempted to worship angels, which even John was tempted to do on the Isle of Patmos. Yet, the angel told him, "See *that you do* not *do that*! I am your fellow servant, and of your brethren who have the testimony of Jesus …" (Rev. 19:10).

Angels Are Different From Human Beings

The triune God created the angels from nothing. They are spirit beings that possess a head, hands, legs and a body, and some have six wings. They can never change their body into the flesh and bones of a human being (Isa. 6:2). When God created the angels, He created them with extraordinary powers. They can cross billions of miles of space within seconds. Even fallen angels have the ability to perform miracles, such as healing disease, walking on fire, making evil spirits appear temporarily to look like fire, telling the future with up to fifty percent accuracy. Particularly, these angels and the former chief of the angels, Lucifer, are able to make the human brain function like a digital recorder, even without our knowing what is being recorded and erased. They also have the ability to create wind and fire. They can survive without food for a long time. Yet, they cannot kill another angel; nor, for the present, can they themselves die. During the creation of the angels, God gave them their powers. All the angels—even the fallen angels have the same powers. If God once decides something, it will remain the same. Holy angels and fallen angels have no power to reproduce in any manner.

The Six Days of Creation

There are many views of the Creation story. However, the best way to understand the six-day creation story is through true science and Bible evidence.

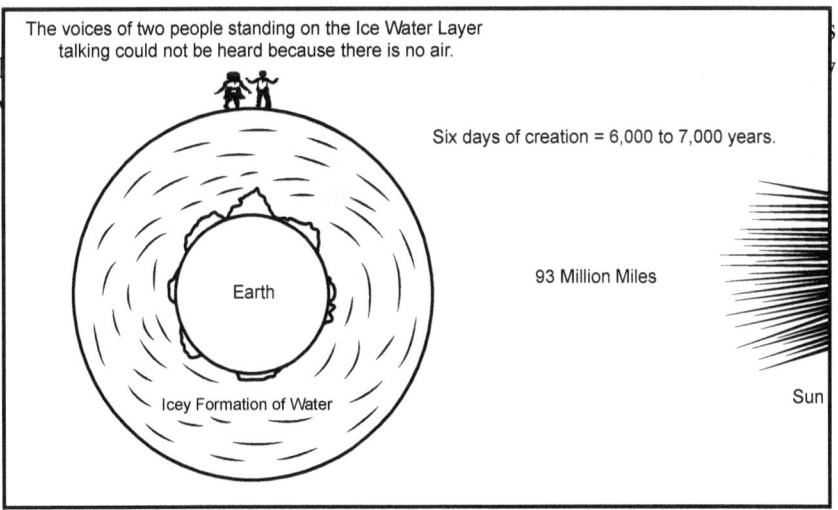

Light Without the Sun

Genesis 1:1 says, "In the beginning God created the heavens and the earth." "In the beginning" does not designate a definite time, but we know that it was before the six days of creation that the earth came into being. The six days of creation were accomplished at the start of the six thousand years. During that time, God created the solar system, which contains the sun, the moon, and the eight planets of (1) Mercury, (2) Venus, (3) Earth, (4) Mars, (5) Jupiter, (6) Saturn, (7) Uranus, and (8) Neptune. (Pluto has been disqualified from being a planet because its orbit crosses over that of Neptune.) These orbit the sun by the power of the triune God who dwells in heaven. If God were not in control of the solar system, the planets would be burnt to ashes.

How did the earth get light on the first day? When God said, "Let there be light," what happened? The simple theory is that, in the prior creation, God placed Earth beyond Pluto—that is, at 12 billion miles' distance. However, during the six days of Creation, when God said, "Let there be light," the orbit of the earth moved from 12 billion miles away from the sun to 9.3 million miles, which is the present distance. The sun started spinning at its present speed the very same instant that the earth began rotating at its present speed of 5.8 miles per second such that it takes twenty-four hours for one day and night rotation. According to Genesis 1, "God divided the light from the darkness. God called the light Day, and the darkness He called Night. So the evening and the morning were the first day" (Gen. 1:4, 5).

Heat or Light

The presence of heat on this earth is a curious matter. It is generally thought, in accordance with Charles' law, that it is the falling of sunlight on earth that produces heat. The intensity of the heat increases as the altitude increases, but due to low atmospheric pressure, the amount of heat present at higher altitudes actually drops. This view prevailed until the 1960s. However, in the late 1970s, scientists discovered that the sun's rays possess radioactive elements and concluded that these elements are the source of heat.

With the aforementioned facts in mind, we need to ask two basic questions: 1. Since the surface of the earth and its atmosphere are convex, which can only refract and produce divergent rays, how can light ever be the source of heat? 2. If the sun's rays contain radioactivity, how is it possible for aircraft to travel in earth's atmosphere?

Sunrays Have Five Directions

If these two questions make sense to you, then you may be interested in identifying the real source of heat formation.

Sunlight can travel in five ways: (1) As a ray of light, (2) as a beam of light, (3) as a parallel beam, (4) as a convergent beam, and (5) as a divergent beam.

Planet earth is orbiting the sun at a distance of 93.3 million miles. The middle of the sun reaches 220,000°C. Every second, 400,000°C of heat is produced. The light of the sun travels at 188,000 miles per second, taking eight seconds to reach the earth. The amount of heat that reaches the earth varies from 72° to 105° F. Though the sun emits

220,000°C of heat, only 72–105º F of heat reaches earth. What happens to the remaining heat?

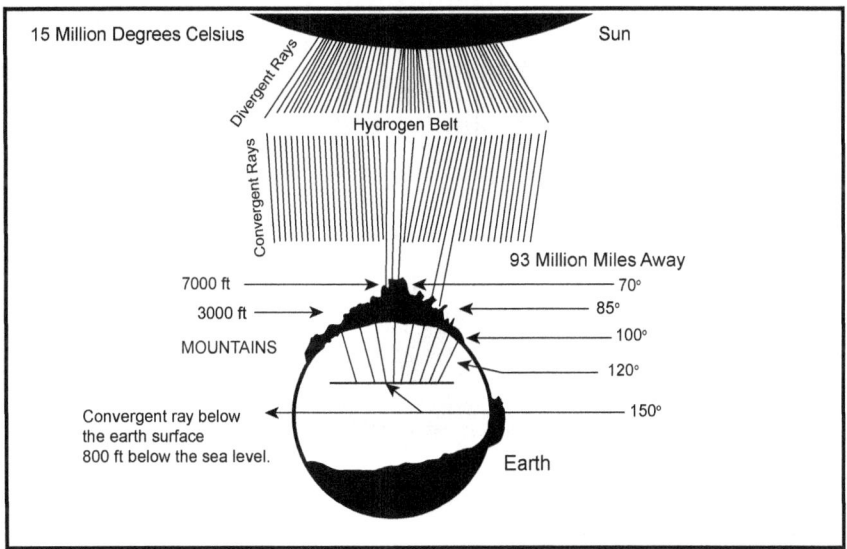

Sunrays passing through a convex lens achieve 220,000°C of heat. When Sunrays that are allowed to pass through a convex lens strike a piece of cotton at the converging point for sufficient time, the cotton will burn completely.

Divergent Rays Passing Through a Convex Lens Will Not Get Hot.

If the same convex lens is placed perpendicularly, the rays pass through and get refracted with only light and no heat. Initially, the sun produces 220,000°C heat. This passes through a hydrogen layer of gasses. The hydrogen molecules filter the heat, causing refraction of the sun's light and reducing the heat to between 72ºF and 105ºF. As the light reaches the earth's surface, the heat can increase to 96ºF at 0–800 feet above sea level, or from 120–150ºF, according to our first diagram. The oxygen layer of gasses reduces the traveling range of sunrays from 120 sq. inches to 1 sq. inch, thereby allowing the earth to get moderate heat.

70 *Amazing Truth!*

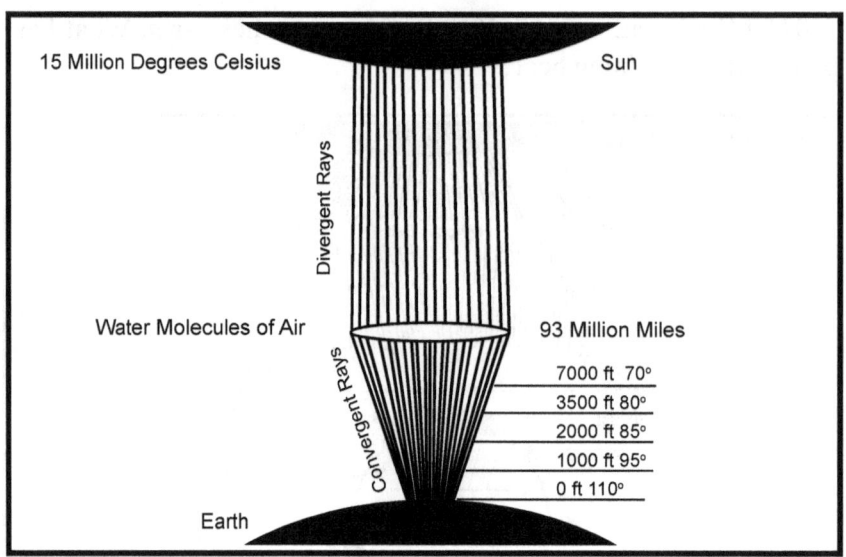

The Reflection of Sunlight

The variation in heat is due to water molecules in the air, which are acting as the medium of transport of heat in sunlight. Placing water molecules of appropriate size in the air places the converging point at a little below the sea level. Being farther from the converging point, the higher altitude has a lower temperature. Therefore, the lower temperature in higher altitudes is not due to lower atmospheric pressure.

How do we get heat? How is Charles' Law involved? We get heat through the air in the atmosphere, but, more specifically, it is through the water molecules in the air. The water molecules in the air act like a convex mirror, turning sunlight into convergent rays and transferring more heat to the earth. The God of heaven is the Creator of the water that was on this earth before the six days of creation. Furthermore, according to Charles' Law, the heat will increase as we go higher and higher. However, in some places, scientists have discovered that, due to the low pressure of the winds, the temperature will drop to 1.8°C. What is the true explanation of this phenomena? Is it possible to use these facts to prove scientifically how the earth got light from the sun in the first four days? We can call this new scientific theory "How we get heat from the sun." Presently, Charles' Law explains that, as the sunrays strike the earth, its being reflected by the refraction causes the heat from the sun. This is an erroneous application of Charles' Law and the science of physics.

Explanation of Charles' Law

Through water molecules in the air, radiant heat is formed in this earth. Until the 1970s, scientists believed, according to Charles' Law, that sunlight reflected from the earth is the source of heat. In the 1980s, scientists postulated that it is the radioactivity of sunrays that gives earth heat. What is the real answer to this quandary of science? Both theories are utterly false.

When sunlight is reflected from the earth, its rays become divergent. Divergence always decreases the amount of light and heat, as it will be defused. How do we get heat? According to a newer theory, it is the radioactivity of sunlight that causes heat. This means the sunrays gain an electric charge. However, if this is true, then how can airplanes, space shuttles, and rockets travel through the atmosphere? Will they not be burned to ashes? This challenge rebuts the second theory. Now let us explore radioactivity.

Scientific Explanation of Radioactivity

Wherever more heat is produced above 80 to 120°C more electricity will be produced. This new theory of physics is being employed in the production of electricity by burning "hardened coal" in Neyveli in the Indian state of Tamil Nadu. The sun is 220,000°C at the surface, and sunlight travels to this earth at the great speed of 186,000 miles per second. That is why scientists are postulating the presence of radioactivity in sunlight.

When sunlight, which travels at 186,000 miles per hour, reaches the earth's atmosphere, water molecules, which are composed of two hydrogen atoms and one oxygen atom, are joined together, causing the light to diverge and reducing the molecule's temperature as it reaches the earth at between 105 and 110ºF. This is evidence of the work of God. The earth is like a big round ball with a radius of 5000 miles. The convex surface area of its atmosphere contains water molecules that refract light and reduce its very high heat, allowing for cool breezes on the earth. This is the handiwork of the God of the Bible whose dwelling place is in heaven. God did not create the sun on the fourth day of His creation of six days. Rather, He created it before the six days of creation, in the period covered by Genesis 1:1. Before the six days of creation, our earth and sun were already created and that the earth orbited in the same solar system that it has been for the last 6,000 to 7,000 years. Yet, at that time, it orbited the sun beyond Pluto, at a distance of twelve billion miles. Pluto orbited the sun in darkness at a distance of more than three billion miles. At the time that God placed the earth at the very great distance of twelve billion miles away from the sun, the earth was a giant, icy ball. If it had been any closer to the sun, the ice would have melted a long time before. That is why God placed the earth so far away from the sun—even beyond Pluto.

The Solar System Hangs in the Universe

The sun is not only hanging in the universe, but it is also rotating around a central point in the heavens. The earth is rotating in the solar system at the same time that the sun is speeding through space at 150 miles per second, taking just over 360 days, or one year, to complete a single orbit around the sun. At the same time, the earth is rotating at the speed of 18.5 miles per second, with one revolution equaling one day. A Biblical year is 360 days and not 365¼ days, which I consider to be false geology and science. Not only is the solar system rotating, but so are all of the heavens. For the past thousands of years, as when it was created during God's first creation of Genesis 1:1, there are seven other solar systems rotating around heaven. *All* solar systems rotate around heaven, for God's dwelling place is the center of the universe amidst its billions of stars and galaxies.

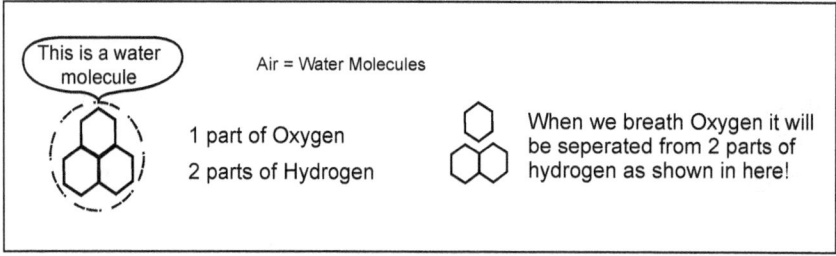

Before the First Day of the Six-day Creation by Jesus Christ

Before the week of Creation, the earth's orbit in this solar system was beyond the present orbit of Pluto. Orbiting the sun at a distance of twelve billion miles, the earth did not get sunlight and it was covered with ten miles of frozen water, which would be deep enough to cover the Himalayans.

The First Day of the Creation

As soon as the sun's light fell on the earth, the ten miles of ice on the giant ice ball began to melt. Prior to the six days of Creation, God had created the earth and its great depths of water ("the deep," Gen. 1:2). (The present shape of the earth, with its mountains, rivers, plains, and ocean depths, is the result of the global flood of Genesis). At that time, if two people holding hands stood on the ten miles of ice covering the earth and looked up, they would not have seen anything—not the sun, not the moon, and not the stars of the night. It has only been for the past thousands of years that the earth has rotated with its darkest night as the above drawing portrays.

Without the sun on the third day, how did the earth bring forth grass, herbs, and the fruit-yielding trees?

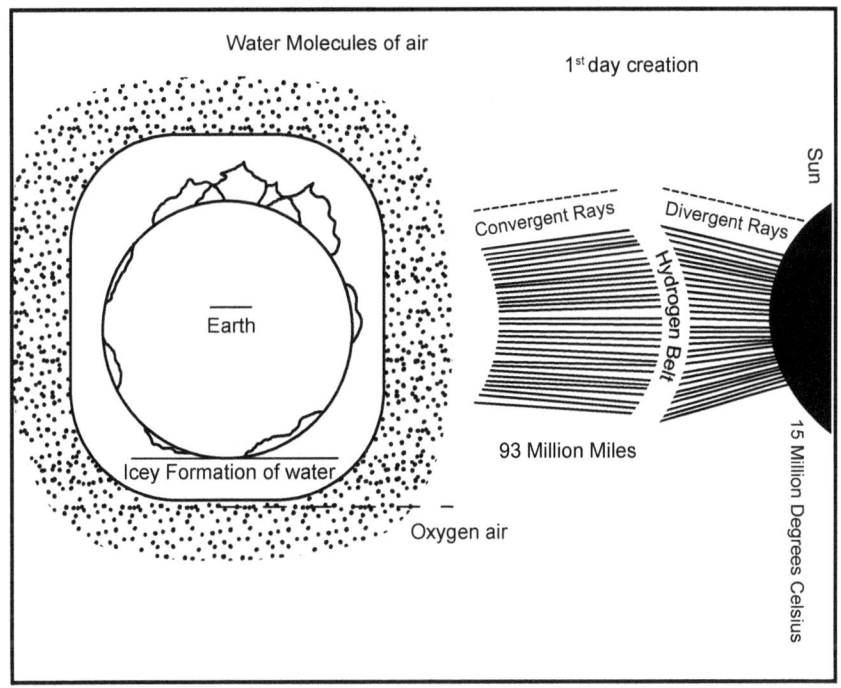

Air

Air contains water molecules. A water molecule contains two elements—oxygen and hydrogen. The air that animals breathe contains trillions and trillions of water molecules.

1. We breathe in oxygen through the nose and mouth.
2. We breathe out carbon dioxide into the air.
3. The carbon dioxide that we breathe out benefits the plants and is taken in by their leaves. In return, the leaves breathe out oxygen for our benefit. This wonderful system is evidence of the wisdom of the living God of heaven.
4. Besides hydrogen, there are other gases, like helium, argon, and nitrogen, in the atmosphere.

The Second Day of the Creation

On the second day of the Creation, as a result of heat from the proximal sunlight, all the ice covering the earth automatically melted into water molecules and some evaporated into the air as hydrogen and oxygen. On this second day of Creation, more than half of the ten miles of ice on the sphere of the earth went into the "firmament" (or atmosphere) that separated the water on earth from the water above the earth (Gen. 1:6).

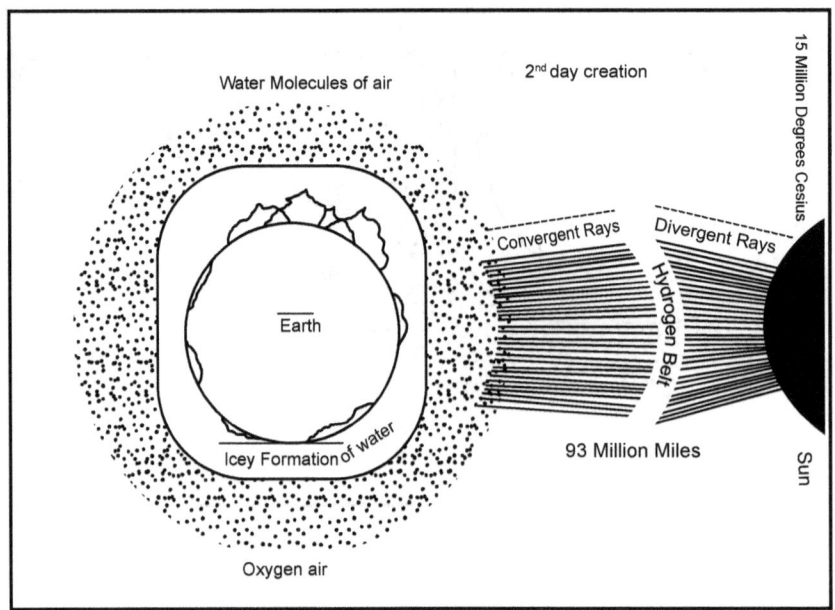

The Third Day of the Creation

Now by the third day, all the ten miles of ice water had evaporated into the air, and the land had become visible. In other places, the rest of the water was as deep as the sea and oceans. Then, once the land became visible, sunlight automatically appeared, producing heat on the second day or, in some places, on the third day. The warmth of the sunlight warmed the soil for all the seeds of the herbs, the grass, and the fruit-yielding trees to germinate. These had been kept in storage for thousands of years when God created the earth and covered it with water. That is what took place on the third day of God's creation.

Some people question how chlorophyll could be produced in earth's vegetation to give it its greenish color without there having been sunlight. The answer is that sunlight would act on the chlorophyll on the third day when all vegetation on the earth began growing.

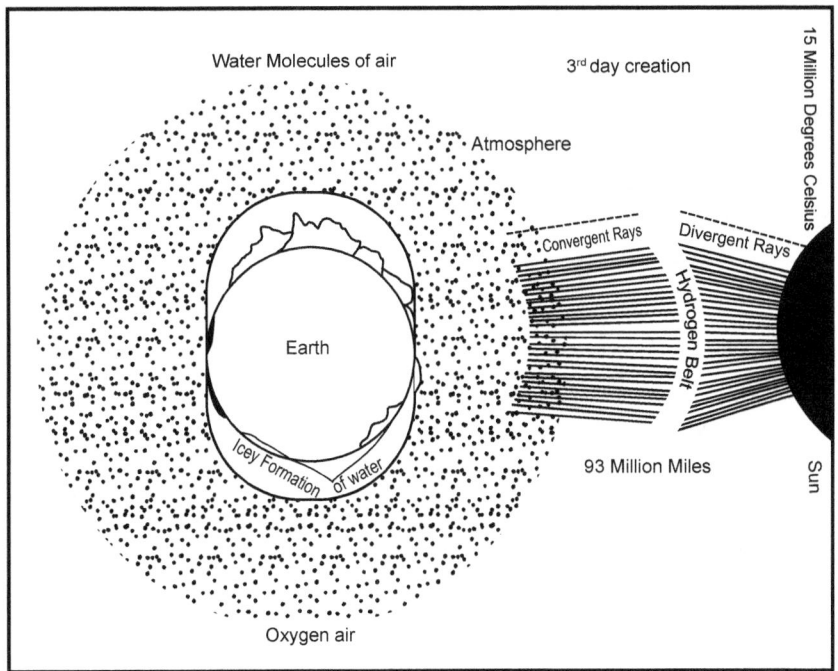

The Fourth Day of the Creation

The earth's atmosphere was created by the sun's heat as the water molecules in the air worked like a mirror, magnifying the heat. As you can see in the accompanying picture, this metaphor is consistent with true science and true knowledge about the world today. On the fourth day of Creation, water molecules in earth's atmosphere, which extended forty miles from the land upwards worked as a gigantic telescope. When the atmosphere reaches a height of 5 to 10 miles above the earth's surface, all of the water molecules of air automatically act as a gigantic telescope for humans and animals to see the moon 240,000 miles away and the sun 93.3 billion miles away. This view of the earth's "telescope" has only been understood since 1960, and it was discovered as a result of Bible study.

How do water molecules work? If we look through a convex lens, very small letters seem much bigger. Not only that but, with our atmospheric telescope, we can see things at a very great distance, such as stars that are more than 25 billion miles from the earth. We use the forty-mile deep atmosphere, with its oxygen and hydrogen, argon, radon, and other gases, like an automatic movable gigantic telescope. It came into existence on the fourth day of Creation, as revealed in the Holy Bible. Job 37:18 says, "With Him, have you spread out the skies, strong as a cast metal mirror?" This is an apt scientific explanation, in keeping with the explanation of Moses, the prophet of God, that "God created the sun, moon, and stars" on the "fourth day." Moses' statement is consistent with what we know of the natural world (Job 36:27–30; see also Jer. 10:13).

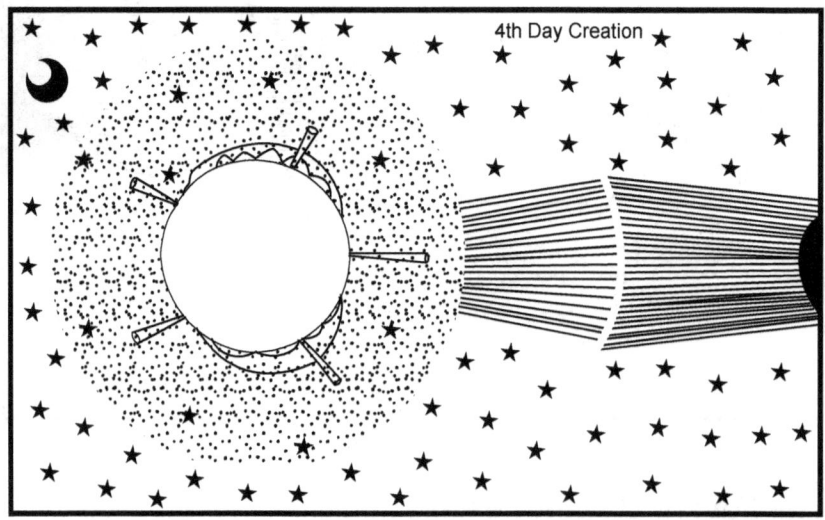

What is the Horizon?

All around the 5,000-mile diameter globe of the earth is an atmosphere of air. It was created by the God of heaven—the God of the

Bible—through a process that extended from the first to the fourth day of the creation of this world.

What is the new theory regarding human eyesight?

The Earth's Amazing Telescope

Applying this theory about the gigantic, moveable telescope, which allows us to see the sun, moon, and stars from the earth, provides new insight into physical science. This is the new theory as applied to human eyesight.

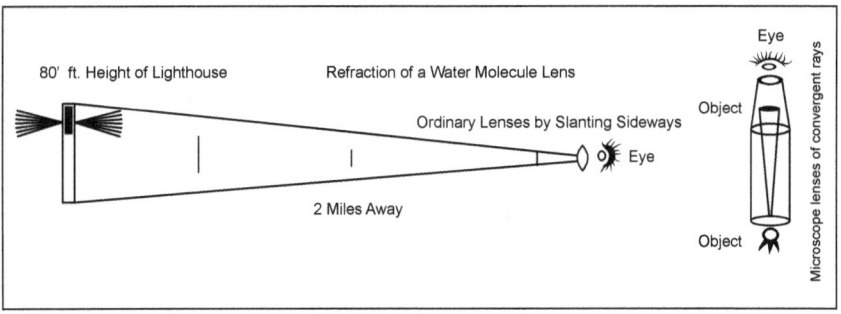

How Lightning and Thunder Occur

It is generally believed that lightning, followed by thunder, is the result of the collision of clouds with different electric charges. Clouds always have positive electricity. It is when negative electricity discharges from the earth that lightning and thunder result. This current scientific theory is wrong.

Benjamin Franklin's Theory of Lightning and Thunder

In 1753, Benjamin Franklin put forth the idea that clouds possess electricity. He drew this conclusion from an experiment he conducted in 1752 in which he experienced an electric shock while flying a kite that was connected to a bare copper wire in a lightning storm. After he invented the lightning rod, he connected a bell to the rod, which sounded every time there was a lightning storm. His experiments provided the basis for his concluding that clouds contain electricity. The result of Franklin's experiment may even be enough to convince you. Yet, in science, results must be carefully evaluated, and even smaller mistakes can lead to major problems. That is why we present our theories so others can evaluate them. If Franklin's conclusion is correct, then let us ask a basic question: If clouds carry electricity, what will happen to aircraft that go through clouds with electricity? What is the true science of lightning and thunder?

During the separation of oxygen and hydrogen, there is a time when the more volatile gases of phosphorous and methane interfere, producing lightning and thunder without an electric current. Water molecules contain two atoms of hydrogen and one atom of oxygen. During condensation, the sun's heat waves split the bonds of the water molecules, separating the hydrogen atoms from the oxygen atom. During this time of separation, if the combustible gases of methane or phosphorous come in contact with the separation point, the water molecules are vigorously separated, producing enormous heat and light with great sound and electricity. The pattern of visible light can be miles long in the sky.

Lightning, Thunder, and Rain

The present theory of physics says that clouds have positive electricity while the earth has negative electricity. Yet, what would happen if an aircraft went through the clouds if they had a positive current? It would mean that any aircraft traveling through the clouds should be burned up. However, so far, nothing like that has happened. Aircraft travel through the clouds safely.

Water molecules in the air are made up of three atoms, one of them is oxygen and the other two are hydrogen. However, air also contains carbon dioxide, methane, phosphorus, radon, argon, and other gases. So, how do we get rain? What is the present scientific theory of rain?

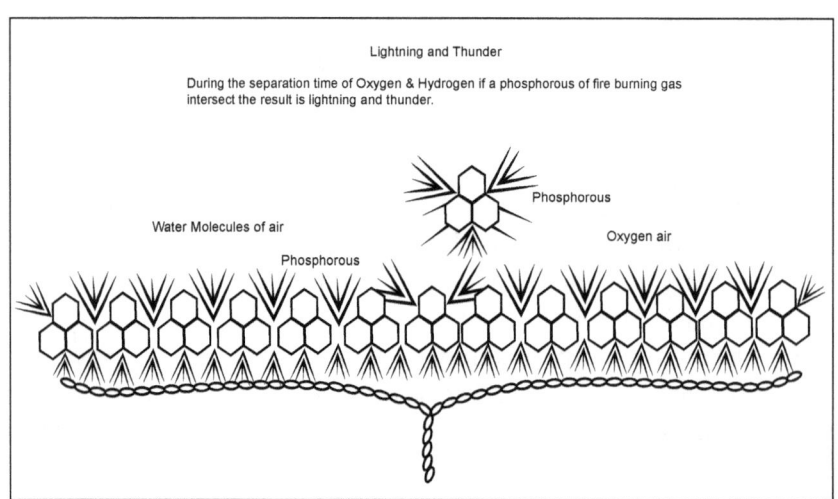

Lightning and Thunder
During the separation time of Oxygen & Hydrogen if a phosphorous of fire burning gas intersect the result is lightning and thunder.

The true theory is that getting rain requires hot and cold air. Sunlight falls upon the water and produces vapor in the form of clouds. Then, as the clouds cool, the water condenses and we get rain. This is a completely erroneous theory, as propagated by schoolteachers and college professors. If this theory is true, then wherever clouds are cooled, that area should get rain. Then why, in the Himalayas and in the Tundra, do they get snow instead of rain? The present theory does not properly answer the question.

1. For snow to fall: During the period of snowfall in the Himalayas and in the Tundra, water molecules in the air get cold and freeze, turning all the water molecules into ice balls of snow. As these fall from the clouds, they are called snowfall.

2. For rain to fall: At the same time, clouds contain hot gasses like argon and radon. The ice balls in the clouds, melt, become water droplets, and fall as rain. The true theory of rain is that, when hot air and cold air are mixed together, then rain falls from the clouds. This conclusion needs to be made clear for scientists and the general populace.

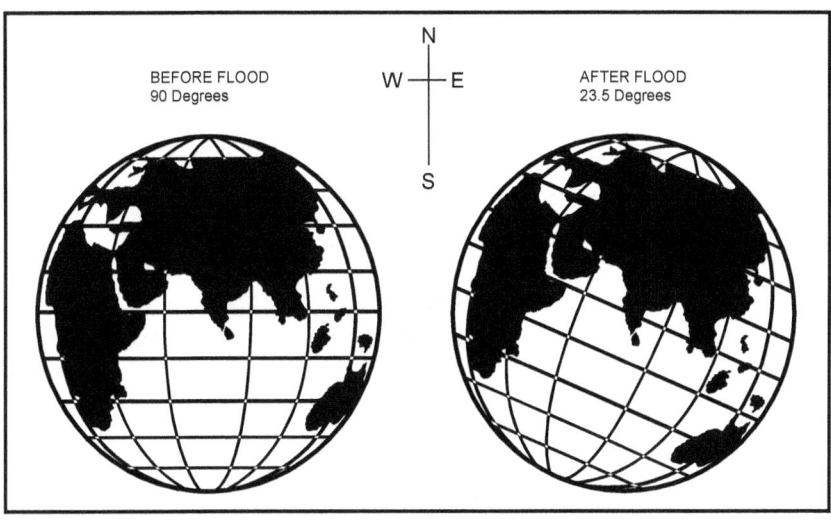

How many gases in the world have been discovered thus far? Who created the gases of this earth? Due to the shift in the earth's tilt, from 90º to 23½º, God created sixty-nine new types of gases. God produced different types of gases through His natural laboratory. God's action of tilting the earth (Heb. 12:27, 28), together with the high speed of the earth's revolution—about 1,000 miles per hour—created a very large vacuum above the earth. The vacuum is a very high-pressure area that is mixed with the oxygen and carbon dioxide layer. When hydrogen is pulled by this vacuum, the same rays of the sun, which penetrated the hydrogen molecules, quickly heat up to more than 2000°C and produce a spark that travels the vacuum gap of nearly 1500 to 2500 miles, and the mixture of gases produces another sixty-nine types of gases.

On the fifth day, God created carbon dioxide on the earth as the animals that inhabited the water and the air breathed out carbon dioxide. Then, the grass and green leaves of the trees and other plants, which were brought into the world on the third day, breathed in the carbon dioxide and produced oxygen for the animals.

Helium, argon, radon, and methane are the heat-producing agents. There are other cooler gases. These were created by the living God of heaven in that one day. The meeting of hot and cold gases produces rain on the earth. This is true science.

How does the rainbow appear in the sky? According to Newton's law, was there a rainbow before the Flood?

This is the fifth new scientific theory, and it concerns the physics of the rainbow. According to Newton's law, sunlight has color and that is the source of rainbows. However, the physics behind rainbows has long been a matter of controversy between theologian and scientist. Scientists have held that the sun's rays contain various colors that produce the rainbow.

Newton's law says that sunlight inherently has seven colors and that rainbows would have been manifest before the Flood. Newton put forward two experiments to determine whether sunlight has the capability to produce the colors of a rainbow.

In the first experiment, he rotated, at great speed, a disc that was painted with seven colors. During its rotation, only one color was visible.

In the second experiment, Newton held up a "prism" to let sunlight pass through it. The light that exited the prism is divided into seven colors. We offer the following experiment as a challenge to the false scientific theory.

1. We place a glass chamber with a prism at its center and, at the exit end of the glass chamber, there is a projection screen. When sunlight is allowed to pass from the other end through the prism, it comes out on the projection screen as seven bands of colored light.

This same experiment was repeated with a vacuum in the glass chamber. The results were the same as in the previous experiment.

Next, the source of light was changed. Rather than sunlight, candlelight was used. The results were the same as with the sunlight.

A torchlight was used as the source, and there was no change in the results.

The following conclusion can be drawn from the experiment.

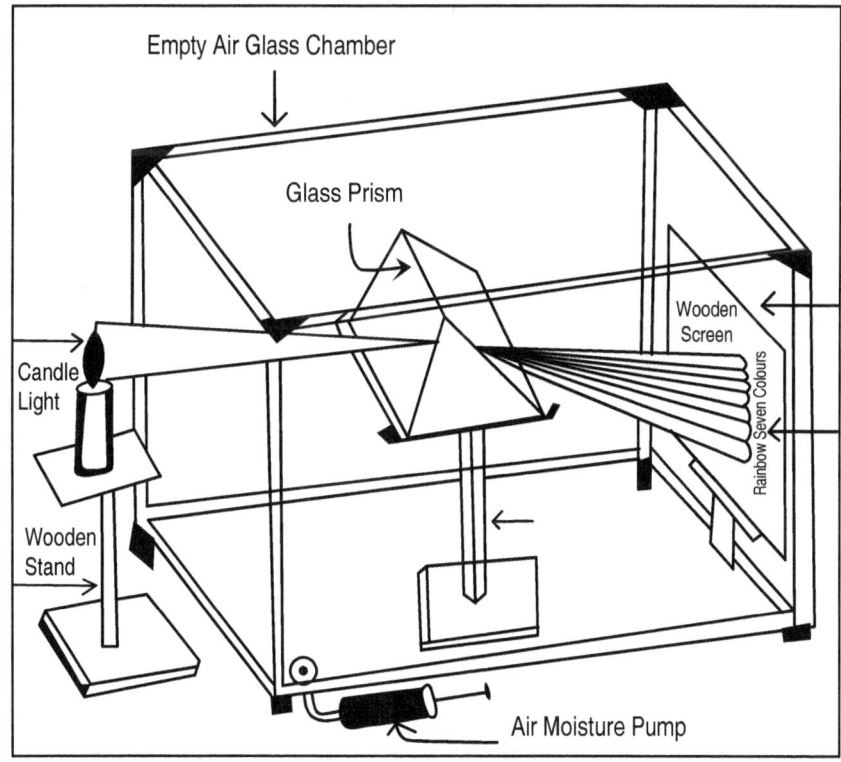

Since sunlight, candlelight, and torchlight produced similar results, it clearly reveals that it is the prism that divides the light into seven colors, irrespective of the source. but not the Newton theory of about sunlight having seven colors.

The true theory of physics is that sunlight has no colors but only heat and that it is the prism that converts sunlight into divergent rays, producing seven colors.

Hence, by these true physics of rain and the rainbow, there was no rain or rainbow before the Flood in 2503 BC.

How We Are Able to See Things at Different Distances

Because water molecules function as very tiny lenses, we cannot see parallel more than two miles or three miles. This would include the very highest pillar or tower even three to four miles away. This is because we see through the edges of each water molecule lens. However, when we look directly upward through the water molecule lenses in the atmosphere, we can see the sun, the moon, and the stars—some of which are nine billion miles away.

When the 24-hour Day Starts and Ends
The day starts every evening at sunset, not at 12 o'clock midnight.

According to Genesis 1, "So the evening and the morning were the first day ... the second day ... the third day ... the fourth day ... the fifth day ... the sixth day" (Gen. 1:5, 8, 13, 19, 23, 31). Then, "on the seventh day, God ended his work which He had done, and He rested on the seventh day from all His work which He had done" (Gen. 2:2). Yet, according to Genesis 1:1, the earth was created to orbit the sun without sunlight falling on it. During the first day of Creation, God allowed the sun's rays to fall upon our earth. This light portion of the 24-hour cycle God called "day." The twelve hours of the earth's rotation when it was in darkness God called "night." For this reason, a day runs from evening to morning—not from midnight to midnight. Not only is the midnight to midnight definition of a day not biblical, but observing Christmas every December 24th at midnight is also not biblical.

God's Amazing Design of the Human Brain
Our brain contains numberless neurons, or nerve cells. No one has been able to make neurons grow. The neurons in our brains work like photocells in a system for digital recording—down our backbone from our head to our leg. The neurons control everything about the body—how we run, how we think, our emotions, our speech, and our reproductive system. The individual movements of our body parts—of our legs, our hands, and every other part of our body—all are controlled by our "motor neurons." Neurons are entirely different from the 182 other types of cells in our bodies. These unique cells are why we humans are different from the other living creatures in the world—and even different from the heavenly angels. Our neurons cannot be divided, and they will not fuse with any of the other 182 types of living cells in our bodies. Brain neurons may die from Alzheimer's disease or a traumatic head injury. That is why no one in the world has been able to stimulate the production of new neurons in the brain.

The Brain as a Digital Recorder

There are photo cells in the brain that work like digital recorders. What we read and see is recorded in the photocells of our brains. In other words, every activity is recorded in the brain by these cells. These cells are 1/50th as thick as a hair. Their length is several miles long. Their total size is that of a cricket ball, weighing about .075 kilograms. When you try to think or remember certain incidents, these cells quickly retrieve the memory of the incident as a picture that is relayed to a small TV-like screen in our brain. Neither animals nor angels have this precise system. Jesus Christ, the second Person of the triune God, created the first man, Adam, from the miry clay. He created him in His own image, likeness, and bodily shape. Best of all, He patterned man's brain after His. We should never forget these things.

The cerebellum is the switchboard of the brain. By the orders of the cerebellum, the brain functions like a digital recorder, capturing sensory information within a second and relaying the sequence of information to the small TV-like screen in our brain in an activity called "thinking."

The brain can be steered by four powers:
1. We have control over our own brain, as was mentioned above.
2. The God of heaven has control over the recording our brain does. Therefore, He can give visions that are recorded in our brain bypassing our will.
3. Similarly, God has given our individual guardian angels control over our brain when He wishes.
4. Finally, Lucifer and his hosts of fallen angels can also control the brain by means of miracles, like the healing of the sick, walking on fire, fortune telling, bringing fire down from heaven. In spite of this power, he can never control the minds of men and women who fear and worship God faithfully. Therefore, Satan and his companions can never overcome the true children of God in any way. Every Christian should always remember this very important truth about the limit of Satan's power.

The Brain Thinks—Not the Heart

No human being understands the correct and real meaning of the holy Ten Commandments of God. We are very sorry to say that none of us has known the seventh sense fully. In using only five of our senses, our knowledge operates at the level of the animals. The sixth and seventh senses separate us from the animals. If we do not know or utilize the seventh sense, we will be leading an animal life. All but the seventh sense—regarding the holy Ten Commandments of God—can be gained in modern universities. Yet, one cannot get the seventh sense from any university. You cannot obtain it from books. Many Christian universities teach biblical theology. Yet, none have fully understood the holy Ten Commandments except the Seventh-day Adventist universities. Other Christian universities teach that the holy Ten Commandments of God were nailed to the cross. In one way it may be true that their knowledge is lower than that of the animals, for even animals do not have any knowledge of killing, raping, or committing adultery (taking one's neighbor's wife). Any theologian teaching against these Ten Commandments (which is the seventh sense) operates below the animals. Yet, some leaders and pastors in the Seventh-day Adventist Church also preach that we cannot keep the Ten Commandments now. But we can go to heaven by the grace of Jesus Christ. Doing so means that there is no actual difference between them and the other Protestant theologians.

Chapter 5

God's Church During the Former and Latter Rain

Many people have great confusion about the work of the Holy Spirit—especially with reference to the former and latter rain. Today, post-modern churches hold different views about God the Holy Spirit and His work. Thousands are deceived because they have not gotten a clear understanding of the truth about this subject from the Bible. In this chapter, we are going to study about God the Holy Spirit, who is the third Person of the triune God, how He guided God's people throughout the Bible, and how the two comings of the Holy Spirit empower the church to this day.

From the book of Genesis to the book of Revelation, the Bible talks about God the Holy Spirit. Genesis 1 says, "The earth was without form, and void; and darkness *was* on the face of the deep. And the Spirit of God was hovering over the face of the waters" (Gen. 1:2). Throughout biblical history, we see how Jesus Christ (1 Cor. 10:1–4) and God the Holy Spirit have worked together (Rev. 2:7). In the book of Revelation, the Holy Spirit speaks even to us, "He who has an ear, let him hear what the Spirit says ..." (Rev. 2:7, 11, 17, 29; 3:6, 13, 22). The prophet Joel speaks about the former and the latter rain as two special comings of the Holy Spirit. Jesus also will have had a first and a second coming. Christ came to offer himself as a sacrifice for the human race at His first coming. Immediately thereafter, God the Holy Spirit came to empower the church in carrying Christ's message of the gospel to the world.

The prophecy about the former and the latter rain says: "And it shall come to pass afterward that I will pour out My Spirit on all flesh; your sons and your daughters shall prophesy. Your old men shall dream dreams. Your young men shall see visions. And also on My menservants and My maidservants, I will pour out My Spirit in those days. And I will show wonders in the heavens and in the earth; blood and fire pillars of smoke. The sun shall be turned into darkness. And the moon into blood; before the coming of the great and awesome day of the LORD" (Joel 2:28–31).

Meaning of the Former Rain

Christ articulated a great vision concerning the harvesting of the church as a result of the resurrection of Jesus Christ. The disciples grasped this concept as we see in James' beautiful description of the early and latter rain. James wrote: "Therefore be patient, brethren, until the coming of the Lord. See *how* the farmer waits for the precious fruit of the earth, waiting patiently for it until it receives the early and latter rain" (James 5:7). James compared the Christian's expectation of the harvest brought about by the Holy Spirit to the farmer's expectation of rainfall upon his field, and he asks that we exercise patience in our impatient world. The former rain helped the crops to begin growing (and also ripened the spring grain harvest), and the latter rain helps produce a better harvest of grain in the fall. The first coming of the Holy Spirit helped to germinate what Jesus taught His disciples. With this goal, Jesus promised His disciples that He was going to send them the Comforter, who would teach them all things (John 14:26). Thus, when they started the ministry of the New Testament church, the guidance of the Holy Spirit was vigorously poured out. This is what is known as the "former rain." In the same way, the latter rain will prepare the world field for the harvest that comes at the end of the church period.

The Former Rain, AD 31—100

Immediately following the death of the Savior, the disciples lost hope in His mission. However, after the Saviour's resurrection and ascension to heaven, hope returned, and they were filled with the Holy Spirit. Jesus had said: "Behold, I send the Promise of My Father upon you; but tarry in the city of Jerusalem until you are endued with power from on high" (Luke 24:49). Peter declared: "But this is what was spoken by the prophet Joel: *'And it shall come to pass in the last days, says God, That I will pour out of My Spirit on all flesh ...*" (Acts 2:16, 17). The beginning of the former rain started on the fiftieth day after Passover, which is Pentecost. On that day, God the Holy Spirit gave them extra power and strength to preach the resurrected Lord Jesus. Peter spoke to the crowd, and everyone heard in his or her own tongue. Acts 2:6, 7 says, "And when this sound occurred, the multitude came together, and were confused, because everyone heard them speak in his own language. Then they were all amazed and marveled, saying to one another, 'Look, are not all these who speak Galileans?'" In other words, when Peter spoke, and the other disciples repeated his message, everyone present understood the message in their own respective language. Acts 2:9–11 says that more than sixteen language groups were present that day, yet everyone understood what was proclaimed. This phenomenon is the hallmark of the former rain.

After this, the Apostles performed great miracles, such as the healing of the lame so they could walk, of those born blind that they could see, the raising of the dead, and the casting out of devils, as well as many other marvels. Though the church was being persecuted at this time, every word of Christ was also being fulfilled, such as, " 'And these signs will follow those who believe: In My name they will cast out demons; they will speak with new tongues; they will take up serpents; and if they drink anything deadly, it will by no means hurt them; they will lay hands on the sick, and they will recover'" (Mark 16:17, 18).

A major product of the former rain was the writing of the New Testament, twenty-seven books written by eight inspired authors (cf. 2 Tim. 3:16). The Holy Spirit inspired them. Some received direct visions, while others carefully collected information under the guidance of the Holy Spirit (see Luke 1:1–4). (For details regarding the authors of each book, see Chapter 1.)

Timeline of the Apostles

The apostles followed all of Jesus' instructions. In particular, they were not confused about obedience to God's law. The apostle John wrote: "And whatever we ask we receive from Him, because we keep His commandments and do those things that are pleasing in His sight" (1 John 3:22). The apostle Peter was bold enough to answer the religious authorities, "we ought to obey God rather than men" (Acts 5:29). Jesus' original eleven disciples (which means "followers," or "students") became His apostles (which means "missionaries," or "sent out ones"). On the day of Pentecost, one hundred and twenty followers of Jesus united in fasting and prayer for the gift of the Holy Spirit and ended up shaking Jerusalem and the surrounding towns.

The pen of inspiration shares that others besides Peter and Paul raised the dead and performed great miracles that are not mentioned in the New Testament. Every day God the Holy Spirit guided them to preach the gospel, and first three thousand and then five thousand souls were added to the church. They preached with authority and commanded the people to trust in God and to be truthful to Him. When Ananias and Sapphire lied to the Holy Spirit, they died before the One they thought to deceive (Acts 5; cf. Matt. 12:32).

The early believers were able to forgive others' sins. "If you forgive the sins of any, they are forgiven them; if you retain the *sins* of any, they are retained" (John 20:23). This was in keeping with Jesus' statement, "Whatever you bind on earth will have been bound in heaven: and whatever you loose on earth shall have been loosed in heaven" (Matt. 18:18, CSB).

Understanding the Work of God and the Holy Spirit

After the Apostles received the power of the Holy Spirit, they lived authentic lives and, for the first time, were called "Christians" in the city of Antioch (Acts 11:26). The work of God the Holy Spirit continued throughout the rest of the Bible. However, this special work required the ascension of Jesus Christ. This work required not only preaching and healing but, in a Greek-speaking world, it also required the earlier translation of the Old Testament from Hebrew and Aramaic into Greek. The Holy Spirit enabled the ministry of the Apostles and the bishops, such as Timothy and Titus, and guided their thoughts that they might write the New Testament books of the Bible. Matthew, Mark, Luke, and John wrote the Gospels; James and others wrote

Chapter 5 God's Church During the Former and Latter Rain

their epistles. The Revelation of John, written during his banishment to the Isle of Patmos, is itself a very large epistle. Owing to the faithful and extraordinary work of the Apostles among the people in Antioch, the apostles were for the first time called "Christians," because all they wanted to talk about was "Christ"—the Messiah.

Until the nineteenth century, such power and the explosive spread of the gospel would not be seen again on the face of the earth. This pointed to the divine source of guidance and power within the movement. Since the apostles obeyed God's holy words and laws, they were able to perform miracles, but not in the way that we see miracles performed today. The church was united, and they were of one accord. Even the deacons were filled with the Holy Spirit, and their ministries were powerful. Stephen preached a powerful message in Jerusalem, and, tragically, he was stoned to death and became the first martyr. Nonetheless, the word of God spread like wildfire. Christians were filled with zeal and shared the gospel story throughout the world, and it was during this time that they collected the thirty-nine books of the Old Testament from synagogues, dungeons, palaces, treasuries, and caves in different countries.

In fulfillment of biblical prophecy, the persecution took place in AD 34 as the Jewish people in Jerusalem stoned Stephen while Saul of Tarsus, who would become the famous apostle Paul, stood by watching. In response to the persecution begun by the stoning of Stephen in AD 34, the Apostles and the new believers in Christ fled from Jerusalem to many other countries. They took their sacred Bible and kept it safe in many places. By the power of the early rain of the Holy Spirit, all 39 of the books of the Old Testament were collected and systematically copied and preserved in different countries. At the same time, after the dispersion of the Christians, many false prophets arose and wrote without the guidance of the Holy Spirit. Today we call them apocryphal writings, which means "hidden" or "doubtful." (These writings should not be confused with the seven books of the Apocrypha in the Catholic Bible, which were written in Greek before the coming of Christ.)

But God has been faithful in preserving His Word. The Bible has been preserved throughout the centuries and, even when it was not available to the people, God was faithful in sharing His love in many ways. The Septuagint was translated by seventy scholars who carefully studied the Bible and separated the Apocrypha, or doubtful books written in Greek, from the true books written in Hebrew. At the same time, they were unable to assign authorship and put them in chronological order. In the Middle Ages, the Albigenses, the Waldenses, and the Huguenots gave their lives to preserve God's Word. God raised "the Morning Star of the Reformation," John Wycliffe, and then William Tyndale, in AD 1430. These two men translated the Bible into the English language. Much of the wording of the Tyndale version is carried over into the King James Version from AD 1611 that is still in use. Many other reformers arose after John Wycliffe, translating the Bible into several other languages.

The Importance of the Latter Rain

The former and the latter rain are a dual prophecy. (You can read about dual prophecy in the section on one hundred and eighty prophecies.) The Scriptures say: "And it shall come to pass afterward that I will pour out My Spirit on all flesh; your sons and your daughters shall prophesy, your old men shall dream dreams, your young men shall see visions. And also on *My* menservants and on *My* maidservants I will pour out My Spirit in those days. And I will show wonders in the heavens and in the earth: blood and fire and pillars of smoke. The sun shall be turned into darkness, and the moon into blood, before the coming of the great and awesome day of the Lord" (Joel 2:28–31).

Part of the prophecy was fulfilled at the time of the apostles, but the rest is yet to be fulfilled. God promised that, when He shows "wonders in the heavens and in the earth," He will pour out the latter rain. Jesus also predicted what would take place in the last days in Matthew, the 24th chapter. These great signs took place in the nineteenth century.

The sun was darkened on May 19, 1780, and the moon became blood red on the same night, and the stars fell on November 13, 1833. The star shower was seen from West Germany to Mexico and was recorded in numerous newspapers and encyclopedias. After the fulfillment of this prophecy, a Baptist preacher named William Miller preached the nearness of the Second Advent of Christ. This proclamation was the roaring of the lion of Revelation 10. Three thousand pastors of the sixth church period of Revelation—the Philadelphia church—caught the vision of God and Christ's return from their study of Daniel 8:14 and the 2300-day prophecy. Though they misunderstood the "cleansing" described in the prophecy and experienced the great disappointment of 1844, they revived the sense of the imminence of Christ's return within Christianity.

With the outpouring of the latter rain came signs and wonders, and God called people who feared Him to bring Christians back to the sixty-six books of the Bible. Among those called to do this work were Ellen G. White, Joseph Bates, James White, Uriah Smith, J. N. Andrews, and Hiram Edson. Through messages received through visions and dreams from God, Ellen G. White called the people back to the teachings of God's Word. This was the beginning of the proclamation of the Laodicean message. Central to this message was the exposition of the books of Daniel and Revelation. Just as the book of Daniel predicted, knowledge of God's Word had increased (Dan. 12:4). Yet, it was not merely biblical and prophetic knowledge that increased but also technological knowledge as well. (I will list some of the inventions of this period later in this book.)

The Advent Movement continued as a group of those who passed through the great disappointment searched the Bible to understand what they had misunderstood about Daniel 8:14, which says, "And he said to me, 'For two thousand three hundred days: then the sanctuary shall be cleansed.' While searching this truth, they also discovered other great truths, such as the Sanctuary, the state of the dead, the Second Coming, the sacredness of God's Law and the Sabbath. Through the help of the latter rain, they were given the wisdom to understand the prophecies and to expound upon the sixty-six books of the Bible. Under the former rain, the apostles drew meaning from the Old Testament, under the latter rain, God's faithful will be able to explain the whole Bible.

Miracles Attributed to the Holy Spirit

Pentecostal churches perform miracles; some Protestant churches also perform miracles in the name of Jesus and the Holy Spirit; millions of Roman Catholics perform miracles in the name of Mary, in the name of the "infant Jesus", in the name of the apostles, or in the name of the Catholic saints. These various Christians perform the miracle of healing in public places as a charismatic movement.

Jim Bakker taught the healing power of the Spirit and hosted a popular television show on which thousands of miracles were said to be performed. Back in the 1980s, his following numbered in the thousands and he operated the 2400-acre "Heritage USA" theme park, water park, and residential complex. A US court convicted Jim Bakker on twenty-four counts of mail and wire fraud, defrauding followers of $158 million for partnerships in the PTL ministry's Heritage USA. He had previously been disgraced by a sex and hush money scandal. His 45-year prison sentence was vacated, and he ended up serving four years. After the ordeal, he asked the forgiveness of those he had wronged: "I want to humbly ask for forgiveness to those I have offended or hurt in any way by my sin and arrogant lifestyle." Do these scandals help us to believe in the miracles performed under his ministry? He himself said in one interview that those who performed miracles on his show "lived like profligates."

What is the explanation for these miracle workers? Is it possible to perform miracles and not be walking with God?

Jesus said, "Many will say to Me in that day, 'Lord, Lord, have we not prophesied in Your name, cast out demons in Your name, and done many wonders in Your name?' And then I will declare to them, 'I never knew you; depart from Me, you who practice lawlessness!" (Matt. 7:22, 23).

The simple truth is that, at the time of the former rain, the apostles were obeying God's law, and they were filled with the Holy Spirit and performed miracles. The same conditions exist during the time of the Laodicean church—the last church before Jesus comes. John wrote: "Here is the patience of the saints; here *are* those who keep the commandments of God and the faith of Jesus" (Rev. 14:12). Sadly, all these vehement proclaimers of the gospel are not willing to accept the law of God as the foundation of God's kingdom. If someone is not willing to accept God's moral law yet performs miracles in the name of Christ, then we can know that the power is not coming from Christ. If the healing is not coming from Christ, then we can figure out where it's coming from.

Lucifer can do the following miracles:

- He can enable those who do not have a child to get a child.
- He can heal cancer, leukemia, and leprosy.
- He can enable people to walk on burning hot coals without it harming their feet.
- He can enable a person to stand on piercing needles with his bare feet without pain or bleeding.
- He can even temporarily deliver men, women, and children under satanic possession from his power.
- He cannot heal those who were born blind or lame.
- He can enable people to temporarily heal those who are

Chapter 5 God's Church During the Former and Latter Rain

possessed and troubled by a demonic spirit, by placing on their body a Bible or a cross made out of wood, steel, or even ordinary cardboard or paper. Once controlling their body, the demonic spirit will come out with shrieks, and they will be delivered temporarily, leaving people to think that the Bible or the cross of Jesus has supernatural power. Such miracles of Satan have deceived many human beings within Christendom.

The Scriptures warn us about the miraculous works of the evil one.

- Paul wrote: "And no wonder! For Satan himself transforms himself into an angel of light" (2 Cor. 11:14).
- Jesus told His disciples, "For false christs and false prophets will rise and show great signs and wonders to deceive, if possible, even the elect" (Matt. 24:24).
- Jesus also warned, "Then many false prophets will rise up and deceive many" (Matt. 24:11).
- Peter warned about false teachers and destructive heresies (2 Peter 2:1, 2).
- John warned believers about antichrists (1 John 2:18).
- Paul talked about "the man of sin," "the mystery of lawlessness," and "the working of Satan" (2 Thess. 2:3–10).
- John warned: "every spirit that does not confess that Jesus Christ has come in the flesh is not of God ..." (1 John 4:3).
- Paul wrote about "deceiving spirits and doctrines of demons" (1 Tim. 4:1). Today we can see the works of the devil in nearly every church in the world.

Yet, no one, without God, can do the following:

- They cannot raise the dead to life as Peter did and as Paul described.
- They cannot cause severed fingers to grow back again.
- They cannot give eyesight to those born blind nor the ability to walk to those born lame (John 10:21).
- They cannot stop cyanide poisoning or the venom of a snakebite from causing death.
- They cannot bring back to life those who were burned to death by fire.
- They cannot reattach leaves that have been plucked from a tree.

If anyone in the world is doing any of the above-mentioned miracles, then you can know that God the Holy Spirit is present and the miracles are performed through His power.

Conclusion: The guidance of the Holy Spirit exists in Scripture from Genesis to Revelation, yet, like the two comings of Jesus Christ, there are to be two comings of the Holy Spirit. These are the former rain, during the time of the seventh and final church. The purpose of the former rain of the Holy Spirit was to fulfill the Bible writings and that of the latter rain is to explain the whole Bible. Does God's Holy Spirit still guide us like Jesus Christ did when He was on earth? Yes, He does. Zechariah 10:1 says, "Ask the LORD for rain in the time of the latter rain. The LORD will make flashing clouds; He will give them showers of rain, grass in the field for everyone."

Chapter 6
Seven Holy Ordinances

Only the Bible defines that which is holy and that which is not. The Lord is very faithful in sharing the holy ordinances in the Holy Bible. The Bible gives seven holy ordinances, which we are going to study in this chapter. Humble yourself before the Lord that He may give you understanding on this subject.

The First Holy Ordinance is Marriage.

Genesis 2:18 says, "And the Lord God said, '*It is* not good that man should be alone; I will make him a helper comparable to him." God desired that Adam have a matching companion. Genesis 2:22, 23 tells how God made Eve and what Adam said in response: "Then the rib which the Lord God had taken from man He made into a woman, and He brought her to the man. And Adam said: 'This *is* now bone of my bones and flesh of my flesh; she shall be called Woman, because she was taken out of Man.' " God instituted holy marriage between Adam and Eve on the sixth day of Creation. Today God wants marriage to be holy and undefiled. The Bible gives seven admonitions regarding marriage.

1. We should not choose our life partner from unbelievers.

    2 Corinthians 6:14 says, "Do not be unequally yoked together with unbelievers." Marriage from outside of the faith brings calamity and sadness in life. If we select unbelievers to wed, the whole marriage life may be miserable.

2. Choose a good woman or man.

    Proverbs 31:10 asks, "Who can find a virtuous wife? For her worth *is* far above rubies." It is a very important step to marry a good woman or a godly man. Deuteronomy 22:13–30 describes the laws of marriage.

3. The married couple should be separated from their parents.

    Genesis 2:24 says, "Therefore a man shall leave his father and mother and be joined to his wife" after they are married.

4. Husbands should honor their wife.

    1 Peter 3:7 says, "Husbands, likewise, dwell with *them* with understanding, giving honor to the wife, as to the weaker vessel, and as *being* heirs together of the grace of life, that your prayers may not be hindered." The Bible calls the woman a "weaker vessel," so the man should take care of his wife. Of the wife, the Bible says, "Your desire *shall* be for your husband, and he shall rule over you" (Gen. 3:16). According to these two verses, the man should treat his wife with understanding and a woman's affections should be for her husband, whom she should accept as leader of the home.

5. Spouses should honor each other.

    God plainly explained that the husband and wife should render to each other due benevolence. "Let the husband render to his wife the affection due her, and likewise also the wife to her husband" (1 Cor. 7:3). Throughout their lifetime, such affection between husband and wife is essential.

6. Spouses should stay together.

    God said that, after getting married, the wife should not depart from her husband. However, if she does leave, she should remain unmarried or be reconciled to her husband, and the husband should not put away his wife.

Divorce and Remarriage

"Now to the married I command, *yet* not I but the Lord: A wife is not to depart from *her* husband. But even if she does depart, let her remain unmarried or be reconciled to *her* husband. And a husband is not to divorce *his* wife" (1 Cor. 7:10, 11).

According to the verses above, a husband should not divorce his wife and the wife should be reconciled to her husband. God ordained that marriage in His church be holy. When Paul writes about remarriage, it is in the context of the death of one's spouse.

1 Corinthians 7:39 says, "A wife is bound by law as long as her husband lives; but if her husband dies, she is at liberty to be married to whom she wishes, only in the Lord." By the same token, if a wife has died, the husband is free to get remarried with another for the rest of his life. This scripture points out that marriage is absolutely holy in this life.

Ellen G. White's Statement on Divorce and Remarriage

Ellen White wrote:

A woman may be legally divorced from her husband by the laws of the land and yet not divorced in the sight of God and according to the higher law. There is only one sin, which is adultery, which can place the husband or wife in a position where they can be free from the marriage vow in the sight of God. Although the laws of the land may grant a divorce, yet they are husband and wife still in the Bible light, according to the laws of God.

I saw that Sister _____, as yet, has no right to marry another man; but if she, or any other woman, should obtain a divorce legally on the ground that her husband was guilty of adultery, then she is free to be married to whom she chooses.

Separation from an Unbelieving Companion—If the wife is an unbeliever and an opposer, the husband cannot in view of the law of God, put her away on this ground alone. In order to be in harmony with the law of Jehovah, he must abide with her unless she chooses of herself to depart. He may suffer opposition and be oppressed and annoyed in many ways; he will find his comfort and his strength and support from God, who is able to give grace for every emergency. He should be a man of pure mind, of truly decided, firm principles, and God will give him wisdom in regard to the course, which he should pursue. Impulse will not control his reason, but reason will hold the lines of control in her firm hand, that lust shall be held under bit and bridle. (*Adventist Home*, p. 344).

Paul wrote: "But if the unbeliever departs, let him depart; a brother or a sister is not under bondage in such *cases*. But God has called us to peace" (1 Cor. 7:15).

The Second Holy Ordinance is the Sabbath.

God rested on the SEVENTH DAY, and He blessed the Sabbath day and sanctified it because He rested on it from all His six days of work (Gen. 2:2, 3; Exod. 20:11). The first six days of the week are defined in Genesis 1:3–5, 6–8, 9–13, 14–19, 20–23, 24–31, and, the seventh day of the week is defined in Genesis 2:2, 3. God created the Sabbath for human beings to observe and keep holy. God Himself declared in the constitution of His kingdom on earth that every man, woman, and child should keep it holy (Exod. 20:8–11). Furthermore, God ordained that six days are for labor and all our work, and the seventh day is the Sabbath of the Lord our God. On the Sabbath, we and all other people in our household are not to do any work. For this purpose, the Lord blessed the Sabbath day and made it holy.

From the beginning of this earth, in 4159 BC, to this day, in Israel and in all the Arab countries, the names of the days of the week have *first* day, *second* day, *third* day, *fourth* day, *fifth* day, *sixth* day and the SEVENTH DAY, or "the Sabbath." However, in 1582, Pope Gregory XIII introduced the Gregorian calendar, which was eventually adopted all over the world. In his calendar, the days of the week received names, taken from seven celestial bodies. Since light comes to earth from the sun, the first day of the week was named Sunday. The second day was named after the Moon. The other days were named after Mercury, Venus, Mars, Jupiter, and Saturn, which were considered gods in the Roman world. In English, the weekday names were replaced by German equivalents—Tuesday, Wednesday, Thursday, Friday, and Saturday. The day names add confusion for Christians.

Many have facetiously asked about the Sabbath day: "Is there any evidence in the Bible that Saturday is the Sabbath day?" We can find the answer in Luke 23. The passage is a portrayal of what took place after the crucifixion of the Lord Jesus Christ.

> ⁵⁰ Now behold, *there was* a man named Joseph, a council member, a good and just man. ⁵¹ He had not consented to their decision and deed. *He was* from Arimathea, a city of the Jews, who himself was also waiting for the kingdom of God. ⁵² This man went to Pilate and asked for the body of Jesus. ⁵³ Then he took it down, wrapped it in linen, and laid it in a tomb *that was* hewn out of the rock, where no one had ever lain before. ⁵⁴ That day was the Preparation, and the Sabbath drew near. ⁵⁵ And the women who had come with Him from Galilee followed after, and they observed the tomb and how His body was laid. ⁵⁶ Then they returned and prepared spices and fragrant oils. And they rested on the Sabbath according to the commandment.

In verses 52 to 54, we see Joseph of Arimathea carefully wrapping the body of Jesus in linen and laying it in a new tomb. The day this took place is called "the Preparation [day]." It is the day immediately before the Sabbath, as verse 54 indicates. Joseph was able to lay Jesus' body to rest just before the Sabbath started. The women who wished to embalm Jesus body kept the fourth commandment, resting on the Sabbath. Luke 24:1 says, "Now on the first day of the week, very early in the morning," the women went to embalm the body of Jesus. To their surprise, His body was no longer there. Jesus was resurrected on the first day of the week. The account shows that Jesus died on the cross on the sixth day (Friday), which is why people observe "Good Friday." Christians also observe the first day of the week (Sunday) as "Easter." These facts testify to Jesus' being laid in the tomb just before the Sabbath day started.

Tithe, the Third Holy Ordinance

Tithe is a holy ordinance between God and humankind. Abraham introduced it in 2136 BC (Gen. 14:20), and Paul repeated the story of its introduction in Hebrews 7:1, 2. Genesis chapter 1, verses 26 and 28, says that God created man. This makes God our Creator. Genesis chapter 2, verse 15, says that God put man in the Garden of Eden and gave him and his descendants the whole earth. In Malachi 3:10, God says, "Bring all the tithes into the storehouse that there may be food in my house." The purpose for this was so people could pay God the tribute of tithe, in stewardship to Him, to demonstrate their belief that He is our Creator and keep His house full of food for His servants. This is God's call to every person in the world. Hence the tithe is holy unto God.

Tithe is one tenth of our income—either in money, grain, oil, or any other material blessing that God has given. 1 Corinthians 9:13 says that the priests who minister in the temple lived by the income that came into the temple. This enabled them to live in this world while doing God's work. The parallel for our time is that church pastors should also live by the tithe income. Paul says, "It pleased them indeed, and they are their debtors. For if the Gentiles have been partakers of their spiritual things, their duty is also to minister to them in material things" (Rom. 15:27). David said: "For all things *come* from You, and of Your own we have given You" (1 Chron. 29:14). God says through Haggai that if we do not return the tithe to God, God will not bless all our land, and we will be unable to cultivate it and bring forth its fruits. Such a curse will always be with us.

Haggai wrote, "You have sown much, and bring in little; you eat, but do not have enough; you drink, but you are not filled with drink; you clothe yourselves, but no one is warm; and he who earns wages, earns wages *to put* into a bag with holes" (Hag. 1:6). "Therefore the heavens above you withhold the dew, and the earth withholds its fruit. For I called for a drought on the land and the mountains, on the grain and the new wine and the oil, on whatever the ground brings forth, on men and livestock, and on all the labor of *your* hands" (Hag. 1:10, 11).

At the same time, to pay tithes on even the smallest of our increase and flaunt it before others while not keeping the rest of God's teachings is useless. Jesus declared: "Woe to you, scribes and Pharisees, hypocrites! For you pay tithe of mint and anise and cummin, and have neglected the weightier *matters* of the law: justice and mercy and faith. These you ought to have done, without leaving the others undone" (Matt. 23:23).

Again, another very important issue is who will return tithes. Not everybody will do so because doing so is a sacred duty like obeying the holy Ten Commandments. Thus, we would expect the tithe payer to also keep all of God's commandments and to respect anything else that belongs to God.

The Fourth Holy Ordinance is Holy Prayer in Christ's Name.

In Old Testament times, blood sacrifices were offered for the forgiveness of sins. However, the value of the sacrifices ended after the cross because of the holy prayer to be offered in Jesus' name consecrated at Jesus' death (John 15:16; 16:23, 24, 26). From the time of Moses until the crucifixion of Jesus (1491 BC to AD 31), all Jewish males were required to go to Jerusalem to offer blood sacrifice for their pardonable sins. If anyone did not go to Jerusalem to sacrifice for their pardonable sins on the tenth day of the seventh month—the Day of Atonement—God would punish him through plagues. No Jew could escape God's judgment. That is why Jesus Christ came to earth in 4 BC—to give free and eternal salvation to all humankind. He came to earth and shed His blood for us, making it unnecessary for people to go to the temple in Jerusalem to offer blood sacrifice in the way that Muslims go on a pilgrimage to Mecca.

Because Jesus came and shed His holy blood to give us forgiveness, He asks that we pray in His name. That He is the lamb of God, sent to take away the sins of the world, was not introduced by Jesus Christ, but by John the Baptist (John 1:29). Since *He* is the means of reconciliation with God, prayer should be offered in His name (Acts 4:12) and not in the name of Mary or any "saint." The Bible clearly declares that Christ is the only mediator between God and man (1 Tim. 2:5). There is no other mediator. The book of Daniel talks about an "abomination" (Dan. 12:11) that purports to stand between God and man. It was inaugurated by Pope Saint Symmachus (498–514) when he set up the papal union of church and state in AD 508—a union that lasted 1290 years. Today millions of Roman Catholics follow the abomination. In Matthew 24:15, Jesus cautioned His followers to be aware of "the abomination of desolation." Daniel predicted the removal of the "daily," which means that the desolating power would intervene in Christ's intercession wit God on man's behalf and would get the people to follow it instead. Daniel 12:11 says, "And from the time *that* the daily *sacrifice* is taken away, and the abomination of desolation is set up, *there shall be* one thousand two hundred and ninety days."

Jesus Christ Himself declared: " 'Therefore when you see the "*abomination of desolation*" spoken of by Daniel the prophet standing in the holy place' (whoever reads, let him understand) 'Then let those who are in Judea flee to the mountains' " (Matt. 24:15, 16).

What is the meaning of the "abomination of desolation" described by Daniel the prophet? It applies to every man, woman, and child who is born in this world up to the present. Jesus Christ Himself established the seven holy ordinances for His one true church. From the day after the crucifixion, Jesus Christ ordained the holy ordinance of praying through His name.

1. Every day until we die, we can immediately receive pardon for our pardonable sins—sins that are not unto death (see 1 John 5:16) through holy prayer, that is, through praying in His name.

2. Yet, there is no forgiveness for unpardonable sins (sins unto death, 1 John 5:16, 17) even though praying in Jesus' holy name. In AD 508, in fulfillment of Daniel's prophecy, the "abomination" established a prayer of desolation, which continued for a period of 1290 years. Who is responsible for the desolating prayer? It is "the beast," which is identified in the prophecy as the Roman Catholic papacy.

According to this abomination prophecy, holy prayer through Jesus Christ was changed in AD 508 by Pope Symmachus of the Roman Catholic Church in AD 508 into prayer to Jesus through the Blessed Virgin Mary. This practice is followed in Roman Catholic churches the world over. Roman Catholics pray to Jesus through Mary to receive forgiveness of their daily sins. Later, the Roman Emperor Justinian commanded that every Roman Catholic use this prayer. The desolating power reigned from AD 538 to AD 1798, when Pope Pious VI was taken captive by the French General Berthier. This abominating power also fulfilled the prophecy of Daniel 12:11 from AD 508 to 1798—the 1290- year prophecy. Even with the ending of Roman Catholic power in 1798, this same abomination, of praying to Jesus through Mary ,continues in the Christian world today.

In saying, "who ever reads, let him understand," Jesus was telling His disciples that the abomination would be very dangerous. He was telling his disciples and all His future disciples to read and understand the prophetic warning, for if we pray otherwise, our eternal salvation will be in doubt.

Holy Baptism

Jesus said: "He who believes and is baptized will be saved; but he who does not believe will be condemned" (Mark 16:16). The obvious implication of this statement is that babies should not be baptized. To do so is an abomination to the Lord because babies do not know the meaning of sin, that is, the difference between good and evil, and they do not have the capacity to respond in belief to a knowledge of Jesus Christ.

Jesus the Messiah received baptism in the River Jordan. The Bible says that, after His baptism, He came straight up out of the water (Mark 1:10). In Luke 3:21, we find that John the Baptist baptized Jesus in water by immersion.

Matthew 3:6 says that people confessed their sins and received baptism, "Now John also was baptizing in Aenon near Salim, because there was much water there. And they came and were baptized" (John 3:23). The fact that there was "much water" is another indication that the people, in baptism, were being immersed in water. If they were being sprinkled, as is now the general practice, they would not need "much water."

Luke 7:29, 30 and Acts 8:12 describe tax collectors, Pharisees, and both men and women receiving baptism. Even the chief minister of Candace, the queen of Ethiopia, received baptism from Philip (Acts 8:12, 26–39). The businesswoman Lydia received the Holy Spirit and baptism (Acts 16:14, 15). Even a jailer received a late-night baptism at the hands of the apostle Paul (Acts 16:33).

The Significance of Baptism

Romans 6:3 says, "Or do you not know that as many of us as were baptized into Christ Jesus were baptized into His death." Galatians 3:27 says, "For as many of you as were baptized into Christ have put on Christ." John 4:2 says that Jesus Christ did not Himself baptize, but that had His disciples baptize for Him. Acts 2:38 indicates that being baptized is an individual matter—we cannot receive baptism for another (much less for the dead). Jesus charged His disciples to go and preach the gospel to all the nations. We are to baptize in the name of the Father, the Son, and the Holy Ghost (Matt. 28:19). Acts 19:1, 5 teaches that, if we have not received baptism in a proper manner, we can be rebaptized. Hebrews 6:1, 2 mentions the doctrine of baptism.

Presently we are living in the seventh and last church period, which is the period of Laodicea. The truth of Jesus to the Laodicean church is based on Revelation 14:12, which identifies God's true people as those who keep the commandments of God and have the faith of Jesus Christ. These spiritual standards are greatly needed in the world today. In holding these standards, the remnant Seventh-day Adventist Church is qualified to baptize. Different than the Seventh-day Adventist Church, at least sixty-five denominations teach that the holy Ten Commandments were nailed to the cross and, thus, the truth is not in them. According to James 2:10, if we violate any one of the commandments, we are guilty of all. Preparations for baptism should be made before the Sabbath begins.

The Real Holy Lord's Supper

The seventh holy ordinance given by Jesus Christ combines the ordinance of foot washing, which represents humility between church members, and holy communion, which reminds us of the death and resurrection of Christ (1 Cor. 11:26). Philippians gives a picture of Jesus humbling Himself as a man and becoming obedient unto death, even the death of the cross (Phil. 2:6–8). Luke says that Jesus Himself explained to the twelve apostles, "I am among you as the One who serves" (Luke 22:27). The ordinance of foot washing teaches that we are all equal in Christ.

John describes how Jesus washed the disciples' feet. "After that, He poured water into a basin and began to wash the disciples' feet, and to wipe *them* with the towel with which He was girded" (John 13:5). When Jesus got to Peter, Peter said, "You shall never wash my feet!" (John 13:8). Jesus answered him, "If I do not wash you, you have no part with Me" (John 13:8). "If I then, *your* Lord and Teacher, have washed your feet, you also ought to wash one another's feet" (John 13:14).

On another occasion, Jesus told Simon, "I entered your house; you gave Me no water for My feet, but she ["this woman"] has washed My feet with her tears and wiped *them* with the hair of her head" (Luke 7:44). "I say to you, a servant is not greater than his master ... If you know these things, blessed are you if you do them" (John 13:16, 17). After explaining these things to them, Jesus showed how to observe the Lord's Supper. Paul wrote the Corinthians, "The Lord Jesus on the same night in which He was betrayed took bread; and when He had given thanks, He broke it and said, 'Take, eat; this is My body which is broken for you; do this in remembrance of Me' (1 Cor. 11:23, 24). Verse 25 says, "In the same manner *He* also *took* the cup after supper, saying, 'This cup is the new covenant in My blood. This do, as often as you drink *it*, in remembrance of Me.'" Then Paul added: "For as often as you eat this bread and drink this cup, you proclaim the Lord's death till He comes" (1 Cor. 11:26). And, last of all, Paul issued a warning: "Therefore whoever eats this bread or drinks *this* cup of the Lord in an unworthy manner will be guilty of the body and blood of the Lord" (1 Cor. 11:27). Unworthy members cannot inherit the kingdom of God. Under the curse of God, some have become sick and have even died. Preparations for the Lord's Supper should be made before the Sabbath begins.

Seven Time Periods in the Health Message

The first time period. Before sin, God gave Adam and Eve water to drink and fruit and seed-bearing plants to eat (Gen. 2:16). There were no dead cells coming from their bodies. Whatever they ate was digested without waste. "And God said, 'See, I have given you every herb *that* yields seed which *is* on the face of all the earth, and every tree whose fruit yields seed; to you it shall be for food. Also, to every beast of the earth, to every bird of the air, and to everything that creeps on the earth, in which *there is* life, *I have given* every green herb for food'; and it was so" (Gen. 1:29, 30).

The second time period. After sin, God added greens and herbs, along with the nuts and fruits, to help excrete the dead cells from the body. Genesis 3:18 says, "Both thorns and thistles it shall bring forth for you, And you shall eat the herb of the field." On this diet, Methuselah lived 969 years.

The third time period. From the time after the Flood until Israel's wilderness wandering, God gave humans permission to eat meat to reduce the age of man from nearly a thousand years to 70–80 years (Ps. 90:10). Genesis 6:3 says, "And the LORD said, 'My Spirit shall not strive with man forever, for he *is* indeed flesh; yet his days shall be one hundred and twenty years."

Ellen White explained: "After the flood the people ate largely of animal food. God saw that the ways of man were corrupt, and that he was disposed to exalt himself proudly against his Creator, and to follow the inclinations of his own heart. And He permitted that long-lived race to eat animal food to shorten their sinful lives. Soon after the flood the race began to rapidly decrease in size, and in length of years" (*Spiritual Gifts*, vol. 4a, 1864, pp. 120, 121).

The fourth time period. While Israel wandered in the wilderness, God gave them only Manna to eat except when they rebelled against Him and He gave them quail (Exod. 16: 16, 35). "And the children of Israel ate manna forty years, until they came to an inhabited land; they ate manna until they came to the border of the land of Canaan."

The fifth time period. God gave a list of clean meats in Leviticus 11. "Now the LORD spoke to Moses and Aaron, saying to them, 'Speak to the children of Israel, saying, 'These *are* the animals which you may eat among all the animals that are on the earth: Among the animals, whatever divides the hoof, having cloven hooves and chewing the cud—that you may eat. Nevertheless these you shall not eat among those that chew the cud or those that have cloven hooves: the camel, because it chews the cud but does not have cloven hooves, *is* unclean to you; the rock hyrax, because it chews the cud but does not have cloven hooves, is unclean to you; the hare, because it chews the cud but does not have cloven hooves, is unclean to you; and the swine, though it divides the hoof, having cloven hooves, yet does not chew the cud, is unclean to you. Their flesh you shall not eat, and their carcasses you shall not touch. They are unclean to you.

'These you may eat of all that *are* in the water: whatever in the water has fins and scales, whether in the seas or in the rivers—that you may eat. But all in the seas or in the rivers that do not have fins and scales, all that move in the water or any living thing which is in the water, they *are* an abomination to you. They shall be an abomination to you; you shall not eat their flesh, but you shall regard their carcasses as an abomination. Whatever in the water does not have fins or scales—that *shall* be an abomination to you.

'And these you shall regard as an abomination among the birds; they shall not be eaten, they are an abomination: the eagle, the vulture, the buzzard, the kite, and the falcon after its kind; every raven after its kind, the ostrich, the short-eared owl, the sea gull, and the hawk after its kind; the little owl, the fisher owl, and the screech owl; the white owl, the jackdaw, and the carrion vulture; the stork, the heron after its kind, the hoopoe, and the bat.

'All flying insects that creep on *all* fours *shall* be an abomination to you. Yet these you may eat of every flying insect that creeps on all fours: those which have jointed legs above their feet with which to leap on the earth. These you may eat: the locust after its kind, the destroying locust after its kind, the cricket after its kind, and the grasshopper after its kind. But all *other* flying insects which have four feet *shall be an abomination to you.*' " (Lev. 11:1–23)

The sixth time period. In 1863, God showed the health message to Ellen G. White, pointing out the superiority of a vegetarian diet for God's people (see *Spiritual Gifts*, vol. 4a, p. 153).

> Flesh was never the best food; but its use is now doubly objectionable, since disease in animals is so rapidly increasing. (*The Ministry of Healing*, 1905, p. 313)

> Animals are becoming more and more diseased, and it will not be long until animal food will be discarded by many besides Seventh-day Adventists. Foods that are healthful and life-sustaining are to be prepared, so that men and women will not need to eat meat. (*Testimonies for the Church*, vol. 7, 1902, p. 124)

> 663. When will those who know the truth take their stand on the side of right principles for time and for eternity? When will they be true to the principles of health reform? When will they learn that it is dangerous to use flesh meat? I am instructed to say that if ever meat eating were safe, it is not safe now. (Manuscript 133, 1902)

> 644. The light given me is that it will not be very long before we shall have to give up using any animal food. Even milk will have to be discarded. Disease is accumulating rapidly. The curse of God is upon the earth, because man has cursed it. The habits and practices of men have brought the earth into such a condition that some other food than animal food must be substituted for the human family. We do not need flesh food at all. God can give us something else. (*Australasian Union Conference Record*, July 28, 1899)

> When flesh is discarded, its place should be supplied with a variety of grains, nuts, vegetables, and fruits, that will be both nourishing and appetizing. This is especially necessary in the case of those who are weak, or who are taxed with continuous labor. (*The Ministry of Healing*, 1905, pp. 316, 317)

Meat is not essential for health or strength, else the Lord made a mistake when He provided food for Adam and Eve before their fall. All the elements of nutrition are contained in the fruits, vegetables, and grains. (*The Review and Herald*, May 8, 1883).

Before the Fall, Adam and Eve had all the elements of nutrition in fruits, vegetables, and grains.

The seventh time period. When God has made new heavens and a new earth, there will be no meat eating then or at any time into eternity. "And he showed me a pure river of water of life, clear as crystal, proceeding from the throne of God and of the Lamb. In the middle of its street, and on either side of the river, *was* the tree of life, which bore twelve fruits, each *tree* yielding its fruit every month. The leaves of the tree *were* for the healing of the nations" (Rev. 22:1, 2).

Chapter 7

God's Unchangeable Law and Its 105 Specifications

Isaiah wrote, "Cry aloud, spare not; lift up your voice like a trumpet; tell My people their transgression, and the house of Jacob their sins" (Isa. 58:1). God is asking us to distinguish between right and wrong, between what is sinful and what is holy. The apostle Paul warned: "For if the trumpet makes an uncertain sound, who will prepare for battle? So likewise you, unless you utter by the tongue words easy to understand, how will it be known what is spoken?" (1 Cor. 14:8, 9). Unless we teach what is right and wrong, people will live and die in fool's paradise. So, let us consider the basics of right and wrong through a series of questions and answers.

Question: What is sin?

Answer: "Whoever commits sin also commits lawlessness, and <u>sin is lawlessness</u>" (1 John 3:4).

Question: What are the wages of sin?

Answer: "The wages of sin *is* death" (Rom. 6:23).

Question: How do we recognize sin?

Answer: "What shall we say then? *Is* the law sin? Certainly not! On the contrary, I would not have known sin except through the law...." (Rom. 7:7).

Question: What is the law, and where is it written?

Answer: "For I would not have known covetousness unless the law had said, *'You shall not covet'* " (Rom. 7:7). This is a reference to the holy Ten Commandments in Exodus 20:3–17.

Question: Is God's law holy?

Answer: "Therefore the law *is* holy, and the commandment holy and just and good" (Rom. 7:12).

Question: What is the nature of God?

Answer: "He who does not love does not know God, for God is love" (1 John 4:8).

Question: How do we show that we love God and man?

Answer: "By this we know that we love the children of God, when we love God and keep His commandments. For this is the love of God, that we keep His commandments. And His commandments are not burdensome" (1 John 5:2, 3).

Question: What did Jesus say about the commandments?

Answer: "Do not think that I came to destroy the Law or the Prophets. I did not come to destroy but to fulfill. For assuredly, I say to you, till heaven and earth pass away, one jot or one tittle will by no means pass from the law till all is fulfilled. Whoever therefore breaks one of the least of these commandments, and teaches men so, shall be called least in the kingdom of heaven; but whoever does and teaches *them*, he shall be called great in the kingdom of heaven." (Matt. 5:17–19). "So He said to him, 'Why do you call Me good? No one *is* good but One, *that is*, God. But if you want to enter into life, keep the commandments' " (Matt. 19:17).

Chapter 7 God's Unchangeable Law and Its 105 Specifications

God did not give the Ten Commandments solely to the children of Israel; He gave them to every human being born on the earth. The Ten Commandments are the only document that was "written with the finger of God." These commandments are fifteen singular verses out of the 31,175 verses that make up the Bible. It was Jesus Christ who wrote the Ten Commandments with His own finger and gave them to Moses. Because He wrote them, the Bible calls them holy. Were it not for God's Holy commandments, the Bible could be like any other book. As we read the Bible, it gives us more detail. Jesus Christ, God the Father, and the Holy Spirit have given us the Bible through 39 authors, writing from 1531 BC to AD 97. Ever since Adam's sin in 4159 BC until John's composing of the Revelation in AD 100, Christ has given the Ten Commandments as a seventh—or moral—sense for human beings to follow. However, throughout the time in the wilderness from Moses to the occupation under Joshua, God introduced a formal system for the forgiveness of sin in the sanctuary service taught by Moses. The various laws were given during this time period: the moral law, the ceremonial law, the physical law, and the civil law.

The following references show that violation of any of the Ten Commandments was a capital offense. Those who disobeyed them were stoned to death.

1. "He who sacrifices to *any* god, except to the LORD only, he shall be utterly destroyed (Exod. 22:20; see also Lev. 20:2; Deut. 13:1–5).

2. "And he said to them, 'Thus says the LORD God of Israel: "Let every man put his sword on his side, and go in and out from entrance to entrance throughout the camp, and let every man kill his brother, every man his companion, and every man his neighbor" ' ... The Moses returned to the LORD and said, Oh, these people have committed a great sin, and have made for themselves gods of gold" (Exod. 32:27, 31).

3. "And whoever blasphemes the name of the LORD shall surely be put to death" (Lev. 24:16).

4. "You shall keep the Sabbath, therefore, for *it is* holy to you. Everyone who profanes it shall surely be put to death; for whoever does *any* work on it, that person shall be cut off from among his people" (Exod. 31:14).

5. "And he who curses his father or his mother shall surely be put

to death" (Exod. 21:17).

6. "He who strikes a man so that he dies shall surely be put to death" (Exod. 21:12).

7. "The man who commits adultery with *another* man's wife, *he* who commits adultery with his neighbors' wife, the adulterer and the adulteress, shall surely be put to death" (Lev. 20:10).

8. "And Joshua said, 'Why have you troubled us? The LORD will trouble you this day.' So all Israel stoned him with stones and they burned them with fire after they had stoned them with stones" (Josh. 7:25).

9. "One witness shall not rise against a man concerning any iniquity ... you shall put away the evil from among you" (Deut. 19:15, 19).

10. "The man who commits adultery with *another* man's wife, *he* who commits adultery with his neighbor's wife, the adulterer and the adulteress, shall surely be put to death" (Lev. 20:10).

But in the New Testament, violators of the Ten Commandments were given the opportunity to receive forgiveness from God as they prayed in the name of Jesus Christ. This provision began the day Jesus died, as He forgave the repentant thief hanging beside him. At the same time, 1 John 5:16, 17 describes two types of sins. These are unpardonable sins, which are sins "leading to death," and pardonable sins, which can be easily forgiven through prayer. Out of the unpardonable sin, there is a total of 105 open sins. 1 John 1:7 says, "And the blood of Jesus Christ His Son cleanses us from all sin." Our sins will be forgiven at the time of baptism, and we will have the assurance of salvation. However, Matthew 12:32 mentions sin against the Holy Spirit that will not be forgiven.

God wants us to keep the law of life that we may have a peaceful life. That was the reason that Jesus said: "If you love Me, [you will] keep my Commandments" (John 14:15, margin).

The Present Trend of the Protestant Churches

There are sixty-five organized churches in the world that claim that the holy Ten Commandments were nailed to the cross. However, when God created Adam and Eve, He blessed them and commanded them to be fruitful and multiply, and He revealed the truth from generation to generation. He commanded Moses to write down the moral law, the holy Ten Commandments, which He first wrote with His own finger as the human's seventh sense. A good example of how it inculcates a moral sense is in the seventh commandment, which says, "You shall not commit adultery." This commandment requires us not to marry our own sisters or brothers, unlike the animals, which have only five senses to employ in multiplying. God had a similar purpose in giving us the other commandments to direct our lives. Yet, if churches preach that the law was nailed to the cross, what morality can they teach this generation and how can they differentiate right from wrong? Today, many Christians promote a flexible view of keeping God's law.

Which is the True Church?

The Seventh-day Adventist Church believes in keeping God's law, and the church that keeps the holy Ten Commandments and its 105 specifications (1 John 5:16, 17) is the true church.

Embodiment of Laws

Apart from the holy Ten Commandments, Jesus Christ gave the Mosaic law, comprising 1,532 verses with the ceremonial, civil, and physical laws. Of these, 1082 verses are ceremonial and were nailed to the cross, while the other 450 verses have practical value and should be followed.

The Moral Law. God wrote the Ten Commandments with His own finger (Exod. 20:1–17; Deut. 9:10). The first four commandments address man's relationship to God, and the last six address man's relationship to man. For example, "You shall not covet" covers such things as: (1) blood relations as close as brothers and sisters should not marry; if they do, their marriage is an abomination unto the Lord; (2) a man should not marry to two wives; (3) likewise, a woman cannot have two husbands; (4) men and women should not have sexual relations with the wives or husbands of others ; (5) nor should they practice homosexual acts or have sex outside of marriage. All such acts violate the moral laws of God.

The Ceremonial Law. Paul wrote: "Having wiped out the handwriting of requirements that was against us, which was contrary to us. And He has taken it out of the way, having nailed it to the cross" (Col. 2:14).

The Physical Laws. 1. Women should not wear men's clothing and men should not wear women's clothing. 2. Women should not cut their hair, according to popular culture, and men should not grow their hair long. Both are an abomination to the Lord because they lead to confusion of the sexes. 3. Both men and women should not poke holes in their body for jewelry; such ornaments are an abomination unto the Lord. 4. God's people should not tattoo their body; nor should they shave off their eyebrows. 5. God's people should not eat unclean animals, birds, or fish, for these will affect their health. 6. God's people should not drink intoxicating liquors or use tea, coffee, tobacco, alcoholic beverages, or dangerous drugs, such as LSD, cocaine, opium, or heroin. These are an abomination unto the Lord, for they violate the physical laws, ordained by God, that govern the body.

These are the three types of laws that were given in the law of Moses. These laws are bylaws to the main constitution of the holy Ten Commandments of God. The 450 verses concerning the bylaws are explanations of the holy Ten Commandments of God. We can understand the 105 specifications with the help of the "Spirit of Prophecy" books, as well as with the assistance of modern medical science and present general knowledge. Prayerfully we will consider the importance of the Ten Commandments and what each commandment teaches us so that we can put them all into practice.

The 105 Specifications of the Holy Ten Commandments

- *The First Commandment and its Thirteen Specifications*

    "You shall have no other gods before Me" (Exod. 20:3).

    1. The God of the Bible is indeed the triune God, but to teach that the Father, the Son, and the Holy Spirit are separate Gods is a violation of the first commandment. Christ said: "I and My Father are one" (John 10:30). He also said: "You call Me Teacher and Lord, and you say well, for *so* I am" (John 13:13). To help the Jews understand how close He is to the first Person of the Godhead, Jesus used relational terms, "Father" and "Son." However, Christ is inherently equal

with the Father. Hebrews 1:9 explains, *"Therefore God, Your God, has anointed you."* There is equality in the triune God. Though the LORD God is rightly "Our Father," as Jesus taught us in His model prayer, yet, this does not imply that Jesus was a "Son" in the same way that human sons are conceived of their fathers and mothers. Such a notion might lead some to believe that Jesus' earthly mother Mary was divine or that she was God's wife. Either of these would be an abomination unto the Lord.

2. There is no inherent hierarchy between the three Persons of the triune God. Many verses in the Bible say that the Father is greater than Jesus Christ and that the Father is the head of Jesus Christ (see John 14:28; 10:29; Luke 22:29; Acts 2:32). However, Jesus Christ is equal to the first Person of the Godhead (1 Cor. 11:3).

3. For those who do not know about the likeness, image, nature, equal powers, and equal reasoning of the biblical triune God, I should say that the three Persons of the triune God were equally involved in the first creation (Gen. 1:1), but only Jesus Christ and the Holy Spirit were involved in the second creation (the six days of creation, 6,000 years ago) (Gen. 1:2, 26, 27; Heb. 1:2).

4. It is a sin to assert that God ever violated His covenants or altered the word that came from His lips (Ps. 89:34; Job 33:14). What God says, He means; He does not need to repeat His words for His words to be true.

5. The very first creation of this world by the triune God, which God created from nothing in the twinkling of an eye, occurred over 6,000 years ago (Gen. 1:1).

6. It is a sin to assert that the first Person of the Godhead is the only God and that Jesus Christ and the Holy Spirit are not fully God. This is a false belief of some groups that call themselves Christian (1 John 5:7).

7. It is a sin to assert that Jesus Christ brought about the virgin birth without the first or third Persons of the Godhead (Phil. 2:5–7, RSV; Matt. 1:18).

8. It is a sin to witness, call on, or pray in the name of the Father and the Son without understanding the triune God (1 John

5:7; Exod. 3:14). There are 211 verses in Scripture that refer to the Father and the Son.

9. It is wrong to promote modern pictures of Jesus Christ (Deut. 4:15–19; Rev. 1:13–17).

10. It is a sin to use the picture of a dove as an example of the Holy Spirit. According to Matthew 3:16; Mark 1:10; and John 1:32, God the Holy Spirit descended more like a helicopter than like a plane. Other pertinent verses on this subject are Luke 3:22; Exod. 20:4; and Deut. 4:15–19.

11. We must be extremely respectful when we call, read, write and sing, "Jesus is our friend and our brother," and, of course, He can call us whatever He wants (Mark 7:7; Matt. 12:18; Heb. 2:11, 12; Rev. 14:7).

12. Worshipping our father and mother —or any other human being—by bowing down before them is directly against God. Our God is a jealous God; He will not have us worshiping anyone else (Exod. 20:6; Matt. 4:10; Rev. 22:8–10).

13. It is a sin to worship anyone other than the God of heaven. This includes the Virgin Mary, Allah (as a God different who is different from the One portrayed in the Bible), fire, water, rain or any angel, whether fallen or unfallen. Whether people worship these entities directly or indirectly, they are violating the first and third commandments.

• *The Second Commandment and Its Five Specifications*

"You shall not make for yourself a carved image—any likeness *of anything* that *is* in heaven above, or that *is* in the earth beneath, or that *is* in the water under the earth" (Exod. 20:4).

14. We should not keep any resemblance of God or any kind of idol, statue, or image (Luke 2:51, Mary kept everything in her heart; Exod. 22:20; Deut. 4:15–19; Rev. 1:13–17).

15. Bowing down to parents and political leaders, bishops and popes is a violation of the second and third commandments of God. We should not even fold our hands in greeting human

beings. All praise should go to Christ alone (Exod. 20:4, 5; Matt. 23:7; 8).

16. We should not pray to modern pictures of Jesus, nor should such a picture come to our minds in prayer. If it does, it is not faith, and our prayers will be an abomination unto the Lord. Our prayer will not be heard, and we will not go to heaven (Acts 4:11, 12; Exod. 20:5; Deut. 4:15, 16; Rev. 1:13, 14).

17. If the picture of a dove flashes into our minds when we think of the Holy Spirit, we are dishonoring God the Holy Spirit (Acts 4:11, 12; Exod. 20:5; Gen. 1:26).

18. No human in the world besides Jesus Christ was or is—or ever has been— holy. We should not call any person a saint, a holy man of God, nor even call Paul "St. Paul" or Peter "St. Peter," because we human beings are only creatures. Only the Creator is holy(Ps. 103:14; Rom. 3:10).

- ## *The Third Commandment and Its Fourteen Specifications*

"You shall not take the name of the LORD your God in vain, for the LORD will not hold *him* guiltless who takes His name in vain" (Exod. 20:7).

19. We should not swear in the name of our biblical God, under any of His titles (Matt. 5:34).

20. During our prayers, we should not mindlessly repeat phrases, such as, "Praise the Lord!" "Hallelujah!" or "the blood of Jesus Christ." (Matt. 6:7).

21. The vain observance of Christmas, Easter, Good Friday, Lent days and the sending of greetings for these holidays and Christmas carol singing are not mentioned in Scripture (Matt. 14:6; Mark 7:7).

22. Observing false sabbaths on Fridays and Sundays, wearing Thali and wedding rings, which are signs of the Hindu snake god, worshipping one's husband like god, using excessive jewels and ornaments, and loving materialism more than God

are violations of the commandment (Exod. 20:8; 1 Peter 3:3; Gen. 1:26; 1 Tim. 2:9; Exod. 33:5, 6).

23. Baptizing babies, baptizing by sprinkling, birthday celebrations, naming and ear-piercing ceremonies, funeral services, prayer vigils, and celebrating memorial services that exceed what God has asked us to do are also violations of the commandment (Col. 2:14; Matt. 6:5; Luke 9:60; Rom. 6:4, 5; Mark 6:21–27).

24. Observing holy communion without foot washing, taking holy communion from the fallen churches, and serving holy communion to unworthy members lead many people to fall sick because they have gone against God (1 Cor. 11:29, 30).

25. All night prayers, healing prayers, fasting prayers, and praying through Mary are an abomination unto the Lord when a person disrespects God's law and practices lawlessness (Matt. 7:22).

26. Preaching that God's law was nailed to the cross while performing all types of miracles of healing on the public stage is not from God but by the power of Satan (Matt. 7:22; Ps. 50:18; Prov. 28:9).

27. In modern times, people who claim to speak in tongues and interpret this experience as their being possessed by "the Spirit" or who conduct meetings using rock music to attract people to church while introducing spirit mind control through sensual movements of the body are violating the third and the seventh commandments of God (Matt. 7:22).

28. Spirit mediums using wizard communication and astrology to tell the future, observing the auspicious and inauspicious days and times, and using spirit mediums to take vengeance on others also violate the third commandment (Rev. 14:12; Mark 7:7; and Lev. 20:27).

29. Men should not wear ladies' garments, and ladies should not wear men's garments like pants, jeans, men's banyans, or tight-fitting chudidhar showing much of themselves to tantalize men. Ladies should cover their head with a veil while going into the church and praying to God with other people (1 Cor. 11:2–15; Deut. 22:5). Also, women who bob their hair

or cut it in a weird way, and men who grow their hair long are committing an abomination to the LORD (Lev. 19:31; Deut. 22:5; 1 Cor. 11:13–15).

30. Neither men nor women should tattoo their bodies. Ladies should not use makeup and shave their eyebrows, wear gold ornaments and jewels, pierce their ears, nose, or other body parts, for these all belong to God, and these things are an abomination to the LORD (1 Cor. 11:14, 15; Deut. 22:5; Lev. 19:28; Deut. 14:1).

31. Establishing false churches with the vain doctrines of men, collecting tithes and offerings from the people and cheating them of their money by the power of Satan is an open violation of the Ten Commandments (Ps. 50:18; James 1:11; 5:1).

32. The use of tobacco, betel nut, or other injurious stimulants, stimulating drinks like tea and coffee, dangerous drugs, and alcoholic beverages are a violation of God's law (Deut. 29:18).

- ## *The Fourth Commandment and Its Fifteen Specifications*

Keeping the Sabbath is about remembering the Sabbath day to keep it holy. The commandment says: "Remember the Sabbath day, to keep it holy. Six days you shall labor and do all your work, but the seventh day *is* the Sabbath of the LORD your God. *In it* you shall do no work: you, nor your son, nor your daughter, nor your male servant, nor your female servant, nor your cattle, nor your stranger who *is* within your gates. For *in* six days the LORD made the heavens and the earth, the sea, and all that *is* in them, and rested the seventh day. Therefore the LORD blessed the Sabbath day and hallowed it" (Exod. 20:8–11).

33. If, rather than observing the seventh day as our Sabbath, we observe the sixth day (Friday) or the first day (Sunday), we are going against God's revelation. Since 1844, the living God of heaven will not forgive willful violation of the true Sabbath (Exod. 20:10; Rev. 14:12).

34. Doing work and earning money on the Sabbath day is against God's will (Exod. 20:9; Jer. 17:27; Matt. 6:19–34).

35. On the Sabbath day, we should not transact any business. To learn how to keep the Sabbath, please read *Testimonies for the Church*, vol. 6, pp. 355, 360, and Matthew 6:25, 34).

36. During the holy Sabbath, we should not speak unnecessary things like gossiping, teasing, quarreling, or fighting. (Isa. 58:13, 14).

37. During the holy hours of Sabbath, we should not make plans for the other six days of work, and we should not have our own pleasure because it is God's day (Isa. 58:13; Matt. 6:34).

38. We should be careful about unnecessary travel on the Sabbath. We should not buy tickets and travel by train or bus, hire a taxi or auto-rickshaw, even for attending church and Sabbath school. However, we can travel by our own car, bus, scooter, cycle, or plane, but all arrangements, including fueling your vehicle and hiring of a taxi or auto-rickshaw, should be done on Friday in anticipation of the Sabbath (Matt. 24:20; *Testimonies for the Church*, vol. 6, pp. 355–360, Exod. 16:29).

39. Our personal interests, like watching TV or videos, listening to radio news and music, watching TV, reading the daily news, magazines, storybooks, personal letters, writing letters to others, sending telegrams, and playing cards and other types of amusement should be strictly avoided (Matt. 5:20; 6:33; *Testimonies for the Church*, vol. 6, pp. 355–360).

40. Preparing food on the Sabbath, going to a hotel and paying money for food, and buying groceries or paying for a hotel room on the Sabbath show carelessness for the holiness of God's Sabbath. Here is an inspired statement about the preparations we should make for the Sabbath: "On Friday let the preparation for the Sabbath be completed. See that all the clothing is in readiness and that all the cooking is done. Let the boots be blacked and the baths be taken. ... The Sabbath is not to be given to the repairing of garments, to the cooking of food, to pleasure seeking, or to any other worldly employment. Before the setting of the sun let all secular work be laid aside" (*Testimonies for the Church*, vol. 6, pp. 355, 356; Exod. 16:23; 35:3).

41. Husbands and wives should give more importance to God than to worldly pleasure. You can avoid pleasure seeking and come closer to God on the Sabbath so that you will have better relations on the other six days (Ps. 84:1, 2, 10; *Testimonies for the Church*, vol. 6, pp. 355–360).

42. Christians should not enlist in the armed forces as a combatant for reasons of keeping the Sabbath and not killing; however, a Christian can serve as a non-combatant (Exod. 20:8, 11, 13).

43. Preparations for baptism and holy communion on the Sabbath day should be done in advance. Otherwise, both services would be better conducted before or after the Sabbath (Neh. 14:17–19).

44. Care should be taken, on the Sabbath, to avoid church board committee meetings, church board elections, elections of delegates, and ordinations of pastors. Even during the Sabbath School or youth meeting, any skits, dramas, quizzes, or biblical amusements should be devoted to the glory of God, and we should be careful to devote our time to fulfilling God's desires rather than our own (Isaiah 6:5, 6; *Testimonies for the Church*, vol. 6, pp. 355–360).

45. The solemnization of holy marriage and funeral services can be done on other days. Other religious activities, including the presentation of welcome or farewell garlands can also be done on other days (Luke 23:53, 54; Matt. 8:22; Isa. 58:13, 14).

46. Taking photographs or videos is often for our own interests rather than for the purpose of giving glory to God (Matt. 21:13; Isa. 56:6, 7;Isa. 58:13, 14).

47. Observance of the holy Sabbath begins Friday evening when sunlight becomes darkness ("from evening to evening, you shall celebrate your sabbath," Lev. 23:32). Until sunlight fades on Saturday evening, all twenty-four hours of the Sabbath are holy—from Friday evening vespers, which welcome the Sabbath, to Saturday evening vespers, which bid the Sabbath farewell (Neh. 13:15; Jer. 17:19–27, Gen. 1:5).

• *The Fifth Commandment and Its Four Specifications*

"Honor your father and your mother, that your days may be long upon the land which the LORD your God is giving you" (Exod. 20:12).

48. It is a sin to disobey one's parents or to irritate or beat them (Lev. 20:9).
49. It is a sin not to ignore our parents' needs (Exod. 20:12).
50. Listen to the advice of the parents and obey them, when others ask you to commit sin (Exod. 21:15; Prov. 23:22).
51. Threatening and abusing one's parents and making them slaves in one's own home is a violation of the fifth commandment (Prov. 30:17).

• *The Sixth Commandment and Its Nine Specifications*

"You shall not murder" (Exod. 20:13).

52. Murdering someone violates the commandment (Exod. 20:13).
53. Abduction with the plan to kill a person violates the commandment (Exod. 21:16; Deut. 24:7).
54. Plotting to kill a person directly violates the commandment (besides, this is a law of every country, 1 Peter 2:13, 14).
55. The intentional shedding of a person's blood violates the commandment (Gen. 9:6).
56. A Seventh-day Adventist church member cannot go to war as a combatant for any nation by joining the army, navy, air force, or any other branch of service, for no true Christian would do so (*Testimonies*, vol. 8, p. 89).
57. Manipulating a person to commit suicide also violates the commandment (besides, this is the law of the land, (1 Peter 2:12–14)
58. The individual who commits suicide violates the commandment, "You shall not murder" (1 Peter 2:12–14)
59. Manufacturing weapons without knowing how they will be used and selling them to others may put those weapons in the hands of those who will murder.

60. The possession or sale of cocaine or other narcotic drugs violates the sixth commandment and makes one guilty before the law of God (besides, this is the law of the land, 1 Peter 2:14, 17)

• *The Seventh Commandment and Its Fourteen Specifications*

"You shall not commit adultery" (Exod. 20:14).

61. Catering the affections of a person of the other sex besides one's own husband or wife is against God's law (Deut. 22:22).
62. If either the wife or the husband continues to live in direct violation of the seventh commandment, God will not forgive this sin (Exod. 20:14).
63. If a person marries the adulterous party, he or she is violating the seventh commandment (Matt. 19:8, 9).
64. The partner who committed adultery of either sex does not have the right to remarry until the death of his or her former spouse. (1 Cor. 7:39; Matt. 5:32).
65. Baseless divorce violates the commandment (1 Peter 3:7; Gen. 3:16).
66. If a couple divorce because one spouse does not believe in God, the believing spouse cannot get re-married. If she or he gets re-married, it is a direct violation of the seventh commandment (1 Cor. 7:39; Mal. 2:15).
67. Provocative dress of both sexes, using see-through clothing , low-cut blouses, low-hip saris and miniskirts to show the midriff or the thighs is against God's commandment (Mal. 2:15).
68. It is inappropriate for teenage boys and girls to hug and kiss. Dating for a long time without deciding to get married, mixed dancing, and attending nightclubs with showgirls are all against God's commandment (1 Cor. 6:9, 10).
69. Those who watch live or recorded pornographic shows or who film sexual acts for pleasure or profit are committing an abomination unto the LORD (Lev. 20:10).

70. The prostitution of women for profit is also an abomination unto the LORD (Lev. 20:10).

71. Both husband and wife should satisfy their partner, but perverted sex is not in keeping with God's plan for marriage (1 Cor. 7:3, 4).

72. Raping girls, women, boys, or men or helping someone else to commit such an act for money or vengeance is an abomination to God (Exod. 22:16).

73. Fornicators, adulterers, the effeminate, abusers of themselves with mankind, including having sexual relations with animals or same gender sexual relations is an abomination to God (1 Cor. 6:9, 10, 18; Deut. 27:21–23; Exod. 22:19; Lev. 20:10–21).

74. Marriage between a brother and a sister, an uncle and a niece, a parent and a child, which would include a mother-in-law and a son-in-law, a father-in-law and a daughter-in-law, a mother-in-law and her husband's son, and a father-in-law and his wife's daughter, are an abomination unto the LORD and a direct violation of the seventh commandment (Lev. 20:17–21).

- ***The Eighth Commandment and Its Fourteen Specifications***

"Thou shall not steal" (Exod. 20:15). Violations include:

75. Stealing or supporting thieves (Gen. 3:17).

76. Plotting to gain possession of another's property (Josh. 7:25; Exod. 22:4).

77. Cheating in business transactions, as did Ananias and Sapphira (Acts 5:5).

78. Lending money with unlawful heavy interest (Exod. 22:25).

79. Entering politics and serving in the ruling government (Deut. 23:14; Ps. 50:18).

80. Plundering and robbing (*Testimonies for the Church*, vol. 7, p.

212; Exod. 20:15).

81. Adulterating oil, milk, grains, foodstuffs, or medicine (1 Peter 2:14, 16; Lev. 19:35).

82. Gambling of all kinds, including betting on the lottery, horse races, and speculating in the stock market, and taking or giving bribes for work contracts (Prov. 13:11; Lev. 19:36).

83. Using false balances, measurements, or producing counterfeit currency (Prov. 11:1; Lev. 19:36).

84. Hiding essential commodities of goods and selling those goods for unlawful gain (1 Peter 2:14).

85. Smuggling goods, without the knowledge of the government and unlawfully exchanging them for money is a direct violation of this commandment (Moreover, this is the law of the land, 1 Peter 2:14).

86. Tax evasion (Matt. 17:27; 22:21; Luke 20:25).

87. Smuggling dangerous drugs, weapons, arms or ammunition against the law and selling them to the public (besides, this is the law of the land, 1 Peter 2:13, 14)

88. Demanding bribes for government or private jobs, earning unlawful money, issuing false certificates or government documents for gain, and manipulating elections are all violations of the eighth commandment (*Testimonies for the Church*, vol. 8, pp. 236, 237).

- ## *The Ninth Commandment and Its Two Specifications*

"You shall not bear false witness against your neighbor" (Exod. 20:16).

89. This includes being a false witness in the case of a murder (Prov. 19:9; Deut. 19:16–19).

90. Instigating others to bear false witness in the case of a murder (1 Peter 2:14; Exod. 20:16).

- ## *The Tenth Commandment and Its Fifteen Specifications*

"You shall not covet your neighbor's house; you shall not covet your neighbor's wife, nor his male servant, nor his female servant, nor his ox, nor his donkey, nor anything that *is* your neighbor's" (Exod. 20:17). Violations include:

91. Coveting others' possessions (Exod. 20:17; Lev. 19:18).

92. Coveting and attempting to steal another's money, property, or belongings (Exod. 20:17; Deut. 5:21; Lev. 19:18).

93. Coveting and beguiling someone else's wife or husband and falling in love with them (Exod. 20:17; Lev. 18:20).

94. Forcibly abducting men, women, or children and threatening them, kidnapping them to get ransom money from their family, or a husband or a wife threatening his or her partner (Exod. 20:17; Matt. 7:12).

95. Selling of men, women, and children for slavery, prostitution, or other purposes (Exod. 21:16; Matt. 5:44).

96. Slavery of men, women, and children for profit or for intimidation, or controlling another person or persons by blackmail or by threatening their loss of a job (Exod. 21:16; Lev. 19:13).

97. Manipulating the vote of an individual or a group in federal, state, local, or church politics by threats, bribes, or deception (*Testimonies for the Church*, vol. 8, pp. 236, 237).

98. A related violation among Christian believers is showing favoritism according to (1) cast, (2) race, (3) language, (4) national identity, or (5) nepotism (2 Thess. 3:6; Gal. 3:28; Col. 3:11; Lev 9:18).

99. Showing favoritism to the wealthy and well connected within church society or any other governmental or private organization (Exod. 20:17; Lev. 19:15, 18).

100. We the people of God's remnant church must focus on transforming our lives to not see death. A part of this effort is to practice a vegetarian diet. Those who want to go to the heavenly Canaan must practice the heavenly diet during this lifetime. This is part of the seasoning for transformation of the mortal body into immortality. Those who still clamor after flesh foods are coveting that which God says does not belong

to them and it is also mistreating the property of the Holy Spirit. Thus, they are in violation of God's commandment (Num. 11:6, 7, 33, 34; *Testimonies for the Church*, vol. 2, p. 60).

101. Every one of the many Christian denominations (by some counts, there are 33,000—22,000 independent denominations, 9,000 Protestant denominations, 1,600 marginal denominations, 781 Orthodox denominations, 242 Catholic denominations, and 168 Anglican denominations) and their leaders misguide their church members, by teaching doctrine according to their own whims and fancies in direct violation of the tenth, eighth, and third commandments (Ps. 50:18; *Testimonies for the Church*, vol. 8, pp. 236, 237)?

102. As stated in James 2:10 and in Psalm 50:18, those who violate one commandment out of the ten holy commandments are guilty of all. If any believer joins that person in violating the tenth commandment, he will automatically be keeping company with an adulteress and violating the seventh commandment. According to the two scriptures, no remnant believer of the Seventh-day Adventist Church is free to violate even one of the 105 open sins of the holy Ten Commandments. To commit a single point of open sin makes a person an open sinner. As the Spirit of Prophecy says, open sinners must be separated from the remnant church (*Christ's Object Lessons*, p. 71). Church authorities have the power to take disciplinary action as ordained by God, and they must take disciplinary action against the violator and send them out of our churches. If any Adventist church is not taking disciplinary actions against its members who are openly sinning, the whole congregation must be dissolved by the next higher level of the organization, the state conference. Our Lord Jesus Christ has given His church authority and ordained this disciplinary action within the Laodicean, remnant Seventh-day Adventist Church. No other church in this world has been authorized by God to take these disciplinary actions. Our biblical God has given counsel through the Spirit of Prophecy books. They advocate a few points of disciplinary action. In this worldwide organization, every individual in the churches must be given two warnings. Those who continue after the warning must be dismissed from any office they hold in the Seventh-day Adventist Church and

then must be disfellowshipped from the church. We must remember that the authority for discipline comes from Jesus Christ.

103. Baptism and union with the remnant church is for the purpose of purifying the members of the church according to Ephesians 5:26, 27. Open sinners must be separated from the church according to the biblical method of giving two warnings before separation (*Christ's Object Lessons*, p. 71).

104. The guidelines for the disfellowshipping of church members from the Seventh-day Adventist Church can only be settled at a General Conference session and then proclaimed to the worldwide church (Ps. 50:18).

105. We must love the Lord in truth.

Twenty Points of Worthiness

Besides the basis of 105 specifications that should not be violated, there are twenty additional principles of worthiness or eligibility for the selection of ordained ministers, and credential missionaries, Conference leaders, church delegates, church deacons, deaconesses, church elders, and church board members. They must be (1) blameless within the community, (2) the husband of one wife, (3) vigilant (4) sensible, (5) of good behavior, (6) hospitable, (7) a good Bible teacher, (8) should not be a drunkard, (9) should not be violent but should be gentle, (10) should not be a lover of money, (11) should not be unruly, (12) should keep his children from being unruly, (13) must not be a recent convert, (14) should not be a proud person, (15) should not practice witchcraft and other devilish practices, (16) should be recommended by the public, (17) should not fall under reproach, (18) should be a faithful steward of God, (19) should be patient, (20) should be able to manage their own house for, if they cannot manage their own house, how can they care for the church of God? (1 Tim. 3:1–7; Titus 1:6–7).

How can we get ourselves to live by these specifications? It is first by having these 105 specifications recorded in our minds and then by receiving power from the Holy Spirit under the latter rain. During the period from 1844 to 1915, God gave more than 3,000 visions and dreams to call attention to the larger picture of the holy Ten Commandments and the 105 specifications under them. Having these 105

Chapter 7 God's Unchangeable Law and Its 105 Specifications

principles of God's holy law in our minds, the evil angels cannot overcome us. Our individual holy angel will help us to drive away the evil angels if we do not commit the 105 unpardonable sins. This is the seventh sense of man, which was given by Jesus Christ, the living God of heaven. We do not need to read all 19,500 pages of the "latter rain" testimonies, written by Sister Ellen G. White, to understand the 105 unpardonable sins of the holy Ten Commandments, for we have given here a summary of her testimonies. When we love the LORD with all our heart, the LORD will give us the conviction and strength to stand firm and not commit any of these 105 unpardonable sins directly or indirectly. We must beware of miracles disguised as blessings. Do not let anything take your eternal salvation! Pastors of the Seventh-day Adventist Church must go carefully through this list of 105 unpardonable sins against God's law, and they must faithfully uphold them as examples to their flock.

Chapter 8
180 Prophecies Concerning Our Eternal Salvation

One of the most impressive features in Scripture is its inclusion of prophecy, which has projected events before they occur. Out of all the prophecies in the Bible, I have selected 180 that have to do with human salvation. Jesus Christ fulfilled thirty of these at His first coming. Before we consider these prophecies in particular, we need to understand the general nature of prophecy.

What is Prophecy?
Prophecy tells what is going to happen, either in a world kingdom, in a nation's history, in church history, or in an individual's life. When God informs a prophet what is going to happen in a particular year in the future, that is called prophecy.

In other words, prophecy is—
1. The foretelling, or predicting, of what is to come;
2. An inspired message declared by a prophet, either prediction, instruction, or exhortation.

Chapter 8 180 Prophecies Concerning Our Eternal Salvation

3. A divinely inspired utterance or revelation: *oracular prophecies*.
4. 4. The action, function, or faculty of a prophet.

What did Habakkuk say about divinely inspired biblical prophecy?
1. 1. That a prophecy will be fulfilled in its appointed time.
2. 2. When its time has come, it will speak.
3. 3. Prophecy never lies.
4. 4. "Though it tarries," it will surely come.
5. 5. We must wait for its fulfillment.
6. 6. "Because it will surely come" (Hab. 2:3).

How did other biblical prophets describe prophecy?
1. 1. Amos wrote: "Surely the Lord GOD does nothing, unless He reveals His secret to His servants the prophets" (Amos 3:7).
2. 2. Peter wrote: "For prophecy never came by the will of man, but holy men of God spoke *as they were* moved by the Holy Spirit" (2 Peter 1:21).
3. 3. Paul wrote that we should not despise prophesying (1 Thess. 5:20), that is, we should not diminish the gift of prophecy or what a prophet communicates.
4. 4. Peter also wrote that, having a surer word of prophecy, "no prophecy of Scripture is of any private interpretation" (2 Peter 1:20).
5. 5. According to Solomon, "Where *there is* no vision [that is, no prophecy], the people perish: but he that keepeth the law happy *is* he" (Prov. 29:18, KJV). "Of this salvation the prophets have inquired and searched carefully, who prophesied of the grace *that would come* to you, searching what, or what manner of time, the Spirit of Christ who was in them was indicating when He testified beforehand the sufferings of Christ and the glories that would follow" (1 Peter 1:10, 11).
6. 6. Paul wrote: "Test all things; hold fast what is good" (1 Thess. 5:21).

How many types of biblical prophecy are there?

There are four types of prophecies in the Bible. Any prophecy falls under one of these four types. To understand a prophecy, you need to know what type of prophecy it is.

1. **Single prophecies.** By definition, this is a prophecy that will have only one fulfillment. An example of this is Isaiah 53, which predicts the crucifixion of Jesus Christ, who "was led as a lamb to the slaughter." This is a single prophecy because Jesus only had to die once to fulfill it. (Some might think of the virgin birth of Isaiah 7:14 as a single prophecy. However, it had two fulfillments—in the birth of Christ and previously in the time of Isaiah, for the Hebrew word translated "virgin" can also be translated as "young woman.") Isaiah wrote his prophecy in 765 BC. The prophecy was fulfilled in AD 31 in Jerusalem. This is a single prophecy.

2. **Two-part prophecies.** A two-part prophecy has either two parts or two fulfillments. Two examples of this type of prophecy are Genesis 3:15 and Joel 2:23.

    Genesis 3:15 says, "I will put enmity between you and the woman, and between your seed and her Seed; He shall bruise your head, and you shall bruise His heel." This prophecy has two phases of fulfillment: first, Jesus was to bruise Satan's head, which means that Jesus Christ overcame him at the cross, yet He will also destroy Satan at his third coming after the millennium, which Jesus will have spent in heaven. Second, Satan was to bruise Jesus' heel. This took place at the crucifixion of Jesus Christ. The two-part prophecy about the former and latter rain of Joel 2 declares, "Be glad then, you children of Zion, and rejoice in the LORD your God; for He has given you the former rain faithfully, and He will cause the rain to come down for you—the former rain, and the latter rain in the first *month*" (Joel 2:23).

3. **Repetitive prophecies.** Prophecies of this type will repeat until the end of this world. For example, Jesus said, "And you will hear of wars and rumors of wars. See that you are not troubled; for all *these things* must come to pass, but the end is not yet. For nation will rise against nation, and kingdom against kingdom. And there will be famines, pestilences, and earthquakes in various places. All these *are* the beginning of sorrows" (Matt. 24:6, 7).

4. **Time prophecies.** This type of prophecy will be fulfilled at a particular time. For example, (1) Daniel 8:14 was to be fulfilled at the end of 2300 prophetic days or a period of 2300

years, (2) Daniel 12:11 was to be fulfilled after 1290 years, and (3) Daniel 12:12 was to be fulfilled after 1335 years. These are prophecies based on specific time frames for their fulfillments.

The following is a chart of prophetic symbols and their meanings.

Chart 8.1. Keys to Understanding Prophetic Symbols

No.	BIBLE REFERENCE	SYMBOL	MEANING
1	Daniel 7:23	beast	a kingdom
2	Daniel 7:24; 8:21	horn	a king and the kingdom he represents
3	Daniel 7:3	from the sea	from a thickly-populated region
4	Revelation 17:15	waters	people, multitudes, nations, and tongues
5	Revelation 16:12	drying of the Euphrates	support of the people, multitudes, nations, and tongues comes to an end
6	Malachi 4:2	Sun of righteousness	Jesus Christ
7	Luke 1:78	Dayspring on high	Jesus Christ
8	Revelation 7:1	four winds	"The farthest part of earth" (Mark 13:27)
9	Revelation 12:1	a woman clothed with the sun	God's church, Jewish or Christian
10	Revelation 14:4; 17:5	defiling women	corrupted churches
11	2 Corinthians 11:2	chaste virgin or pure bride	the true church
12	Revelation 14:4	"They are virgins"	pure church members have not violated the Ten Commandments

Chart 8.1. Keys to Understanding Prophetic Symbols

No.	BIBLE REFERENCE	SYMBOL	MEANING
13	Ephesians 5:23	Head of the church	Jesus
14	Revelation 12:1	crown of twelve stars	the twelve apostles
15	Acts 4:11 (see also Matt. 21:42; Mark 12:10; Luke 20:17)	the cornerstone	Jesus Christ—not Peter
16	Eph. 2:20; 1 Peter 2:6	Chief cornerstone	Jesus Christ
17	Daniel 2:34, 44	a stone cut out without hands	Jesus Christ
18	1 Corinthians 10:4	the spiritual Rock	Jesus Christ
19	Revelation 12:5	the male Child born of the woman in white	Jesus Christ
20	Romans 11:17	olive branches	1. ancient Israel made up of Jews 2. the Apostolic church and its descendants
21	Revelation 2:1	angel of the church	head of, or messenger to, the church
22	Revelation 18:2, 3	Babylon (Rome)	head of the church, kingly power influencing other nations for evil
23	Revelation 2:20	Jezebel	a corrupted church

Chart 8.1. Keys to Understanding Prophetic Symbols

No.	BIBLE REFERENCE	SYMBOL	MEANING
24	1 Corinthians 14:8	uncertain trumpet sound	corrupted doctrine, uncertain dogmatic principles
25	Ezekiel 4:6	a day	one year
26	Daniel 7:25	a time	one year
27	Daniel 7:25	times	two years
28	Daniel 7:25	dividing of time	half a year
29	Revelation 9:15	an hour (one twenty-fourth of a day)	15 days
30	Revelation 8:1	half an hour	7½ days
31	Daniel 8:14	2300 days	2300 years
32	Joel 2:23, 28–30	former, or early, rain	the first *outward* appearance of God's Holy Spirit
33	Joel 2:23	latter rain	the second *inward* appearance of God's Holy Spirit
34	Esther 8:10	sealed	the symbol of kingly power
35	Revelation 7:2 (see also Isa. 8:16; Exodus 20:3–17)	the seal of the living God	observing the seventh-day Sabbath
36	Revelation 13:17; 15:2	mark of the beast, number of the beast and the number of his name—666	the Sunday sabbath numerical equivalent of *VICARIUS FILII DEI* (vicar of the Son of God)

Chart 8.1. Keys to Understanding Prophetic Symbols

No.	BIBLE REFERENCE	SYMBOL	MEANING
37	Revelation 12:13	dragon	Lucifer, Satan, the devil
38	Revelation 12:14	wilderness	the virgin land that became the United States of America
39	Revelation 12:14	two wings of a great eagle	The United States of America (the nation's emblem has eagle wings)
40	Revelation 6:2; 9:17; 19:11	horse	speed of battle or accomplishment
41	Revelation 6:4	the color red	blood-shedding war
42	Revelation 6:2	the color white	pure or clean
43	Revelation 6:5	the color black	death or mourning
44	Revelation 6:8	a pale color	severe persecution
45	Revelation 8:5	fire from the altar	natural disasters, like earth quakes and pestilence
46	Revelation 8:13	inhabiters of the earth	people living on the planet
47	Revelation 10:1	another mighty angel	William Miller of the United States of America
48	Revelation 10:2	little book	the book of Daniel

Chart 8.1. Keys to Understanding Prophetic Symbols

No.	BIBLE REFERENCE	SYMBOL	MEANING
49	Revelation 10:3	a roaring lion	William Miller's call about the second coming of Jesus Christ in 1844
50	Revelation 13:13; 20:9	fire came down from heaven	fire from the sky as in war or even a nuclear blast

God's Declarations Are Sure

Moses wrote in the book of Job regarding what God declares: "For God may speak in one way, or in another, *yet man* does not perceive it" (Job 33:14). This means that Jesus Christ and God the Holy Spirit will speak once, and whatever They have spoken they will not alter. David declared on God's behalf: "My covenant I will not break, nor alter the word that has gone out of My lips" (Ps. 89:34). This means that, when God makes a covenant, no matter what, He will not change it.

150 Selected Prophecies Connected with Eternal Salvation

1. The prophecy to introduce the plan of salvation:

Genesis chapter 1. In the six days' creation, God took six days to create this world to teach Satan and the fallen angels that Jesus Christ is God and Creator. God created Adam and Eve to obey God's word and to lead the fallen angels to God for their salvation. I have contended that the first plan of salvation was offered to Satan and the fallen angels, but Satan deceived Adam and Eve, so God had to offer a second plan of salvation for them. By creating this world in six days and showing the power to Satan and fallen angels, the first prophecy was fulfilled.

2. The prophecy that predicts life or death as a consequence of sin:

"But of the tree of the knowledge of good and evil you shall not eat, for in the day that you eat of it you shall surely die" (Gen. 2:17). God taught them what is good and what is evil, and He told them that, if they ate the fruit in disobedience, they would die. Since Adam and Eve violated God's law—God's rule over their lives—they both had to die a physical death. This prophecy was fulfilled.

3. The prophecy about marriage:

"Therefore a man shall leave his father and mother and be joined to his wife, and they shall become one flesh" (Gen. 2:24). Here God prophesied that husband and wife will live together. Paul uses this as a metaphor for the remnant church, for the members' love is like that which is between husband and wife. They must show their love for one another in spiritual fellowship. Before loving their neighbor, they first have to keep the first four commandments to show to God Almighty that they love Him. Secondly, they have to keep the other six commandments to demonstrate God's love to their fellow church members and to the sinful world. In the continuing relationship between husbands and wives, we see this prophecy being fulfilled.

4. The prophecy about the enmity between Christ and Satan:

"And I will put enmity between you and the woman, and between your seed and her Seed; He shall bruise your head, and you shall bruise His heel" (Gen. 3:15). This is a two-part prophecy. It must be fulfilled twice. As we read in the beginning: (1) "He shall bruise your head" points to Jesus Christ's overcoming Satan at the cross and also His destroying of Satan at His third coming to this earth after He has spent a thousand years in heaven; (2) "and you shall bruise His heel" points to the crucifixion of Jesus Christ fulfilled in AD 31.

The second part of the two-part prophecy will be fulfilled during the third coming of Jesus Christ after the millennium when Jesus Christ destroys Lucifer and the angels who fell with him as well as all of wicked humanity. (One part of this prophecy has been fulfilled—with the second part left to be fulfilled.)

5. The prophecy of the clothing made of skins:

"Also for Adam and his wife the Lord God made tunics of skin, and clothed them" (Gen. 3:21). God offered sacrifices, shedding innocent blood, to clothe Adam and Eve with the skins of the animals that were sacrificed. The sacrifices pointed forward to the way that His Son was going to die in humankind's place. At the cross, this prophecy was fulfilled when God covered humans with His righteousness, for the righteousness of humans is fig leaves and filthy rags. The sacrifice will cover humans' sins until the second coming of Jesus Christ when every one of Adam's sins will have been washed away by the blood of Jesus Christ, and the great multitude will praise Him. "After these things I looked, and behold, a great multitude which no one could number, of all nations, tribes, peoples, and tongues, standing before the throne and before the Lamb, clothed with white robes, with palm branches in their hands, and crying out with a loud voice, saying, 'Salvation *belongs* to our God who sits on the throne, and to the Lamb!' " (Rev. 7:9, 10).

6. The prophecy of pain in childbirth:

"To the woman He said: 'I will greatly multiply your sorrow and your conception; in pain you shall bring forth children; your desire *shall be* for your husband, and he shall rule over you' " (Gen. 3:16). God blessed Eve and mothers after her to give birth to children and multiply and fill the earth. No doubt children are a blessing. Yet, every woman has to endure pain in childbirth and a woman's desire is to her husband. God gave human beings the sexual feelings we have towards the opposite sex, and He created Adam from the dust of the ground, and He created Eve from Adam's rib. This prophecy has been fulfilled.

7. The prophecy about the Flood:

And God said to Noah, "The end of all flesh has come before Me, for the earth is filled with violence through them; and behold, I will destroy them with the earth. Make yourself an ark of gopherwood; make rooms in the ark, and cover it inside and outside with pitch. And this is how you shall make it: The length of the ark *shall be* three hundred cubits, its width fifty cubits, and its height thirty cubits. You shall make a window for the ark, and you shall finish it to a cubit from above; and set the door of the ark in its side. You shall make it *with* lower, second, and third *decks.* And behold, I Myself am bringing floodwaters on the earth, to destroy from under heaven all flesh in which *is* the breath of life; everything that *is* on the earth shall die. But I will establish My covenant with you; and you shall go into the ark—you, your sons, your wife, and your sons' wives with you. And of every living thing of all flesh you shall bring two of every *sort* into the ark, to keep *them* alive with you; they shall be male and female. Of the birds after their kind, of animals after their kind, and of every creeping thing of the earth after its kind, two of every *kind* will come to you to keep *them* alive. And you shall take for yourself of all food that is eaten, and you shall gather *it* to yourself; and it shall be food for you and for them." Thus Noah did; according to all that God commanded him, so he did. (Gen. 6:13–22)

God foretold the great Flood, by which He would destroy the wicked world. Modern atheistic scientists do not believe the Flood history of the Holy Bible, and that history is even challenged among Christians. They also question why rain should not have fallen before the Flood, and they insist that rainbows were manifest before the Flood. But the word of God declares that the Flood did occur and that the rainbow is a sign of mercy following the Flood.

8. The prophecy of Canaan's curse:

"Then he said: 'Cursed *be* Canaan; A servant of servants He shall be to his brethren.' And he said: 'Blessed *be* the LORD, the God of Shem, and may Canaan be his servant. May God enlarge Japheth, and may he dwell in the tents of Shem; and may Canaan be his servant' " (Gen. 9:25–27). Ham's descendants were cursed as a result of his disrespect for his father when he laughed at his father's nakedness after Noah had become inebriated from drinking wine, thereby violating God's law. Egypt is the land of Ham, as we see in the following Hebrew parallelism: "Israel also came into Egypt; and Jacob dwelt in the land of Ham" (Ps. 105:23). This prophecy has been fulfilled.

9. The prophecy of four hundred years until freedom from slavery:

"Then He said to Abram: 'Know certainly that your descendants will be strangers in a land *that is* not theirs, and will serve them, and they will afflict them four hundred years' " (Gen. 15:13). God predicted that the descendants of Abraham would be slaves in Egypt because of their disobedience to God's commandments. This prophecy has been fulfilled. Those who disobey God's law, after knowing His love and mercy, you will become slaves. "If man had kept the law of God, as given to Adam after his fall, preserved by Noah, and observed by Abraham, there would have been no necessity for the ordinance of circumcision. And if the descendants of Abraham had kept the covenant, of which circumcision was a sign, they would never have been seduced into idolatry, nor would it have been necessary for them to suffer a life of bondage in Egypt; they would have kept God's law in mind, and there would have been no necessity for it to be proclaimed from Sinai or engraved upon the tables of stone. And had the people practiced the principles of the Ten Commandments, there would have been no need of the additional directions given to Moses" (*Patriarchs and Prophets*, p. 364).

10. The prophecy of Ishmael, the father of Islam:

"He shall be a wild man; his hand *shall be* against every man, and every man's hand against him. And he shall dwell in the presence of all his brethren" (Gen. 16:12). God predicted that Abraham's son Ishmael would be an uncontrollable force with enemies on all sides. This prophecy has been fulfilled.

11. The pharaoh's dream and Joseph's interpretation of it:

Genesis, chapters 41 and 42, recounts the significant dream the pharaoh had and its interpretation by Joseph, God's servant. When it came to pass as he predicted, Joseph became the prime minister of Egypt. This prophecy was fulfilled.

12. The prophecy of the multitude of the children of Israel:

"The Angel who has redeemed me from all evil, bless the lads; let my name be named upon them, and the name of my fathers Abraham and Isaac; and let them grow into a multitude in the midst of the earth" (Gen. 48:16). When Abraham was as yet without children, God told him that his descendants would be multiplied. This prophecy has been fulfilled.

13. The prophecy of the character of the children of Israel:

Genesis, chapter 49, tells how Jacob called his twelve sons to his side and blessed them, foretelling how the Messiah would come through Judah. "The scepter shall not depart from Judah, nor a lawgiver from between his feet, until Shiloh comes; and to Him *shall be* the obedience of the people" (Gen. 49:10). This prophecy was fulfilled in Christ.

14. The prophecy of forty years in the wilderness:

"According to the number of the days in which you spied out the land, forty days, for each day you shall bear your guilt one year, *namely* forty years, and you shall know My rejection" (Num. 14:34). Since the children of Israel did not believe in the power of God, they had to wander forty years in the wilderness, and all those who murmured died in the wilderness and fulfilled the prophecy.

15. The prophecy against Eli and his sons:

"And you will see an enemy *in My* dwelling place, *despite* all the good which God does for Israel. And there shall not be an old man in your house forever" (1 Sam. 2:32). God was not happy with Eli the high priest and his sons, and He foretold that they would be destroyed because of their arrogant disobedience. This prophecy was fulfilled to the letter.

16. The prophecy against David because of his adultery:

"Thus says the LORD: 'Behold, I will raise up adversity against you from your own house; and I will take your wives before your eyes and give *them* to your neighbor, and he shall lie with your wives in the sight of this sun. For you did *it* secretly, but I will do this thing before all Israel, before the sun'" (2 Sam. 12:11, 12). This prophecy was fulfilled to the letter.

"So they pitched a tent for Absalom on the top of the house, and Absalom went in to his father's concubines in the sight of all Israel" (2 Sam. 16:22).

17. The prophecy of Solomon's temple:

"And it came to pass in the four hundred and eightieth year after the children of Israel had come out of the land of Egypt, in the fourth year of Solomon's reign over Israel, in the month of Ziv, which *is* the second month that he began to build the house of the LORD. Now the house which King Solomon built for the LORD, its length *was* sixty cubits, its width twenty, and its height thirty cubits" (1 Kings 6:1, 2). The specific numbers of this prophecy are very interesting. In 1015 BC, Solomon was ordained as king, and in the fourth year of his reign—1011 BC—Solomon began to build the temple, completing the work in 1004 BC. Going back 480 years from 1011 BC takes us to 1491 BC, which was the year the children of Israel left Egypt. Only the Bible gives this kind of chronology. More importantly, God predicted that David's son would build the temple, and Solomon did indeed build the temple, fulfilling the prophecy.

18. The prophecy that Israel will become a proverb and a byword:

"*But* if you or your sons at all turn from following Me, and do not keep My commandments *and* My statutes which I have set before you, but go and serve other gods and worship them, then I will cut off Israel from the land which I have given them; and this house which I have consecrated for My name I will cast out of My sight. Israel will be a proverb and a byword among all peoples" (1 Kings 9:6, 7). God expected Solomon to keep His law against worshipping idols, but Solomon was not willing to follow the Lord and he ended up fulfilling the prophecy through his disobedience.

19. The prophecy of a divided kingdom:

"Therefore the LORD said to Solomon, "Because you have done this, and have not kept My covenant and My statutes, which I have commanded you, I will surely tear the kingdom away from you and give it to your servant" (1 Kings 11:11). Again God punished Solomon by giving his kingdom to a servant because of his willful disobedience of God's law. This prophecy was fulfilled to the letter when Jeroboam, Solomon's servant, took over the ten-tribe northern kingdom of Israel (1 Kings 11:26).

20. The prophecy of the condition for the building of Solomon's temple:

"And it came to pass in the four hundred and eightieth year after the children of Israel had come out of the land of Egypt, in the fourth year of Solomon's reign over Israel, in the month of Ziv, which *is* the second month, that he began to build the house of the LORD. Now the house which King Solomon built for the LORD, its length *was* sixty cubits, its width twenty, and its height thirty cubits" (1 Kings 6:1, 2).

"*But* if you or your sons at all turn from following Me, and do not keep My commandments *and* My statutes which I have set before you, but go and serve other gods and worship them, then I will cut off Israel from the land which I have given them; and this house which I have consecrated for My name I will cast out of My sight. Israel will be a proverb and a byword among all peoples" (1 Kings 9:6).

God told Solomon that the temple would not be destroyed if Israel were faithful in keeping God's law. Since Israel turned against God, Nebuchadnezzar destroyed the golden temple, and the prophecy was fulfilled to the letter.

21. The prophecy against the king of Baasha:

"Then the word of the LORD came to Jehu the son of Hanani, against Baasha, saying: 'Inasmuch as I lifted you out of the dust and made you ruler over My people Israel, and you have walked in the way of Jeroboam, and have made My people Israel sin, to provoke Me to anger with their sins, Surely I will take away the posterity of Baasha and the posterity of his house, and I will make your house like the house of Jeroboam the son of Nebat. The dogs shall eat whoever belongs to Baasha and dies in the city, and the birds of the air shall eat whoever dies in the fields' " (1 Kings 16:1–4).

"Now the rest of the acts of Baasha, what he did, and his might, *are* they not written in the book of the chronicles of the kings of Israel? So Baasha rested with his fathers and was buried in Tirzah. Then Elah his son reigned in his place" (1 Kings 16:5, 6).

"And also the word of the LORD came by the prophet Jehu the son of Hanani against Baasha and his house, because of all the evil that he did in the sight of the LORD in provoking Him to anger with the work of his hands, in being like the house of Jeroboam, and because he killed them" (1 Kings 16:7). Elah reigned in Israel seven years. "In the twenty-sixth year of Asa king of Judah, Elah the son of Baasha became king over Israel, *and reigned* two years in Tirzah" (1 Kings 16:8). This prophecy was fulfilled to the letter.

22. The prophecy regarding drought and Ahab and his wife Jezebel:

"And Elijah the Tishbite, of the inhabitants of Gilead, said to Ahab, '*As* the Lord God of Israel lives, before whom I stand, there shall not be dew nor rain these years, except at my word' " (1 Kings 17:1).

God sent Elijah to warn Ahab about the drought that would be brought to the land because of idol worship. This prophecy was fulfilled to the letter.

"You shall speak to him, saying, 'Thus says the Lord: "Have you murdered and also taken possession?" ' And you shall speak to him, saying, 'Thus says the Lord: "In the place where dogs licked the blood of Naboth, dogs shall lick your blood, even yours." '... 'The dogs shall eat whoever belongs to Ahab and dies in the city, and the birds of the air shall eat whoever dies in the field' " (1 Kings 21:19, 24).

Ahab and his wicked wife killed Naboth and took his land. Consequently, God sent Elijah to give them a fatal curse. This prophecy has been fulfilled to the letter.

23. The prophecy against the drought and an unbelieving officer:

"Then Elisha said, 'Hear the word of the Lord. Thus says the Lord: "Tomorrow about this time a seah of fine flour *shall be sold* for a shekel, and two seahs of barley for a shekel, at the gate of Samaria"' " (2 Kings 7:1).

"Then that officer had answered the man of God, and said, 'Now look, *if* the Lord would make windows in heaven, could such a thing be?' And he had said, 'In fact, you shall see *it* with your eyes, but you shall not eat of it.' And so it happened to him, for the people trampled him in the gate, and he died" (2 Kings 7:19, 20).

This prophecy was fulfilled to the letter.

24. The prophecy of adding fifteen years to the life of Hezekiah the king:

"And I will add to your days fifteen years. I will deliver you and this city from the hand of the king of Assyria; and I will defend this city for My own sake, and for the sake of My servant David" (2 Kings 20:6).

This prophecy was fulfilled to the letter.

25. The prophecy of God's judgment:

"And I will add to your days fifteen years. I will deliver you and this city from the hand of the king of Assyria; and I will defend this city for my own sake, and for the sake of My servant David" (2 Kings 20:6). "Say among the nations, 'The LORD reigns; the world also is firmly established, it shall not be moved; He shall judge the peoples righteously' " (Ps. 96:10; see also Ps. 9:7, 8). God is indeed the righteous judge, and this prophecy was fulfilled.

26. The prophecy about the virgin birth of Jesus Christ:

"Therefore the Lord Himself will give you a sign: Behold, the virgin shall conceive and bear a Son, and shall call His name Immanuel" (Isa 7:14). "For unto us a Child is born, unto us a Son is given; and the government will be upon His shoulder. And His name will be called Wonderful, Counselor, Mighty God, Everlasting Father, Prince of Peace" (Isa 9:6).

The prophecy regarding the virgin birth of Jesus Christ was fulfilled to the letter, for not only did a young woman conceive (the Hebrew word *'almah* in Isaiah 7:14 can be translated "young woman of marriageable age or newly married") but a virgin (Greek, *parthenos*)—Mary—conceived and gave birth to Jesus.

27. The prophecy of the former and latter rain:

"Be glad then, you children of Zion, and rejoice in the LORD your God; for He has given you the former rain faithfully, and He will cause the rain to come down for you—the former rain, and the latter rain in the first *month*. The threshing floors shall be full of wheat, and the vats shall overflow with new wine and oil" (Joel 2:23, 24). "And I will show wonders in the heavens and in the earth: blood and fire and pillars of smoke. The sun shall be turned into darkness, and the moon into blood, before the coming of the great and awesome day of the LORD" (Joel 2:30, 31; see also Isa. 13:10).

This prophecy about the former and the latter rain will have been fulfilled by the two public ministries of the Holy Spirit—in the former rain, from AD 31 to AD 100 and in the latter rain, from AD 1833 to until the coming of the Lord. (See the exposition on the former and the latter rain.)

28. The prophecy against false prophets:

"For the LORD has poured out on you the spirit of deep sleep, and has closed your eyes, namely, the prophets; and He has covered your heads, *namely,* the seers" (Isa. 29:10).

According to this prophecy, many organized Christian churches are not willing to see the real truth of God in the Bible.

29. The prophecy of the seven last plagues:

"Moreover the light of the moon will be as the light of the sun, and the light of the sun will be sevenfold, as the light of seven days, in the day that the LORD binds up the bruise of His people and heals the stroke of their wound" (Isa. 30:26). According to this prophecy, during the period of the seventh of the seven last plagues, the heat of the sun will be increased seven times greater than it is now—from 110º F to 770º F. However, the God of heaven will protect His children and cover them completely. He will fulfill the prophecy regarding the last of the seven plagues after He has sealed the 144,000. The seven last plagues will last just one year of 360 days. (This prophecy is not yet fulfilled.)

30. The prophecy that God's children will be cared for:

"He will dwell on high; His place of defense *will be* the fortress of rocks; bread will be given him; his water *will be* sure" (Isa. 33:16). During the seven last plagues, God's children will move from the very big cities to the villages and will get their food and water without contamination from nuclear radiation; it will not affect the vegetation where God's people live. This prophecy is not yet fulfilled.

31. The prophecy about a new heaven and a new earth:

" 'For behold, I create new heavens and a new earth; and the former shall not be remembered or come to mind. But be glad and rejoice forever in what I create; for behold, I create Jerusalem *as* a rejoicing, and her people a joy. I will rejoice in Jerusalem, and joy in My people; the voice of weeping shall no longer be heard in her, nor the voice of crying. No more shall an infant from there *live but a few* days, nor an old man who has not fulfilled his days; for the child shall die one hundred years old, but the sinner *being* one hundred years old shall be accursed. They shall build houses and inhabit *them;* they shall plant vineyards and eat their fruit. They shall not build and another inhabit; they shall not plant and another eat; for as the days of a tree, *so shall be* the days of My people, and My elect shall long enjoy the work of their hands. They shall not labor in vain, nor bring forth children for trouble; for they *shall be* the descendants of the blessed of the LORD, and their offspring with them.

" 'It shall come to pass that before they call, I will answer; and while they are still speaking, I will hear. The wolf and the lamb shall feed together, the lion shall eat straw like the ox, and dust *shall be* the serpent's food. They shall not hurt nor destroy in all My holy mountain,' says the LORD" (Isa. 65:17–25).

The new heaven and new earth will be created, as was the first creation, by Jesus Christ and the Holy Spirit during the period of Christ's third coming to this earth after the millennium in heaven. This prophecy is not yet fulfilled.

32. The prophecy about the twelve disciples:

" 'Behold, I will send for many fishermen,' says the LORD, 'and they shall fish them; and afterward I will send for many hunters, and they shall hunt them from every mountain and every hill, and out of the holes of the rocks' " (Jer. 16:16).

"Then they will deliver you up to tribulation and kill you, and you will be hated by all nations for My name's sake" (Matt. 24:9; see also Luke 21:20–25).

This prophecy has to do with the twelve disciples who were called by Jesus Christ and the Holy Spirit from AD 27 to 100 to do God's work as Jesus said, "Follow me, and I will make you fishers of men" (Matt. 4:19). These were the same disciples whom Satan doggedly persecuted. In accordance with this prophecy, all twelve disciples were martyred before AD 65 except for John, who died after AD 96–97, when he served on the island of Patmos as a prisoner and wrote the twenty-two chapters of Revelation—God's final word in the Bible. This prophecy has been fulfilled to the letter.

33. The prophecy about the destruction of Jerusalem:

"But if you will not heed Me to hallow the Sabbath day, such as not carrying a burden when entering the gates of Jerusalem on the Sabbath day, then I will kindle a fire in its gates, and it shall devour the palaces of Jerusalem, and it shall not be quenched" (Jer. 17:27). In AD 609 Jeremiah prophesied regarding the Sabbath violation of the descendants of Israel's third king— Solomon, and Jeremiah wrote that fire would destroy Jerusalem, which would be captured by the Babylonian king Nebuchadnezzar. Before the golden temple in Jerusalem was destroyed by fire, God commanded the prophet Jeremiah to remove the holy Ten Commandments in the ark and all the holy articles from the Most Holy Place and hide them in Mount Nebo. (The precise location is not listed in the text.) This prophecy was fulfilled to the letter.

34. The prophecy about the captivity of Jerusalem:

"For thus says the LORD: 'Behold, I will make you a terror to yourself and to all your friends; and they shall fall by the sword of their enemies, and your eyes shall see it. I will give all Judah into the hand of the king of Babylon, and he shall carry them captive to Babylon and slay them with the sword. Moreover I will deliver all the wealth of this city, all its produce, and all its precious things; all the treasures of the kings of Judah I will give into the hand of their enemies, who will plunder them, seize them, and carry them to Babylon" (Jer. 20:4, 5).

Jeremiah prophesied that the Babylonian king Nebuchadnezzar would capture Judah. Not only that but, according to Jeremiah 52:12–34, the city would be burnt and Judah's possessions would be carried to Babylon. This prophecy was fulfilled to the letter.

35. The prophecy about the Time of Jacob's Trouble:

"For thus says the LORD: 'We have heard a voice of trembling, of fear, and not of peace. Ask now, and see, whether a man is ever in labor with child? So why do I see every man *with* his hands on his loins like a woman in labor, and all faces turned pale? Alas! For that day *is* great, so that none *is* like it; and it *is* the time of Jacob's trouble, but he shall be saved out of it" (Jer. 30:5–7).

According to this statement, Jeremiah prophesied that, during the time of the seven last plagues, the children of God will undergo the trials of the time of Jacob's trouble. This prophecy has not yet been fulfilled.

36. The prophecy about one day equaling one year:

"According to the number of the days in which you spied out the land, forty days, for each day you shall bear your guilt one year, *namely* forty years, and you shall know My rejection" (Num. 14:34). In this text, God gives the key to understanding time prophecy, and that is, one day equals one year. (Daniel's contemporary gave the same key in Ezekiel 4:6.) Whenever we calculate the length of biblical prophecy given in days—as, for example, 2300 days, 1260 days, 1290 days, and 1335 days—we find that they are years. This prophecy has been fulfilled.

37. The prophecy of world history:

"But there is a God in heaven who reveals secrets, and He has made known to King Nebuchadnezzar what will be in the latter days. Your dream, and the visions of your head upon your bed, were these: … And in the days of these kings the God of heaven will set up a kingdom which shall never be destroyed; and the kingdom shall not be left to other people; it shall break in pieces and consume all these kingdoms, and it shall stand forever" (Dan. 2:28, 44).

The God of heaven foretold the five parts of world history, including four world kingdoms that would begin with the first world empire of Babylon. This prophecy, delivered by the prophet Daniel, would be an outline of world history. The part of the prophecy regarding the image has been fulfilled. The stone that was cut out from the mountain, which dashed the statue to pieces, is the second coming of Jesus Christ. This part of the prophecy is not yet fulfilled.

38. The prophecy about king Nebuchadnezzar and his pride:

"That very hour the word was fulfilled concerning Nebuchadnezzar; he was driven from men and ate grass like oxen; his body was wet with the dew of heaven till his hair had grown like eagles' *feathers* and his nails like birds' *claws*" (Dan. 4:33).

Nebuchadnezzar lived out in the fields seven years before returning to his throne. The previous three chapters describe the first world emperor—the Babylonian king Nebuchadnezzar, who ruled the world from 606 to 538 BC, a period of 78 years. During this time, Daniel, the twenty-third biblical prophet, was raised up by God to reveal many spiritual truths and to foretell the history of the world. This prophecy has been fulfilled.

39. The prophecy about the fall of Babylon:

" '… And this is the inscription that was written: MENE, MENE, TEKEL, UPHARSIN. This *is* the interpretation of *each* word. MENE: God has numbered your kingdom, and finished it; TEKEL: You have been weighed in the balances, and found wanting; PERES: Your kingdom has been divided, and given to the Medes and Persians.'… That very night Belshazzar, king of the Chaldeans, was slain. And Darius the Mede received the kingdom, *being* about sixty-two years old" (Dan. 5:25–28, 30, 31).

After the first world empire, the Babylonian kingdom, ruled from 606 to 538 BC, the Medo-Persian kingdom, which was divided into 127 provinces and included India and Ethiopia, took the world stage from 538 to 331 BC. Esther was queen during the Medo-Persian period. The third world empire was that of Greece under Alexander the Great. It lasted from 331 to 168 BC when it was overtaken by the Roman Empire, whose emperors held world dominance from 168 BC to AD 476, a period of well over six centuries. The empire that was begun by Julius Caesar broke into the ten kingdoms of Europe. This prophecy has been fulfilled.

40. The prophecy about the changing of times and God's law:

"The ten horns *are* ten kings *who* shall arise from this kingdom. And another shall rise after them; he shall be different from the first *ones,* and shall subdue three kings. He shall speak *pompous* words against the Most High, shall persecute the saints of the Most High, and shall intend to change times and law. Then *the saints* shall be given into his hand for a time and times and half a time" (Dan. 7:24, 25).

In fulfillment of this prophecy, Constantine changed the day of worship from the Sabbath to Sunday in AD 321. Later, in AD 583, which was during the time of the divided ten kingdoms, the Roman Emperor Justinian introduced the Pope as a Roman emperor to rule the church and the nation. During the period of AD 538 to AD 1798, covering exactly 1260 years, 192 popes ruled the nations and the Catholic Church ("The List of Popes," *Catholic Encyclopedia*). During this period of 1260 years, the pope functioned as an antichrist, bringing many new doctrines into the Christian church. Principal among these changes of God's law was the removal of the second commandment, allowing the use in worship of images for Jesus Christ, Mary, the apostles, and other Christians who were considered saints. Another change has to do with the sanctity of the seventh-day Sabbath. Church authorities claimed that the sanctity of the seventh day was transferred to Sunday, the first day of the week. Besides these changes, the Church inaugurated other festivals, such as Christmas on the 25th of December, and instituted child baptism and forgiveness of sin through priestly confession. It also moved the beginning of the day from sunset to 12 o'clock midnight, contrary to what the Bible teaches about the day beginning at evening and continuing through the night into the light part of the day (Gen. 1:5, 8, 13, 19, 23, 31). Last of all, in AD 1811, Pope Gregory added five days in to the year when he introduced the Gregorian calendar with 365 days, in contrast to the biblical year which had 360 days. Those who rejected Pope Gregory's authority were persecuted. This prophecy has been fulfilled.

41. The prophecy about the seventy weeks:

"Seventy weeks are determined for your people and for your holy city, to finish the transgression, to make an end of sins, to make reconciliation for iniquity, to bring in everlasting righteousness, to seal up vision and prophecy, and to anoint the Most Holy."

Chapter 8 180 Prophecies Concerning Our Eternal Salvation 153

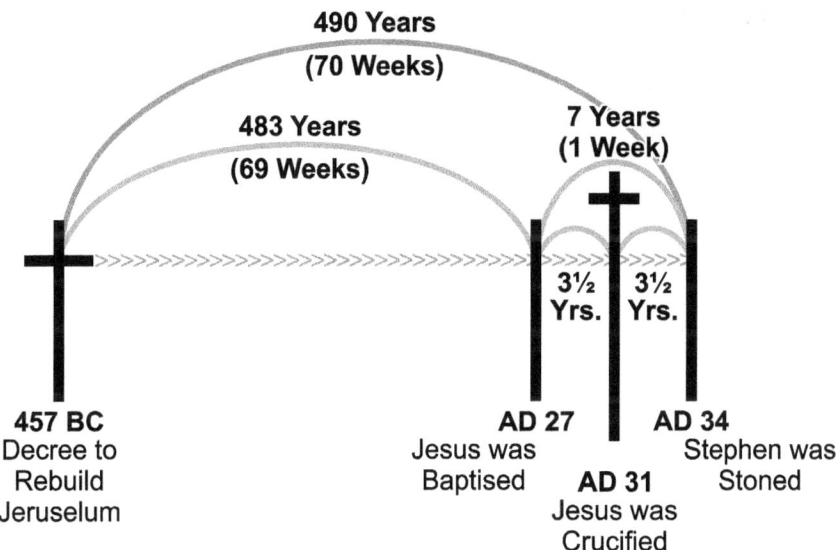

"Know therefore and understand, *that* from the going forth of the command to restore and build Jerusalem until Messiah the Prince, *there shall be* seven weeks and sixty-two weeks; the street shall be built again, and the wall, even in troublesome times."

"And after the sixty-two weeks Messiah shall be cut off, but not for Himself; and the people of the prince who is to come shall destroy the city and the sanctuary. The end of it *shall be* with a flood, and till the end of the war desolations are determined. Then he shall confirm a covenant with many for one week; but in the middle of the week he shall bring an end to sacrifice and offering. And on the wing of abominations shall be one who makes desolate, even until the consummation, which is determined, is poured out on the desolate." (Dan. 9:24–27)

This prophecy points to the crucifixion of Jesus Christ in the last of the seventy weeks and the propagation of the gospel message to the gentiles at the close of the seventy weeks. In taking the gospel to the Gentiles, church leaders taught the believers to pray in Christ's name and to be baptized with the baptism that was introduced by John the Baptist and Jesus Christ for the forgiveness of sins. From the crucifixion on, sins were forgiven by taking baptism and offering holy prayer in the name of Jesus Christ without the blood of sacrifices and going to Jerusalem once a year to offer sacrifices on the Day of Atonement. This prophecy has been fulfilled to the letter.

42. The prophecy of Daniel, chapter 11:

The second verse of Daniel, chapter 11, tells about Alexander the Great. The fourth verse describes the division of the Greek empire into four kingdoms, one of which was Egypt in the south. Verse 15 describes Julius Caesar in 44 BC, emperor of Pagan Rome. Verse 17 points to Cleopatra of Egypt, and verse 18 describes the death of Julius Caesar at the hands of Anthony his general. This prophecy was fulfilled.

43. Prophecy about the divided kingdoms:

Daniel 11, verse 4, describes the dividing of the Greek Empire of Alexander the Great into four kingdoms. Of these, Egypt will be in the south.

And now I will tell you the truth: Behold, three more kings will arise in Persia, and the fourth shall be far richer than *them* all; by his strength, through his riches, he shall stir up all against the realm of Greece. Then a mighty king shall arise, who shall rule with great dominion, and do according to his will. And when he has arisen, his kingdom shall be broken up and divided toward the four winds of heaven, but not among his posterity nor according to his dominion with which he ruled; for his kingdom shall be uprooted, even for others besides these. (Dan. 11:2–4)

Julius Caesar established Rome in 44 BC. "So the king of the North shall come and build a siege mound, and take a fortified city; and the forces of the South shall not withstand *him*. Even his choice troops *shall have* no strength to resist" (Dan. 11:15).

Cleopatra was to rule in Egypt. "He shall also set his face to enter with the strength of his whole kingdom, and upright ones with him; thus shall he do. And he shall give him the daughter of women to destroy it; but she shall not stand *with him,* or be for him" (Dan. 11:17).

Roman general Marcus Anthony killed Julius Caesar. "After this he shall turn his face to the coastlands, and shall take many. But a ruler shall bring the reproach against them to an end; and with the reproach removed, he shall turn back on him" (Dan. 11:18). These prophecies were fulfilled to the letter.

44. The prophecy of the special resurrection:
"And many of those who sleep in the dust of the earth shall awake, some to everlasting life, some to shame *and* everlasting contempt." (Dan. 12:2). The people who crucified Jesus Christ will be resurrected to everlasting contempt. This will take place when Jesus returns. "Behold, He is coming with clouds, and every eye will see Him, even they who pierced Him. And all the tribes of the earth will mourn because of Him. Even so, Amen" (Rev. 1:7). This prophecy has not yet been fulfilled.

45. The prophecy about knowledge in the modern world:
"But you, Daniel, shut up the words, and seal the book until the time of the end; many shall run to and fro, and knowledge shall increase" (Dan. 12:4). Overall knowledge in the world has increased as well as prophetic knowledge. This prophecy has been fulfilled.

46. The prophecy about the Wisdom of God's children:
"Many shall be purified, made white, and refined, but the wicked shall do wickedly; and none of the wicked shall understand, but the wise shall understand" (Dan. 12:10). Not everyone can understand God's Word. Only those who accept Jesus Christ as their personal Savior and who are willing to obey His Word will understand, from God's perspective, what is happening and what will take place in the world in the future. This prophecy has been fulfilled.

47. The prophecy about the book of sin:
"The iniquity of Ephraim *is* bound up; his sin *is* stored up" (Hosea 13:12). Hosea spoke about a record, or book, of sins. Joel described the early and latter rain.

"Be glad then, you children of Zion, and rejoice in the Lord your God; for He has given you the former rain faithfully, and He will cause the rain to come down for you—the former rain, and the latter rain in the first *month*" (Joel 2:23). It is my view that this prophecy has been fulfilled.

48. The prophecy of the scarcity to the word of God:

" 'Behold, the days are coming,' says the Lord GOD, 'That I will send a famine on the land, not a famine of bread, nor a thirst for water, but of hearing the words of the LORD' " (Amos 8:11). Throughout the Dark Ages, the Bible was not in the hands of the people. This prophecy has been fulfilled.

49. The prophecy about the destruction of Nineveh and the repentance of people:

"Yet forty days, and Nineveh shall be overthrown" (Jonah 3:4). The people of Nineveh repented. The fulfillment of this prophecy was that it led the people to repentance, showing the conditional nature of prophecy.

50. The prophecy about the character of the 144,000 of the remnant church:

"I will leave in your midst a meek and humble people, and they shall trust in the name of the LORD. The remnant of Israel shall do no unrighteousness and speak no lies, nor shall a deceitful tongue be found in their mouth; for they shall feed *their* flocks and lie down, and no one shall make *them* afraid" (Zeph. 3:12, 13). Revelation, chapter 14, talks about the character of the 144,000 "saints." This prophecy has not yet been fulfilled.

51. The prophecy about landing of New Jerusalem:

"And in that day His feet will stand on the Mount of Olives, which faces Jerusalem on the east. And the Mount of Olives shall be split in two, from east to west, *making* a very large valley; half of the mountain shall move toward the north and half of it toward the south" (Zech. 14:4). This prophecy tells where the golden city of the New Jerusalem will land at the third coming of Jesus Christ. It will be in the middle of the Mount of Olives in Jerusalem. This prophecy is not yet fulfilled.

52. The prophecy about the book of remembrance:

"Then those who feared the LORD spoke to one another, and the LORD listened and heard *them;* so a book of remembrance was written before Him for those who fear the LORD and who meditate on

His name" (Mal. 3:16). This prophecy, regarding the book of remembrance in heaven, is not yet fulfilled.

53. The two-part prophecy about the destruction of this world:

"For behold, the day is coming, burning like an oven, and all the proud, yes, all who do wickedly will be stubble. And the day which is coming shall burn them up," says the LORD of hosts, "That will leave them neither root nor branch" (Mal. 4:1). Some destruction will take place at Jesus' second coming (2 Thess. 2:8). However, at Jesus' third coming, the earth will be burnt up. This prophecy has not yet been fulfilled.

54. The prophecy about John the Baptist:

" 'Behold, I will send you Elijah the prophet before the coming of the great and dreadful day of the LORD. And he will turn the hearts of the fathers to the children, and the hearts of the children to their fathers, lest I come and strike the earth with a curse' " (Mal. 4:5, 6). John the Baptist came in the spirit of Elijah and fulfilled this prophecy to the letter. (Matt. 11:14, 15; 17:12)

55. The prophecy of the modern Pentecostal and charismatic churches

"Many will say to Me in that day, 'Lord, Lord, have we not prophesied in Your name, cast out demons in Your name, and done many wonders in Your name?' And then I will declare to them, 'I never knew you; depart from Me, you who practice lawlessness!'" (Matt. 7:22, 23).

This prophecy talks about a counterfeit latter rain as millions of Pentecostal, charismatic, and Roman Catholic believers perform miracles in these days while openly denying God's law. This prophecy is being fulfilled.

56. The prophecy that the divinity of Christ would not die on the cross

"For as Jonah was three days and three nights in the belly of the great fish, so will the Son of Man be three days and three nights in the heart of the earth" (Matt. 12:40). Jesus died as a human being, but His divinity did not die, and Jesus changed His human body into a spirit body, which only God can have, and after three days changed back to a human body when He was resurrected from the tomb. This prophecy has been fulfilled.

57. The prophecy against the Ten Commandments being nailed to the cross

" '*And in vain they worship Me, teaching as doctrines the commandments of men'* " (Matt. 15:9). Instead of preaching God's commandments and His love, men will preach the commandments of men by declaring that the law was nailed to the cross. (Compare Col. 2:14 and Eph. 2:15 for what was nailed to the cross, in the context of Col. 2:22, which condemns the teaching of the commandments of men.) This prophecy has been fulfilled to the letter.

58. The prophecy that Jesus is the Cornerstone

"And I also say to you that you are Peter, and on this rock I will build My church, and the gates of Hades shall not prevail against it" (Matt. 16:18). Jesus Christ is the "rock" (*petra*), or Cornerstone, and Peter is merely a pebble (*petros*) according to the Greek translation (Eph. 2:20; 1 Cor. 10:4; Ps. 18:2; Dan. 2:34; Acts 4:11, 12; Isa. 28:16). This prophecy has been fulfilled.

59. The prophecy about the holy prayer

"And I will give you the keys of the kingdom of heaven, and whatever you bind on earth will be bound in heaven, and whatever you loose on earth will be loosed in heaven" (Matt. 16:19). From the crucifixion on, every time we pray in the name of Jesus Christ our sins will be forgiven. This prophecy has been fulfilled.

60. The prophecy of last-day events

"And you will hear of wars and rumors of wars. See that you are not troubled; for all *these things* must come to pass, but the end is not yet. For nation will rise against nation, and kingdom against kingdom. And there will be famines, pestilences, and earthquakes in various places" (Matt. 24:6, 7). This is a repetitive, ongoing prophecy, with elements that will recur until the coming of the Lord.

61. The prophecy of the false prophets
"Then many false prophets will rise up and deceive many" (Matt. 24:11). Many false prophets have arisen throughout history. This prophecy has been fulfilled.

62. The prophecy about the fulfillment of the gospel
"And this gospel of the kingdom will be preached in all the world as a witness to all the nations, and then the end will come" (Matt. 24:14). The everlasting gospel has been preached and will be preached throughout the world until the end of the world. Remarkably, the Gregorian calendar has aided in the preaching of the gospel of the kingdom. This prophecy is being fulfilled.

63. The prophecy about the prayer of abomination
"Therefore when you see the '*abomination of desolation*,' spoken of by Daniel the prophet, standing in the holy place" (whoever reads, let him understand)" (Matt. 24:15). The prophecy points to holy prayer being changed from the name Jesus Christ to prayer through the Virgin Mary, facilitated through Pope Symmachus in AD 508. The prophecy has been fulfilled.

64. The prophecy about the destruction of Jerusalem:
"Then let those who are in Judea flee to the mountains. Let him who is on the housetop not go down to take anything out of his house. And let him who is in the field not go back to get his clothes. But woe to those who are pregnant and to those who are nursing babies in those days! And pray that your flight may not be in winter or on the Sabbath. For then there will be great tribulation, such as has not been since the beginning of the world until this time, no, nor ever shall be. And unless those days were shortened, no flesh would be saved; but for the elect's sake those days will be shortened" (Matt. 24:16–22). This prophecy talks about the destruction of Jerusalem, which took place in AD 70 by the Roman general Titus before he became emperor of

Rome. This prophecy has been fulfilled word for word. (See *The Great Controversy*, pp. 30–38.)

65. The prophecy about the second coming of Jesus Christ not being in secret:

"For as the lightning comes from the east and flashes to the west, so also will the coming of the Son of Man be. Christ coming will never be secret, everyone will be able to see" (Matt. 24:27). This prophecy has not yet been fulfilled.

66. The prophecy about the last days being like Noah's days:

"But as the days of Noah *were,* so also will the coming of the Son of Man be. For as in the days before the flood, they were eating and drinking, marrying and giving in marriage, until the day that Noah entered the ark" (Matt. 24:37, 38). This prophecy tells about people's behavior in the last days. This prophecy is being fulfilled.

67. The prophecy about Judas' betrayal of Jesus:

"He answered and said, 'He who dipped *his* hand with Me in the dish will betray Me' " (Matt. 26:23). Jesus predicted that Judas would betray Him. This prophecy has been fulfilled.

68. The prophecy about Peter's denial:

"Jesus said to him, 'Assuredly, I say to you that this night, before the rooster crows, you will deny Me three times' " (Matt. 26:34). Jesus made this prediction to Peter about his denial of his Lord. This prophecy has been fulfilled.

69. The prophecy about salvation only through Jesus:

"This is the '*stone which was rejected by you builders, which has become the chief cornerstone.*' Nor is there salvation in any other, for there is no other name under heaven given among men by which we must be saved" (Acts 4:11, 12).

"So they said, 'Believe on the Lord Jesus Christ, and you will be saved, you and your household' " (Acts 16:31). Faith in Jesus Christ and holy prayer in Jesus' name are enough for eternal life. This prophecy declares that salvation is only in the name of Jesus Christ. This prophecy has been fulfilled.

70. The prophecy about salvation to the Gentiles:

"Then he became very hungry and wanted to eat; but while they made ready, he fell into a trance and saw heaven opened and an object like a great sheet bound at the four corners, descending to him and let down to the earth. In it were all kinds of four-footed animals of the earth, wild beasts, creeping things, and birds of the air. And a voice came to him, 'Rise, Peter; kill and eat.' But Peter said, 'Not so, Lord! For I have never eaten anything common or unclean.' And a voice *spoke* to him again the second time, 'What God has cleansed you must not call common.' This was done three times. And the object was taken up into heaven again" (Acts 10:10–16). God revealed that the apostles were to turn to the Gentiles in preaching the gospel. This prophecy has been fulfilled.

71. The prophecy about the remnant:

"Isaiah also cries out concerning Israel: *'Though the number of the children of Israel be as the sand of the sea, the remnant will be saved'* " (Rom. 9:27). The prophecy about the remnant church being saved is being fulfilled.

72. The prophecy of the great multitude:

"For I do not desire, brethren, that you should be ignorant of this mystery, lest you should be wise in your own opinion, that blindness in part has happened to Israel until the fullness of the Gentiles has come in. And so all Israel will be saved, as it is written: *'The Deliverer will come out of Zion, and He will turn away ungodliness from Jacob; for this is My covenant with them, when I take away their sins.'* Concerning the gospel *they are* enemies for your sake, but concerning the election *they are* beloved for the sake of the fathers. For the gifts and the calling of God *are* irrevocable. For as you were once disobedient to God, yet have now obtained mercy through their disobedience, even so these also have now been disobedient, that through the mercy shown you they also may obtain mercy. For God has committed them all to disobedience, that He might have mercy on all" (Rom. 11:25–32). This prophecy about a great multitude has been fulfilled.

73. The prophecy about the resurrection:

"Now this I say, brethren, that flesh and blood cannot inherit the kingdom of God; nor does corruption inherit incorruption. Behold, I tell you a mystery: We shall not all sleep, but we shall all be changed—in a moment, in the twinkling of an eye, at the last trumpet. For the trumpet will sound, and the dead will be raised incorruptible, and we shall be changed. For this corruptible must put on incorruption, and this mortal *must* put on immortality. So when this corruptible has put on incorruption, and this mortal has put on immortality, then shall be brought to pass the saying that is written: *'Death is swallowed up in victory.' 'O Death, where is your sting? O Hades, where is your victory?'* The sting of death *is* sin, and the strength of sin *is* the law. But thanks *be* to God, who gives us the victory through our Lord Jesus Christ. Therefore, my beloved brethren, be steadfast, immovable, always abounding in the work of the Lord, knowing that your labor is not in vain in the Lord" (1 Cor. 15:51–58).

"For the Lord Himself will descend from heaven with a shout, with the voice of an archangel, and with the trumpet of God. And the dead in Christ will rise first. Then we who are alive *and* remain shall be caught up together with them in the clouds to meet the Lord in the air. And thus we shall always be with the Lord. Therefore comfort one another with these words" (1 Thess. 4:16–18).

This is regarding the first resurrection at the second coming of Jesus Christ. This prophecy has not yet been fulfilled.

74. The prophecy that saints will judge:

"Do you not know that we shall judge angels? How much more, things that pertain to this life?" (1 Cor. 6:3). God's people will perform this judgment during the millennium (see Rev. 10:4). This prophecy is not yet fulfilled.

75. The prophecy of the pure church:

"For I am jealous for you with godly jealousy. For I have betrothed you to one husband, that I may present *you as* a chaste virgin to Christ"

(2 Cor. 11:2). The prophetical code of the virgin woman represents the church. This prophecy is not yet fulfilled.

76. The prophecy of the glorious church:
"Husbands, love your wives, just as Christ also loved the church and gave Himself for her, that He might sanctify and cleanse her with the washing of water by the word, that He might present her to Himself a glorious church, not having spot or wrinkle or any such thing, but that she should be holy and without blemish" (Eph. 5:25–27). The prophecy of a "glorious church" is not yet fulfilled.

77. The prophecy about the Birth of Jesus Christ:
The Son of God "made Himself of no reputation, taking the form of a bondservant, *and* coming in the likeness of men" (Phil. 2:7). (Rather than "made Himself of no reputation," the RSV has "emptied himself.") This prophecy was fulfilled when Jesus chose to come to earth to be delivered by virgin birth.

78. The prophecy about ungodly people:
"Whose end *is* destruction, whose god *is their* belly, and *whose* glory *is* in their shame—who set their mind on earthly things" (Phil. 3:19). The belly of ungodly people is their god. This is a repetitive prophecy.

79. The prophecy about open sinners in the church:
"But we command you, brethren, in the name of our Lord Jesus Christ, that you withdraw from every brother who walks disorderly and not according to the tradition which he received from us" (2 Thess. 3:6). Open sinners must be separated from the church. This prophecy has not yet been fulfilled.

80. The prophecy that the earth will be tilted back to 90 degrees:
"Whose voice then shook the earth; but now He has promised, saying, '*Yet once more I shake not only the earth, but also heaven.*' Now this, '*Yet once more,*' indicates the removal of those things that are being shaken, as of things that are made, that the things which cannot

be shaken may remain" (Heb. 12:26, 27). The earth will be tilted from 23½ degrees to 90 degrees. This prophecy is not yet fulfilled.

81. The prophecy about wives:

"Husbands likewise, dwell with *them* with understanding, giving honor to the wife, as to the weaker vessel, and as *being* heirs together of the grace of life, that your prayers may not be hindered" (1 Peter 3:7). Women are the weaker vessel and must be protected and cared for. This prophecy is being fulfilled.

82. The prophecy about the beginning of God's judgment in 1844:

"For the time *has come* for judgment to begin at the house of God; and if *it begins* with us first, what will *be* the end of those who do not obey the gospel of God?" (1 Peter 4:17). In the year 1844, the investigative phase of the heavenly judgment began. Throughout Scripture, God always investigated before He executed judgment. This prophecy is being fulfilled.

83. The prophecy about the blood of Jesus Christ:

"But if we walk in the light as He is in the light, we have fellowship with one another, and the blood of Jesus Christ His Son cleanses us from all sin" (1 John 1:7). Forgiveness comes only through the blood of Jesus Christ. This prophecy is being fulfilled.

84. The prophecy about the triune God:

"For there are three that bear witness in heaven: The Father, the Word, and the Holy Spirit; and these three are one" (1 John 5:7). This text is an evidence for the triune nature of the GOD of heaven. The equation, "one by one by one equals ONE GOD," means they are EQUAL IN ALL RESPECTS. Jesus Christ is described as being the "Everlasting Father" (Isa. 9:6). Jesus Christ is not less than the Father, neither is He more than the Father, and their divinity is equal in all respects because what Jesus thinks, the first Person of the Godhead also thinks, and what the first Person of the Godhead thinks the Holy Spirit also thinks since the mind of all three is synchronized.

85. The prophecy about the seven churches:

"Saying 'I am the Alpha and the Omega, the First and the Last,' and, 'What you see, write in a book and send *it* to the seven churches which are in Asia: to Ephesus, to Smyrna, to Pergamos, to Thyatira, to Sardis, to Philadelphia, and to Laodicea' " (Rev. 1:11). This prophecy started in AD 31 and the final period of the seven churches will end at the second coming of the Lord. As we are living in the last church time period, this prophecy has been partially fulfilled. (See Chapter 9 of this book for details on the seven churches .)

86. The prophecy about the persecution during the Dark Ages:

"Do not fear any of those things which you are about to suffer. Indeed, the devil is about to throw *some* of you into prison, that you may be tested, and you will have tribulation ten days. Be faithful until death, and I will give you the crown of life" (Rev. 2:10).

Emperor Diocletian persecuted the believers of Jesus Christ during the ten years from AD 303 to 313, and many followers of Christ made the ultimate sacrifice as they were thrown to wild animals. This period was also notorious for the false teachings that the Nicolaitans, the Balaamites, and Jezebel brought into the church, compromising the truth.

God's promise to those who overcame under the church of Thyatira is that they will rule over the nations "'… *with a rod of iron; they shall be dashed to pieces like the potter's vessels'*—as I also have received from My Father; and I will give him the morning star" (Rev. 2:27, 28). Two hundred two popes persecuted God's people during the 1260 years of the Thyatira church period (AD 538–1798), killing millions of spiritual descendants of the twelve apostles. Yet, God raised up John Wycliffe, "the Morning Star of the Reformation," to bring God's Word to the people. God also raised up Melanchthon, Martin Luther, and others to launch the Reformation and prepare the church for the latter rain. This prophecy has been fulfilled.

87. The prophecy about the lukewarm condition of the last church:

"So then, because you are lukewarm, and neither cold nor hot, I will vomit you out of My mouth" (Rev. 3:16). These words of the

True Witness describe the "lukewarm" condition of the Seventh-day Adventist Church. According to this prophecy, the church has been spewed out of Christ's mouth because of the many compromises the Church has made with the fallen Protestant churches. Nonetheless, God will have a faithful remnant from this last church to welcome the Lord Jesus at the Second Coming.

88. The prophecy of the beginning of the investigative judgment in Heaven:

"After these things I looked, and behold, a door *standing* open in heaven. And the first voice which I heard *was* like a trumpet speaking with me, saying, 'Come up here, and I will show you things which must take place after this.' Immediately I was in the Spirit; and behold, a throne set in heaven, and *One* sat on the throne" (Rev. 4:1, 2). This prophecy points to judgment commencing in heaven according to the prophecy of Daniel 8:14. In 1844, the investigative judgment was to begin and was to continue until the second coming of Jesus Christ. Revelation, chapter 5, deals with the judgment also. This prophecy has now been partially fulfilled, and it will continue to be fulfilled until the Second Coming.

89. The prophecy of the seven seals:

"Now I saw when the Lamb opened one of the seals; and I heard one of the four living creatures saying with a voice like thunder, 'Come and see.' And I looked, and behold, a white horse. He who sat on it had a bow; and a crown was given to him, and he went out conquering and to conquer" (Rev. 6:1, 2).

The Holy Spirit gave this special seven-seal prophecy with its "seals" and "horses." As the first seal opens, a white horse appears. The white horse represents the first of the seven churches—the church of Ephesus. Since white is a symbol of purity, the white horse under the first seal represents the purity of the people of that church. The twelve apostles were empowered by the outpouring of the "former rain," a period of time under the control of the Holy Spirit, to produce God's written word and then to do God's work. During the period of the "former rain" power of the Holy Ghost, the church was pure and kept the commandments of God. The speed of a galloping horse symbolizes the rapid grown of the church as millions of people became Christians during the Ephesian church period (AD 31–100). This prophecy is being fulfilled to the letter.

90. The prophecy of Revelation 6:3, 4:

The second seal and the second horse represent the second period of the church— the "Smyrna" period, which lasted from AD 100 to 313, a period during which God's people would suffer periodic persecution.

The red horse of this period that gallops across the page of Revelation represents the rapid shedding of the blood of the faithful to their eternal salvation. During this period six pagan Rome emperors persecuted the church: (1) Trajan (AD 98–117), (2) Hadrian (AD 117–138), (3) Marcus Aurelius (AD 161–180), (4) Decius (AD 249–259), (5) Valerian (AD 253–259), and (6) Diocletian (AD 284–305). The ten years from 303 to 313 were a ten-year period during which millions died to their eternal salvation in the "baptism of blood." This prophecy has been fulfilled.

91. The prophecy of Revelation 6:5, 6:

When the third seal is broken, it releases the black horse and its rider. This church period corresponds to Pergamos (AD 313–538), a time period during which Constantine and the emperors who followed him ruled over the Roman Empire, later joining the leaders of the Christian church in praying through the Virgin Mary and the infant Jesus. Instead of honoring God by remembering the seventh-day Sabbath in their churches, they denigrated the Sabbath and worshipped on the first day of the week of Sunday instead. Under Constantine's dynasty, millions of God's people—the descendants of the Apostolic church—lost their lives as martyrs from AD 313 to 538. The color black is a more ominous color than red, for it symbolizes the great many from the apostolic church who were tortured to death as they held to Christ for their eternal salvation. This prophecy has been fulfilled.

92. The prophecy of Revelation 6:7, 8, the fourth seal and the pale horse:

The fourth seal corresponds to the church period of Thyatira, which lasted from AD 538 to AD 1798. It fulfilled the latter part of the prophecy of Jeremiah that says: " 'Behold I will send for many fishermen,' says the LORD, 'and they shall fish them; and afterward I will send for many hunters, and they shall hunt them from every mountain and every hill, and out of the holes of the rocks" (Jer. 16:16).

1. **The pale horse** under the fourth seal reminds us of death and of the pale color of the leaves after they fall from a tree. The vast number of dead leaves reminds us of the vast number of God's people who were killed during the 1260-year period of AD 538 to 1798.

2. **Travel by horse** points to the rapid spreading persecution and martyrdom of the faithful. According to this prophecy, 192 popes of the Roman Catholic Church with the Roman emperors killed many of God's people, fulfilling the prophecy of Jeremiah 16:16. In the dark days of the Dark Ages between AD 538 and 1798, three major groups were under attack: (1) the Waldenses, (2) the Albigenses, and (3) the Huguenots. These fled to the relative safety of the mountains and hills and hid themselves. Yet, the armies of the church pursued these descendants of the apostolic church and hunted them with arrows, swords, and spears. Many of God's people gave their lives for the sake of God's Word, fulfilling this prophecy to the letter.

93. The prophecy of the great multitude:

"When He opened the fifth seal, I saw under the altar the souls of those who had been slain for the word of God and for the testimony which they held. And they cried with a loud voice, saying, 'How long, O Lord, holy and true, until You judge and avenge our blood on those who dwell on the earth?' Then a white robe was given to each of them; and it was said to them that they should rest a little while longer, until both *the number of* their fellow servants and their brethren, who would be killed as they *were,* was completed" (Rev. 6:9–11).

Where did the multitude come from? They came from the great persecution beginning in the time of Stephen until 1844. In this book, I have asserted that there are two plans of salvation. The first plan of salvation was for Lucifer and the fallen third of the angels of heaven, who violated God's law in heaven and were to see the creatorship of Jesus Christ when He created this earth in six days. Adam and Eve were to demonstrate that God's law could be obeyed. However, due to their disobedience, the demonstration could not take place, and the first plan of salvation had to be curtailed.

After they fell in disobedience, God introduced the plan of salvation for humankind, which was symbolized by the blood of a sacrifice. From Adam to Jesus Christ, God has required believers to keep God's law by the power of His grace in being saved. God knew that few people would be eligible for heaven according to this plan. Yet, He reserved a prophecy—Daniel 7:25—that would cover the great multitude. Its meaning would only be understood after the year 1800, though multitudes before that time would enter the kingdom of God through the shedding of blood. During the Dark Ages, the people did not have a whole Bible to read, and they did not even know about the Sabbath much less keep it. Yet, they were still able to enter the kingdom of God. They are the great multitude that John saw standing before God's throne (Rev. 7:9).

God knew before the creation of Lucifer and the other angels who rebelled against God that Lucifer would try to keep others from going to heaven, believing that God's creation could not be restored once spoiled. According to Lucifer's plan, God was acting against Lucifer in this world. Yet, God adapted His plan to accomplish the salvation of the great multitude (Dan. 7:25; Rev. 6:9–11) through the baptism of blood. (This prophecy is in process of being fulfilled.)

Three Ways of Salvation

God introduced three ways of salvation for Adam and Eve's progeny, combating Lucifer's plan to keep people from going to heaven. All are accomplished through faith; all require obedience to God's commands.

The first way of salvation. From Adam to the cross, blood sacrifice was necessary for the forgiveness of sin and for securing eternal salvation. Even still, those who are saved are expected to keep the ten holy commandments. God judged His people for violating the commandments, and He promised them the Messiah. How did God's people understand the forgiveness of sins? With Elijah on Mount Carmel, God sent fire from heaven to consume the blood sacrifice before the people. All those who violated God's law received a just reward according to their deeds. During the forty years of wilderness wandering, very few people were eligible for salvation.

The second way of salvation. All who believe in the name of Jesus Christ will be saved (Acts 16:31). They receive salvation through (1) the faith of Jesus Christ, (2) holy prayer, and (3) baptism. But, from the death of Stephen to the sixth church period ending in 1843, many experienced (4) the baptism of blood, dying as martyrs. Yet, these were all saved by faith and, the best they knew, kept God's commandments. During the Dark Ages, Papal Rome introduced many traditions into the church corrupting it. The people had no access to the Bible, and the Sabbath commandment was already made to apply to Sunday.

The third way of salvation. "Here is the patience of the saints; here *are* those who keep the commandments of God and the faith of Jesus" (Rev. 14:12). The holy ones of God are described as (1) keeping the holy Ten Commandments and (2) having the faith of Jesus Christ. (3) They also glorify God in their bodies (Rev. 14:7; see also 1 Cor. 6:20) through health reform in anticipation of the transformation of their bodies at the second coming of Jesus Christ (1 Cor. 15:51, 52). This prophecy is in the process of being fulfilled.

94. The prophecy of the signs in the sun and the moon:

"I looked when He opened the sixth seal, and behold, there was a great earthquake; and the sun became black as sackcloth of hair, and the moon became like blood. And the stars of heaven fell to the earth, as a fig tree drops its late figs when it is shaken by a mighty wind. Then the sky receded as a scroll when it is rolled up, and every mountain and island was moved out of its place" (Rev. 6:12–14).

The prophecy of the sixth seal predicts earthquakes and signs in the sun, moon and stars as well as the beginning of the latter rain with direct visions being given to the children of God. These signs were fulfilled in their order.

1. The great Lisbon Earthquake occurred November 1, 1755. It was twenty times stronger than the 1906 San Francisco earthquake and was felt as far away as Finland, Martinique, Barbados across the Atlantic, and North Africa.

2. On May 19, 1780, the sun was darkened from sunrise until the next day.

3. That same night, the moon became bloody red in color.

4. On November 13, 1833, the stars fell in the Leonid star shower like unripe figs falling from a fig tree. This prophecy has been fulfilled.

95. The prophecy of the 144,000 and the great multitude:

"And I heard the number of those who were sealed. One hundred *and* forty-four thousand of all the tribes of the children of Israel *were* sealed" (Rev. 7:4).

"After these things I looked, and behold, a great multitude which no one could number, of all nations, tribes, peoples, and tongues, standing before the throne and before the Lamb, clothed with white robes, with palm branches in their hands" (Rev. 7:9).

Revelation 7 describes the great multitude and the 144,000 from this world who go to heaven. This prophecy is not yet fulfilled but is in the process of being fulfilled. (Please read the full chapter about the 144,000.)

96. The prophecy about half an hour silence:

"When He opened the seventh seal, there was silence in heaven for about half an hour" (Rev. 8:1). This half hour of silence in heaven under the seventh seal represents the time after the second coming of Jesus Christ when the saints will be traveling with Jesus Christ seven and a half days (a day equals a year, thus one half hour is 1/48th of a 360-day year) before reaching heaven. We learn this from Ellen G. White, who saw this and wrote: "We all entered the cloud together, and were seven days ascending to the sea of glass, when Jesus brought the crowns, and with His own right hand placed them on our heads" (*Early Writings*, p. 16). In time, we will be privileged to visit other planets like our own. This prophecy is not yet fulfilled.

97. The prophecy about the first trumpet:

"So the seven angels who had the seven trumpets prepared themselves to sound. The first angel sounded: And hail and fire followed, mingled with blood, and they were thrown to the earth. And a third of the trees were burned up, and all green grass was burned up" (Rev. 8:6, 7).

Seven Trumpets: First Trumpet

The seven trumpets were intended to wake up the world before Christ's return. They are seven military conflicts involving seven nations or kingdoms of this world. This prophecy started during the fourth—and last—world empire, that of Rome, which ruled the whole world under one umbrella. The ten divided kingdoms were established by AD 476. From 49 to 44 BC, Julius Caesar was the greatest leader of pagan Rome and established his rule over the whole world. Read the next prophecy.

98. The prophecy of ten European countries:

This prophecy explains that this last and greatest empire would be divided into ten kingdoms—the ten nations of Europe. The northern portion of this great Roman Empire had to fall. Under the first trumpet (Rev. 8:6, 7), the French-speaking Franks started the very first war with Pagan Rome and won, establishing the nation of "France" as the very first European country. Next, the English-speaking Anglo-Saxons began battling Pagan Rome in AD 385 and ultimately overcame it, establishing an independent nation in England. Lastly, in AD 396, the German-speaking Alemanni Goths waged war with Rome and established the German nation, completing the fulfillment of this first trumpet prophecy.

99. The prophecy of the second trumpet:

"Then the second angel sounded: and *something* like a great mountain burning with fire was thrown into the sea, and a third of the sea became blood. And a third of the living creatures in the sea died, and a third of the ships were destroyed" (Rev. 8:8, 9).

With the fulfillment of the second trumpet, the southern parts of Pagan Rome fell, according to Revelation 8:8, 9. The Vandals exercised their power from AD 410–429 and were descendants of Ham who learned shipbuilding directly from Noah. They were the sea warriors of the ancient world. Under the Vandals, Pagan Rome lost (1) Egypt, (2) Libya, (3) Somalia, (4) Sudan, (5) Ethiopia, (6) Algeria, (7) Tunisia, (8) Morocco, and (9) Turkey. Thus, these Negro countries became the fourth "nation" to be carved out of Rome. Then, from AD 430 to 432, the Lombards of Italia waged war with Rome and established the fifth European nation. Thus, this prophecy has been fulfilled.

100. The prophecy about the third and the fourth trumpet:

"Then the third angel sounded: And a great star fell from heaven, burning like a torch, and it fell on a third of the rivers and on the springs of water. The name of the star is Wormwood. A third of the waters became wormwood, and many men died from the water, because it was made bitter" (Rev. 8:10, 11).

The third trumpet portrays the fall of the western parts of Rome. This prophecy predicted the rise, in AD 437 to AD 476, of the sixth nation of "Hungary" (which included the Czech Republic and Poland), the rise of the seventh nation of "Spain," and the rise of the eighth nation of the Burgundians, or Portugal.

Revelation 9:1–12 describes the spiritual darkness of the Middle Ages, which covered a third part of the world. Mohammed preached against idol worship and sought to eradicate it in the world, making war with nations that worshiped idols. Mohammadism started in Mecca and Medina and spread to the other countries of the Middle East.

101. The prophecy of the fifth trumpet of Revelation 9:

The first twelve verses of Revelation 9, under the fifth trumpet, predict the total fall of the eastern part of the mighty Roman Empire. In fulfillment of this prophecy, from AD 470–476, the tribe of the Ostrogoths carved out a ninth nation, occupying the territories of (1) Austria, (2) Yugoslavia, and (3) Albania. Last of all, the tribe of the Heruli took portions of the Roman Empire in the east and, becoming the tenth nation to emerge from the mighty Roman Empire, occupying the territories of (1) Romania, (2) Bulgaria, and (3) the northern part of Greece. Each of these tribes established its own nation in Europe, from AD 380 to AD 476, fulfilling the prophecy of Revelation 9:6–12, in keeping with the statue's feet of iron and clay in Daniel 2:31–44,. The next prophecy is a warning.

102. The prophecy of torment:

"Then the fifth angel sounded: and I saw a star fallen from heaven to the earth. To him was given the key to the bottomless pit" (Rev. 9:1).

The star that fell from heaven is the invasion of Islam. The fifth verse, which talks about the five months of torment, is a prophecy of Islam and its religious rule in the world. Five months, at thirty days per month, means 150 days. So this prophecy, when days are converted to years, signifies 150 years of war. The 150 years of war were a punishment for those who persecuted God's children. These included:

1. The Roman Emperor Julius Caesar and his successors who persecuted the early believers and their descendants from AD 31 to 313.
2. The successors of the Jewish Pharisees and Sadducees who killed the successors of the twelve apostles.
3. The Roman Catholic popes, bishops, cardinals, and priests who killed the followers of Jesus Christ. God allowed the Islamic nations to take revenge.

According to this violent prophecy of the God of heaven, for exactly 150 years—from AD 1299 to 1449—the Islamic kings tormented the descendants of (1) pagan Rome, (2) the Jewish people, and (3) the pope and his followers. Millions of Gentile Christians were killed from AD 31–1798, and they are waiting for the Lord's return. This prophecy is being fulfilled to the letter.

103. Continuation of iniquity prophecy of Revelation 9:13–21:

Revelation 9:15 says that four angels, who had been prepared for the hour and day and month and year, were released to kill a third of mankind.

The Sixth Trumpet of Iniquity Prophecy of 391 years of war

Using the day for a year key, "an hour [15 days], a day [1 year], a month [30 days], and a year [360 days]" (Rev. 9:15) equals a total of 391 years of war. According to Revelation 9:14, the sixth angel is commanded: "Release the four angels who are bound at the great river Euphrates," which is a river in the present countries of Iran and Iraq. The present River Euphrates has been flowing since 2503 BC—just after the Flood. It is the only river mentioned in Genesis that remains and that is used as a symbol in prophecy. For 391 years, forces in the world were at war with (1) the Jewish people, (2) what was left of the Roman Empire, and (3) the Catholic popes, bishops, cardinals, and priests. During this longest war in this world of 391 years, the kings of the Ottoman Empire fought with firearms rather than with knives, swords, spears, and arrows. Not only that, but, for these 391 years of wars, the three groups of people mentioned above were tormented, and many succumbed to extreme pressure becoming followers of Islam. Because of the wars now taking place in the Middle East, the Islamic nations that exist in this world are fulfilling the prophecy to the letter.

104. The prophecy about William Miller:

"The angel whom I saw standing on the sea and on the land raised up his hand to heaven" (Rev. 10:5). Revelation, chapter 10, talks about an angel, or messenger, to the sixth church of Revelation, Philadelphia. The messengers to the Philadelphia church were William Miller and the three thousand ministers who preached the return of Christ with Miller. The little book, mentioned in Revelation 10, is the book of Daniel. It was "sweet," as John described it, to understand the 2300-day prophecy, as proclaimed by William Miller, connected with the second coming of Jesus Christ. In mid-summer 1844, S. S. Snow set the date for Christ's return as October 22, 1844. More than 50,000 Adventist believers eagerly awaited the second coming of Jesus Christ. Yet, Miller misinterpreted the 2300 days (literally "evening-morning two thousand three hundred") of Daniel 8:14, and Jesus Christ did not come in AD 1844. That was a very great disappointment. John wrote: "But when I had eaten it, my stomach became bitter." (Rev. 10:10). The experience the Millerites went through was very bitter. This prophecy is being fulfilled to the letter.

105. The prophecy about the measuring rod:

"Then I was given a reed like a measuring rod. And the angel stood, saying, 'Rise and measure the temple of God, the altar, and those who worship there' " (Rev. 11:1).

The measuring rod in the Bible is the holy Ten Commandments. After the arrival of the period of the latter rain, God revealed the explanation of the Ten Commandments. This prophecy is being fulfilled in these last days.

106. The prophecy about the great multitude:

"But leave out the court which is outside the temple, and do not measure it, for it has been given to the Gentiles. And they will tread the holy city underfoot *for* forty-two months" (Rev. 11:2). This prophecy tells how eternal salvation was extended to the Gentiles as a great multitude that are baptized by blood under the persecution of pagan and papal Rome from AD 538 to AD 1798. This prophecy was fulfilled.

107. The prophecy of the two olive trees and the two candlesticks:

"These are the two olive trees and the two lampstands standing before the God of the earth" (Rev. 11:4). These two witnesses represent the testimonies of the Old and New Testaments. "Your word *is* a lamp to my feet and a light to my path" (Ps. 119:105). "You search the Scriptures, for in them you think you have eternal life; and these are they which testify of Me" (John 5:39). "And this gospel of the kingdom will be preached in all the world as a witness to all the nations, and then the end will come" (Matt. 24:14). This is an ongoing prophecy.

108. The prophecy of the French Revolution:

"When they finish their testimony, the beast that ascends out of the bottomless pit will make war against them, overcome them, and kill them. And their dead bodies *will lie* in the street of the great city which spiritually is called Sodom and Egypt, where also our Lord was crucified" (Rev. 11:7, 8).

This prophecy uses the symbolism of spiritual Sodom and Egypt to portray the persecution of the faithful descendants of the apostles. It pictures their dead bodies lying in the street of the great city.

The Catholic church of France supported the pope during the 1260 years by persecuting and martyring the faithful Huguenots in the horrible St. Bartholomew's Day massacre of 1572. Thousands were killed, and the streets of Paris flowed with blood. The persecutions continued until 1797, driving the productive Huguenots out of the country. The rabble remaining in France were aptly called Sodom for the license they gave to prostitution and other sexual perversions. This prophecy has been fulfilled.

109. The prophecy of the French Revolution:

"Now after the three-and-a-half days the breath of life from God entered them, and they stood on their feet, and great fear fell on those who saw them. And they heard a loud voice from heaven saying to them, 'Come up here.' And they ascended to heaven in a cloud, and their enemies saw them" (Rev. 11:11, 12).

John portrayed the three and a half days (or years) that the bodies of the witnesses were disrespectfully treated. This could symbolize the massacre of Protestants in France from November 1793 to June 1797 and the final denouncement of atheism and Catholicism in favor of Protestantism, or it can point to the annulment of the two witnesses of the Old and New Testaments of the Bible. (See below.) The French Revolution commenced under the rabble citizenry that had driven out the Huguenots and then turned their resentment on the aristocracy and the church. A member of a minor aristocratic family, Charlotte Corday assassinated Jacobin Jean-Paul Marat, who had taken the revolution in a most violent direction. In 1798, during the final two years of the French Revolution, Napoleon Bonaparte became emperor of France.

110. The prophecy of the French persecution:

"In the same hour there was a great earthquake, and a tenth of the city fell. In the earthquake seven thousand people were killed, and the rest were afraid and gave glory to the God of heaven" (Rev. 11:13).

In the same year that Napoleon became emperor (and dictator) of France, his general Berthier arrested Pope Pious VI, who had condemned the Revolution, and put him in the island prison of St. Helena where the pope died in 1799. In taking the pope captive, Napoleon amalgamated the power of Rome with that of France. The French Revolution introduced the guillotine, which took the lives of more than seven thousand people and fulfilling the image of the great earthquake.

The two witnesses, representing the Old and New Testaments of the Bible, were publicly burned, and the French assembly prohibited the printing and reading of the Bible. This prohibition was reversed on June 17, 1797. The first Bible society was started in England in 1816. The American Bible Society was also started and, by 1942, had printed and circulated millions of copies of the Scriptures. This prophecy has been fulfilled.

111. The prophecy about the last trumpet:

"Then the seventh angel sounded: And there were loud voices in heaven, saying, 'The kingdoms of this world have become *the kingdoms* of our Lord and of His Christ, and He shall reign forever and ever!' " (Rev. 11:15).

The seventh—and last—trumpet refers to the second coming of Jesus Christ. This prophecy will soon be fulfilled as the present church has the task of proclaiming the gospel in all the world before Christ returns. The sixth trumpet prophecy about the Islamic nation ended August 11, 1840, and the church of Laodicea started in 1844. During the period of the last trumpet, the three angels' messages will be proclaimed, and, at their close, Christ will come the second time. Part of this prophecy has been fulfilled.

112. The prophecy about the great controversy portrays Christ and His church:

"Now a great sign appeared in heaven: a woman clothed with the sun, with the moon under her feet, and on her head a garland of twelve stars. Then being with child, she cried out in labor and in pain to give birth" (Rev. 12:1, 2).

The woman clothed with the sun symbolizes the faithful people of Israel and the early church. The child who went to heaven, Jesus Christ, is also the church's head. The twelve stars are the twelve disciples of Jesus Christ; the moon represents the Old Testament, which reflects the radiance of Jesus through symbols. The second verse tells about Jesus Christ who came from heaven, was born on this earth, and gained the victory over the devil.

113. The prophecy about Satan, the dragon:

"And another sign appeared in heaven: behold, a great, fiery red dragon having seven heads and ten horns, and seven diadems on his heads" (Rev. 12:3).

This is a two-part prophecy that links first with pagan Rome with its seven heads, which are "seven hills," and ten horns, which are ten kingdoms. After AD 400, pagan Rome was divided into ten kingdoms. During this time, France arose among the ten kingdoms, and a new little horn arose, uprooting three of the first ten and beginning the papal Roman empire, under the headship of the pope in Italy. The red dragon itself represents Satan, "the ancient serpent," who controls the whole world. This prophecy has been fulfilled to the letter.

114. The prophecy about war in Heaven:
"His tail drew a third of the stars of heaven and threw them to the earth. And the dragon stood before the woman who was ready to give birth, to devour her Child as soon as it was born" (Rev. 12:4).

This prophecy explains about the fallen third of the angels of heaven who were driven out of heaven to this earth by Jesus Christ. That could be as many as 33.5 billion angels, who are plotting and acting against God's church today.

115. The prophecy about the apostolic church fleeing from Europe to America:
"Then the woman fled into the wilderness, where she has a place prepared by God, that they should feed her there one thousand two hundred and sixty days" (Rev. 12:6).

The true church of God under the period of the seventh church of Laodicea was birthed in the wilderness of the United States, after believers from the church of Sardis fled from Europe to America in the latter part of the 1260-year prophecy. In this way, God provided a means of protection from the papal beast power for His church. It was the new land of North America. Crossing the Atlantic Ocean in the Mayflower, the Puritans established colonies in the new land. According to Revelation, the churches of Sardis, Philadelphia, and Laodicea would be nourished in the wilderness. This prophecy has been fulfilled.

116. The prophecy about the two wings representing the United States:
"But the woman was given two wings of a great eagle, that she might fly into the wilderness to her place, where she is nourished for a time and times and half a time, from the presence of the serpent" (Rev. 12:14).

The "two wings of a great eagle" in the prophecy of Revelation 12 uniquely correspond to the declaration of the independence of the nation of the United States in 1776. At that time, the newly formed Congress chose the "two wings of a great eagle" as their new nation's emblem. To this day, the emblem appears on all U.S. passports, pointing to America's role in fulfilling this prophecy to the letter through George Washington and the early American patriots.

117. The prophecy of American freedom from the slavery:

"So the serpent spewed water out of his mouth like a flood after the woman, that he might cause her to be carried away by the flood. But the earth helped the woman, and the earth opened its mouth and swallowed up the flood which the dragon had spewed out of his mouth" (Rev. 12:15, 16).

This prophecy speaks about the civil war that ended slavery in the United States in 1865. Through the efforts of Abraham Lincoln, slavery in America was abolished and the country started on the road to equality for everyone.

118. The prophecy about the Remnant church:

"And the dragon was enraged with the woman, and he went to make war with the rest of her offspring, who keep the commandments of God and have the testimony of Jesus Christ" (Rev. 12:17).

According to this prophecy, the remnant of the woman's seed, which emerge from the Laodicean church, are those who follow the commandments of God and the testimony of Jesus Christ. The "testimony of Jesus Christ is the spirit of prophecy" (Rev. 19:10). A parallel passage (Rev. 22:9) links those who have "the spirit of prophecy" with the prophets. Thus, the remnant will have a prophetic messenger of the Lord. Seventh-day Adventists recognize the prophetic gift in the sermons and writings of Ellen G. White. However, not everyone will accept Ellen G. White's writings as divinely inspired, particularly when they have a different theological lens that dismisses certain teachings of Scripture that she upholds.

119. The prophecy of Papal Rome:

"Then I stood on the sand of the sea. And I saw a beast rising up out of the sea, having seven heads and ten horns, and on his horns ten crowns, and on his heads a blasphemous name. Now the beast which I saw was like a leopard, his feet were like *the feet of* a bear, and his mouth like the mouth of a lion. The dragon gave him his power, his throne, and great authority" (Rev. 13:1, 2).

This prophecy employs the symbolism of a beast with seven heads, ten horns, and ten crowns. The beast looked like a leopard with the feet of a bear and the mouth of a lion. This beast represents the papal power, which amalgamated aspects of Rome, Greece (represented by the leopard), Medo-Persia (represented by a bear), and Babylon (represented by a lion). Daniel and John prophesied that the popes of papal Rome would receive their power from the dragon, which is Satan, and would rule for 1260 years.

This prophecy in Revelation builds on the prophecy of Daniel 7:3–8, which pictures four beasts coming out of the sea. The fourth of these beasts, a mighty dragon, represents the Roman Empire of Julius Caesar, which would be divided into ten kingdoms. Of these ten kingdoms, three kingdoms would be displaced by another kingdom that group up among them. In fulfillment of this prophecy, Justinian of France conquered the three kingdoms of the Ostrogoths, the Heruli, and the Vandals from AD 527 to 538, partially restoring the western portion of the Roman Empire. It was the implementation of Justinian's edict of AD 538, regarding the supremacy of the Bishop of Rome over the Church, that began the prophetic 1260 years of temporal rule by the Roman Catholic Church. This prophecy has been fulfilled.

120. The prophecy of the wounding of the beast:

"And *I saw* one of his heads as if it had been mortally wounded, and his deadly wound was healed. And all the world marveled and followed the beast" (Rev. 13:3).

This is a two-part prophecy. The first part of the prophecy is the wounding of the beast, and the second part of the prophecy is the healing of the wound.

For a kingdom to be wounded means that it has temporarily suffered a defeat, though the kingdom can be reinstated in some capacity later on. In fulfillment of this prophecy, in AD 1798, Napoleon Bonaparte's mighty General Berthier declared war on the papacy, arresting Pope Pius VI, imprisoning him on the island of St. Helena where the pontiff later died. At the same time, Napoleon amalgamated the Roman Empire into the nation of France. This fulfilled the part of the prophecy that had to do with the "wound."

121. The prophecy of the regeneration of the Papacy:

"And *I saw* one of his heads as if it had been mortally wounded, and his deadly wound was healed" (Rev. 13:3).

In fulfillment of the prophecy regarding the healing of the beast's head, the Italian dictator Benito Mussolini restored Vatican City to the Pope of Rome in 1929. Vatican City is just one square mile in area (or 110 acres), and it had only 1,000 people living in its limits at the time. This mile-square city was established as a sovereign nation—the State of Vatican City. Since that time, every pope has lived in Vatican City and has reigned over the kingdom of the Roman Catholic Church. This prophecy has been fulfilled.

122. The prophecy of the buffalo beast of the United States:

"Then I saw another beast coming up out of the earth, and he had two horns like a lamb and spoke like a dragon" (Rev. 13:11).

We can describe the two-horned lamb-like beast in the prophecy as a buffalo, or American bison. John could not label it as such since he had never seen a buffalo. He described it as a lamb-like beast. In 1776, George Washington assigned the buffalo as the United States' national animal. The buffalo lives only in America, and a buffalo's character is entirely different from other animals.

1. Though it is a huge animal, a boy can handle a buffalo. It will follow the boy without doing him any harm. That is why John the Revelator used a buffalo to represent the United States of America in his vision from God, for it very aptly represented the character of the nation. The biggest and greatest nation acts calmly without harming other nations in the world. Without considering this biblical prophecy, the United States senate automatically introduced and accepted the eagle as the national bird and the buffalo, or American bison, as the national animal for the United States.

2. We have already recognized that the two wings of an eagle are on the United States passport.

3. The buffalo has two horns, which aptly represent its two fundamental features, which were voted and accepted by the

United States Congress in 1776—civil and religious liberty. To put it another way, it is a nation without a king, a church without a pope. This prophecy was fulfilled to the letter.

4. God had a divine purpose in keeping the American continent a wilderness. It was for the benefit of His "true church." The Lord Jesus Christ limited the number of human beings on this continent until AD 1564 when Christopher Columbus crossed the Atlantic Ocean and discovered the vast continent of America. Sadly, the United States has accepted the way of Rome and will end up speaking like the dragon—the symbol of Rome—fulfilling the prophecy to the letter.

123. The prophecy of United States as a super power:

"And he exercises all the authority of the first beast in his presence, and causes the earth and those who dwell in it to worship the first beast, whose deadly wound was healed. He performs great signs, so that he even makes fire come down from heaven on the earth in the sight of men" (Rev. 13:12, 13).

The prophecy foretells the stance of the United States in not yielding allegiance to the pope for that would be contrary to its constitution and the principle of having a church without a pope. However, according to this prophecy, the United States would ultimately yield to public pressure to honor the Roman Catholic tradition of Sunday worship by enacting a Sunday law. By this means it will yield sovereignty to the pope and the Roman Catholic Church over this nation as they already have sovereignty over the world. The Protestant churches of America gradually fulfilled the first part of this prophecy from 1776 onwards. On every Sunday, they gathered in their respective Protestant churches and worshiped God on the very day championed by the Roman Catholic Church, not seeing the serious challenge this would bring to the United States Constitution

The second part of this prophecy took some time to be fulfilled. It was not until 1987 that the United States president, Ronald Reagan, recognized Vatican City as a nation through the appointment of an ambassador to the pope, the head of the Roman Catholic Church. In so doing, this prophecy has been fulfilled.

124. The prophecy about the American super power:

"He performs great signs, so that he even makes fire come down from heaven on the earth in the sight of men" (Rev. 13:13).

Evidence of the United States' superpower status could include:

1. American President Truman's ordering of the military to break the backbone of Japan and its aggression against other nations in 1945, during World War II, by dropping the atomic bomb on the Japanese cities of Hiroshima and Nagasaki. With the decimation of these cities, Japan surrendered to the allied nations without any condition.

2. America response to Iraq's attack of Kuwait in 1992 with 6,000 warheads and 100,000 tons of ammunition, chasing Saddam Hussein back to Iraq in just 42 days.

3. The Federation of American Scientists estimates that there were more than 17,000 nuclear warheads in the world as of 2012, with around 4,300 of them considered operational and ready for use. This was enough to destroy our planet sixteen times over. Besides the nuclear warheads, there are hydrogen bombs and cobalt bombs with nearly 2,500 intercontinental ballistic missiles that can hit their target 3,400 miles away. There are also stealth bombers, patriot missiles and laser guided interceptors, which can attack the launching pad of the nuclear warheads of an inter-continental ballistic missile that travels at the speed of up to four miles per second. The prophecy is in the process of fulfillment.

125. The prophecy about the Sunday law:

"He was granted *power* to give breath to the image of the beast, that the image of the beast should both speak and cause as many as would not worship the image of the beast to be killed. He causes all, both small and great, rich and poor, free and slave, to receive a mark on their right hand or on their foreheads, and that no one may buy or sell except one who has the mark or the name of the beast, or the number of his name" (Rev. 13:15–17).

The Sunday law in the United States fulfills this prophecy. Representing the mark of the beast, the Sunday law requiring Sunday worship will be fulfilled in the United States and the world. By 1890, the majority of the states in America (excluding Arizona, California, and Idaho) had Sunday laws that controlled buying and selling. Many workshops and printing presses were also mandated to be closed across the land. This even had an effect on the Pacific Press Publishing house, where Ellen G. White's son W. C. White was taken into custody in 1882 for supposed violation of the Sunday law. The Sunday laws affected other Seventh-day Adventists as well. (Compare Uriah Smith, *Thoughts on Daniel and Revelation*, chapter 13.) This prophecy has been fulfilled in part.

126. The prophecy of the number 666:

"Here is wisdom. Let him who has understanding calculate the number of the beast, for it is the number of a man: His number *is* 666" (Rev. 13:18). This prophecy is for information purposes to help identify the beast.

127. The prophecy of the 144,000 and their four identifying characteristics:

"Then I looked, and behold, a Lamb standing on Mount Zion, and with Him one hundred *and* forty-four thousand, having His Father's name written on their foreheads" (Rev. 14:1).

Revelation 14:4, 5: "These are the ones who were not defiled with women, for they are virgins. These are the ones who follow the Lamb wherever He goes. These were redeemed from *among* men, *being* first fruits to God and to the Lamb. And in their mouth was found no deceit, for they are without fault before the throne of God."

The 144,000 are the "firstfruits unto God and to the Lamb" (Rev. 14:4) who will welcome Jesus Christ at His second coming to this earth. This is the final prophecy to be fulfilled by the final church as it welcomes Christ back to earth to take them back with Him to heaven. There are four identifying characteristics of the 144,000. The first of these is that they are not defiled with women; the second is that they are virgins; the third is that they have no guile in their mouths; and the fourth is that they are without fault (Rev. 14:4, 5).

The Four Identifying Characteristics:
1. "These are the ones who were not defiled with woman" means that they have remained faithful to Christ and have not engaged in spiritual idolatry.

2. "For they are virgins" means that they have the purity of believing and following God's holy law.

3. "And in their mouth was found no deceit" means that they do not speak lies (Zeph. 3:12, 13).

4. "For they are without fault before the throne of God" means that they have been reconciled to God and that their lives have been brought into line with His requirements.

In Revelation 7:9–14, John describes seeing a great multitude immediately after hearing the number of people who will be sealed—144,000. These are those who will be alive to meet the Lord in the air when He comes.

128. The prophecy of the first angel's message:
"Then I saw another angel flying in the midst of heaven, having the everlasting gospel to preach to those who dwell on the earth—to every nation, tribe, tongue, and people—saying with a loud voice, 'Fear God and give glory to Him, for the hour of His judgment has come; and worship Him who made heaven and earth, the sea and springs of water' " (Rev. 14:6, 7).

Jesus gave His disciples the great commission, which is to preach the gospel to the whole world before He returns. In addition to the proclamation of the everlasting gospel to every nation, tribe, tongue and people, Jesus told John to call all people to worship Him alone, for He is the Creator, Redeemer, and Sustainer. Belief is the fundamental means of accepting the gospel, as we find in Acts 16:31. Obedience is the natural outgrowth of receiving the everlasting gospel, as we find in Revelation 14:12. The book of Revelation reveals God's intent to join the Old and the New Testaments, with the exception of the ceremonial laws, which were nailed to the cross.

Revelation 14:6, 7 brings to view the hour of judgment that was to begin in the sanctuary in heaven in 1844 (and not on earth). It is a judgment that God foretold in Daniel 8:14. This prophecy was to be proclaimed by the fifth church of Sardis (from 1798 to 1844). However, the Christians of Sardis did not do as they should have done, so they become Babylon while the church of Philadelphia proclaimed the judgment hour message.

129. The prophecy of the second angel's message:

"And another angel followed, saying, 'Babylon is fallen, is fallen, that great city, because she has made all nations drink of the wine of the wrath of her fornication' " (Rev. 14:8).

Babylon represents confusion. The sixth church, Philadelphia, proclaimed the heavenly judgment prior to the second coming of Jesus Christ. William Miller and three thousand other ministers, with thousands of other adherents, were disappointed in their expectation of the return of Christ on March 31, 1844 and October 22, 1844. From 1833 to 1844 they had preached the advent message while the other churches came into more confusion and the church became Babylon as the prophecy predicted.

130. The prophecy of the third angel's message:

"Then a third angel followed them, saying with a loud voice, "If anyone worships the beast and his image, and receives *his* mark on his forehead or on his hand, he himself shall also drink of the wine of the wrath of God, which is poured out full strength into the cup of His indignation. He shall be tormented with fire and brimstone in the presence of the holy angels and in the presence of the Lamb. . . . Here is the patience of the saints; here *are* those who keep the commandments of God and the faith of Jesus" (Rev. 14:9, 10, 12).

The third angel's message was to be proclaimed in all the world by the time of the seventh—and last—church, the Laodicean church of the Seventh-day Adventist Church. The Seventh-day Adventist Church was to proclaim the message of Revelation 14:12: "Here is the patience of the saints, here *are* those who keep the commandments of God and the faith of Jesus." Of particular importance are the Ten Commandments with their 105 specifications.

The second part of the third angel's message is the faith of Jesus Christ (Rev. 14:6; Acts 16:31). Through holy prayer in Jesus' name (Acts 4:12), pardonable sins will be forgiven. However, when someone openly violates God's eternal law without contrition, they will not be forgiven.

131. The prophecy about the great Middle East war:

"Then the sixth angel poured out his bowl on the great river Euphrates, and its water was dried up, so that the way of the kings from the east might be prepared" (Rev. 16:12).

This prophecy describes what is to take place before the battle of Armageddon, as the river Euphrates dries up. Its drying up means that Babylon's system of support will be withdrawn. The region of the original Babylon has been a place of conflict. War began between Iraq and Iran from 1981 to 1987. Then, from 1990 to 1991, war broke out between Iraq and Kuwait, the latter having support from Saudi Arabia. During these two wars, thousands of people died with a final war still coming. Yet, the stirring of the Middle East has energized radical Islam. This prophecy is ongoing and is not completely fulfilled.

132. The prophecy of the war of Armageddon:

"And they gathered them together to the place called in Hebrew, Armageddon" (Rev. 16:16).

This prophecy, which talks about the final (possibly nuclear) war, is not yet fulfilled.

133. The prophecy of the fourth angel's message:

"After these things I saw another angel coming down from heaven, having great authority, and the earth was illuminated with his glory. And he cried mightily with a loud voice, saying, 'Babylon the great is fallen, is fallen, and has become a dwelling place of demons, a prison for every foul spirit, and a cage for every unclean and hated bird!' " (Rev. 18:1, 2).

This additional angel comes down from heaven after the three angels of Revelation 14. When the scripture says that he is "coming down from heaven, having great authority, and the earth was illuminated with his glory," it shows that the Word of God will be magnified more than ever before. The Bible and Bible alone was the watchword of the Reformation. The watchword under this angel is: "Here is the patience of the saints; here *are* those who keep the commandments of God and the faith of Jesus." This means that, "while conflicting doctrines and theories abound, the law of God is the one unerring rule by which all opinions, doctrines, and theories are to be tested"

(*The Great Controversy*, p. 452). This prophecy includes not only the Protestant movement, but also the Seventh-day Adventist movement as well. Everyone who is confused over the role of God's law in the life of the believer should consider the law in one's heart and mind to be a power that enables us to fulfill Jesus' command in John 14:15: "If you love Me, keep My commandments."

134. The prophecy about the prelude of the seven last plagues:

"And I heard another voice from heaven saying, "Come out of her, my people, lest you share in her sins, and lest you receive of her plagues" (Rev. 18:4).

This prophecy explains what will happen to all who refuse to heed the warning of the third angel's message. Those who violate God's eternal law will suffer the seven last plagues. This includes those who violate God's law while they are either leaders or members of the Christian church. As Ellen White wrote: "But I saw that the ministers did not escape the wrath of God. Their suffering was tenfold greater than that of their people" (*Early Writings*, p. 282).

135. The prophecy about the seven last plagues and their duration:

"Therefore her plagues will come in one day—death and mourning and famine. And she will be utterly burned with fire, for strong *is* the Lord God who judges her" (Rev. 18:8).

The suffering of the seven last plagues in that one year, represented by a day in prophecy, will be tenfold greater for the ministers who did not warn their flocks than for those who follow them (*Early Writings*, p. 282). This prophecy is not yet fulfilled.

136. The prophecy about the third coming:

"Then he said to me, 'Write: "Blessed *are* those who are called to the marriage supper of the Lamb!" ' And he said to me, 'These are the true sayings of God' " (Rev. 19:9). This prophecy refers to events that will take place after God's judgment and Jesus' third coming. It is not yet fulfilled.

137. The prophecy of the millennium:

"But the rest of the dead did not live again until the thousand years were finished. This *is* the first resurrection. Blessed and holy *is* he who has part in the first resurrection. Over such the second death has no power, but they shall be priests of God and of Christ, and shall reign with Him a thousand years" (Rev. 20:5, 6).

At the time of Christ's second coming, all the saints will be resurrected, including the great multitude, and they will ascend to heaven with the Lord. The judgment of the millennium is yet to take place. This prophecy is not yet fulfilled.

138. The prophecy about the period after the millennial judgment:

"Now when the thousand years have expired, Satan will be released from his prison" (Rev. 20:7). At the end of the millennium, Satan will be freed to work with his armies on this earth before the saints descend from heaven in the holy city. This prophecy is not yet fulfilled.

139. The prophecy of the New Jerusalem:

Revelation 21 and 22 describe the New Jerusalem. It is a golden city that is 375 miles wide by 375 miles long, a multi-story structure in which the 144,000 will dwell. When it descends to earth, there will be no more sorrow, sickness, pain, or death, and the devil will be no more. This prophecy is not yet fulfilled.

140. The prophecy about the character of the people in the last days:

"'He who is unjust, let him be unjust still; he who is filthy, let him be filthy still; he who is righteous, let him be righteous still; he who is holy, let him be holy still'" (Rev. 22:11). This prophecy will be fulfilled when Jesus returns.

Time Prophecies

141. The prophecy of one day equaling a year:

"According to the number of the days in which you spied out the land, forty days, for each day you shall bear your guilt one year, *namely* forty years, and you shall know My rejection" (Num. 14:34).

Because of Israel's being faithless for forty days, the prophecy specified that they would spend forty years wandering in the wilderness—from 1491 to 1451 BC.

142. The prophecy about the time duration of the seven plagues:

"For thus the LORD has said to me: 'Within a year, according to the year of a hired man, all the glory of Kedar will fail' " (Isa. 21:16). One day equals a year of 360 days. Revelation 18:8 says that the seven plagues are to fall within a year on many who will be killed by them. This is not yet fulfilled.

143. 1260 days' prophecy:

"He shall speak *pompous* words against the Most High, shall persecute the saints of the Most High, and shall intend to change times and law. Then *the saints* shall be given into his hand for a time and times and half a time" (Dan. 7:25).

During the Dark Ages, predicted by the 1260-day (1260-year) prophecy, 192 popes reigned over the church while killing the descendants of the apostles by the millions. This prophecy has been fulfilled.

144. The prophecy of the seven weeks:

"Know therefore and understand, *that* from the going forth of the command to restore and build Jerusalem until Messiah the Prince, *there shall be* seven weeks ..." (Dan. 9:25).

Seven weeks (7 days x 7 weeks = 49 days, which represent 49 years) is the period of time required for the building of Jerusalem's compound wall, which was constructed for their safety. This prophecy has been fulfilled.

145. The prophecy about the date of the Messiah's coming:

"And after the sixty-two weeks Messiah shall be cut off, but not for Himself ..." (Dan. 9:26).

Sixty-two weeks by seven days per week equals 434 days (or 434 years) until the time when Jesus Christ would be baptized and show Himself publicly giving public service for three and half years. This prophecy has been fulfilled.

146. The prophecy about 3½ days equaling 3½ years:

"But in the middle of the week He shall bring an end to sacrifice and offering" (Dan. 9:27).

To the middle of the week is half a week or three and a half days, which prophetically is three and a half years. After three and a half years, Jesus Christ would give His life on the cross and then be resurrected from the grave, bringing an end to the system blood sacrifice in the temple in Jerusalem. This prophecy was fulfilled.

147. The prophecy of the close of probation to Jewish history:

"Seventy weeks are determined [lit. "cut off"] for your people and upon your holy city, to finish the transgression, to make an end of sins, to make reconciliation for iniquity, to bring in everlasting righteousness, to seal up the vision and prophecy, and to anoint the Most Holy.... And on the wing of abominations shall be one who makes desolate, even until the consummation, which is determined, is poured out on the desolate" (Dan. 9:24, 27).

The final week of the seventy weeks were seven days—or seven years—that commenced with Jesus' baptism and ended with the close of God's probation for the Jewish nation. As the gospel went to the Gentiles, the gospel message would need to be preached in 2000 languages that people might obtain eternal salvation. This prophecy has been fulfilled.

148. The prophecy of the 2300 days:

"And he said to me, 'For two thousand three hundred days; then the sanctuary shall be cleansed' " (Dan. 8:14).

2300 days (literally "evening morning two thousand three hundred") equal 2300 years, starting in 457 BC and ending in AD 1844, when the heavenly judgment of human beings started in heaven. This prophecy has been fulfilled.

149. The blessed prophecy:
"Blessed *is* he who waits, and comes to the one thousand three hundred and thirty-five days" (Dan. 12:12).

The prophecy of the 1335 days, with its promised blessing, is a prophecy of 1335 years that stretch from AD 508, with the prayer of abomination instituted by Pope Symmachus, until 1844, when the last church of Laodicea in the Seventh-day Adventist Church commenced. This prophecy has been fulfilled.

150. The last prophecy about the Jewish nation:
There are 5005 verses—from Isaiah to Malachi—that God has given to cover the history and destruction of the Jews. These verses cover their blessing and punishment, and particularly the destruction of the city of Jerusalem and its golden temple. This prophecy has been fulfilled.

Of these 150 prophecies ...
96 are already fulfilled
25 are not yet fulfilled
12 are for information
12 are in the process of fulfillment
3 are time period prophecies
2 are symbolic

Thirty Messianic Prophecies
The following prophecies cover the birth, crucifixion, resurrection, and second coming of Jesus Christ. These include:

- The prophecy that Jesus would overcome the serpent. A two-part prophecy, it has been partially fulfilled through Jesus' death on the cross (Gen. 3:15; see Rom. 16:20).

- The prophecy that Jesus Christ would be the prophet of Israel (Deut. 18:15; see Luke 24:19; John 4:19; 6:14; 7:40; 9:17).

- The prophecy that Jesus would come "out of Jacob" (Num. 24:17, 19).

- The prophecy that Jesus would be the Redeemer (Job 19:25; see Gal. 3:4, 5).

- The prophecy, "thou art my son. This day I have begotten thee" (Ps. 2:7; see John 3:16).

- The prophecy that Jesus would be the "Rock of our salvation" (Ps. 95:1; see also Ps. 18:2; see Matt. 16:18; 1 Peter 2:8).

- The prophecy, "Why hast thou forsaken me?" (Ps. 22:1; fulfilled in Matt. 27:46; Mark 15:34).

- The prophecy that the people would shake their heads and taunt Jesus about calling for God to deliver Him (Ps. 22:7, 8; fulfilled in Matt. 27:43).

- The prophecy that Jesus' crucifiers would pierce His hands and feet (Ps. 22:16; fulfilled in Matt. 27:35; Mark 15:25; Luke 23:33).

- The prophecy that His crucifiers would cast lots for His clothes (Ps. 22:18; fulfilled in Matt. 27:35; Luke 23:34; John 19:34).

- The prophecy, "Into your hand I commit my spirit" (Ps. 31:5; fulfilled in Luke 23:46).

- The prophecy, "In the scroll of the book *it is* written of me. I delight to do Your will, O my God, and Your law *is* within my heart," regarding His willingly coming to fulfill God's purpose (Ps. 40:7; see Heb. 10:7).

- The prophecy that they would give Him vinegar to drink (Ps. 69:21; fulfilled in Matt. 27:34, 48; Mark 15:36; Luke 23:36; John 19:29, 30).

- The prophecy that Jesus Christ would be the Cornerstone rather than Peter (Ps. 118:22, 23; see Eph. 2:20; 1 Peter 2:6).

- The prophecy that a virgin would conceive and bear a son (Isa. 7:14; fulfilled in Matt. 1:23; Luke 1:27; see also Phil. 2:7).

- The prophecy, "For unto us a Child is born," which indicates that Jesus would come into the world through birth (Isa. 9:6; fulfilled in Luke 2:11).

- The prophecy that Jesus Christ would be a precious Cornerstone (Isa. 28:16; fulfilled in Matt. 21:42; Eph. 2:20; 1 Peter 2:6).

- The prophecy that He would not cry (Isa. 42:2; see Matt. 12:19).

- The prophecy about the nature of Jesus' crucifixion, having been beaten, He would be led without complaint to His death (Isa. 53:2–8; see Acts 8:32).

- The prophecy about Jesus' garments being red (Isa. 63:2; fulfilled in Matt. 27:28).

- The prophecy that Jesus would be the seed of Jacob, from the royal tribe of Judah (Isa. 65:9; see Luke 2:4).

- The prophecy that Jesus' crucifiers would give him gall to drink (Jer. 8:14; fulfilled in Matt. 27:34).

- The prophecy that Jesus would be like a Lamb of slaughter (Jer. 11:19; see Acts 8:32).

- The prophecy that Jesus would be the Branch of righteousness to grow up to David (Jer. 33:15).

- The prophecy that symbolized the establishment of Christ's kingdom on earth by a stone carved from a mountain (Dan. 2:34, 44).

- The prophecy, "Out of Egypt I called My son," which predicted that God's Son would dwell in Egypt and be called to leave it (Hos. 11:1; fulfilled in Matt. 2:14, 15, 19).

- The prophecy, "Bethlehem ... you are little among the thousands of Judah," which predicts the place of Christ's birth (Micah 5:2; Matt. 2:5–8).

- The prophecy that Jesus would come as a king riding upon a donkey (Zech. 9:9; Matt. 21:7; Mark 11:7; John 12:14, 15).

In reviewing these texts, we must ask: How likely is it that one individual could fulfill all of these prophecies if He was not truly the Christ, the Anointed One of God, sent to save humankind?

Chapter 9
Church History

In the whole Bible, God has given sixteen time periods, stretching from the Garden of Eden to the new heaven and new earth. The first part of the Bible contains seven of these time periods, from the Garden of Eden to the cross (see Chapter 2). In the second part of the Bible, God gave seven more time periods in the prophecy of the seven churches in Revelation 2 and 3. This prophecy outlines periods of world history that will take place but once. Their significance is revealed by the clues in the passages, the Spirit of Prophecy books, and church history. The prophecy of the seven churches is connected with our eternal salvation.

The First Three Churches

Modern historians reject the biblical testimony about the beginning of the world. Yet, we have provided in this book the major events that have occurred on earth from the beginning of human history until the present. There was no Stone Age or Bronze Age, as we have noted. We have provided evidence that takes us up to the war between Iraq and Kuwait. According to Daniel 2, modern history began with Babylon and continues through the modern European nations. The same ten nations of Europe were also prophesied in the book of Revelation.

The Ephesus Church Period (AD 31–100)

Fifty days inclusive after the Crucifixion came the day of Pentecost. It was the beginning of the fulfillment of Joel 2:23, 28, 29 when the Holy Spirit came upon the apostles and early believers in Jesus Christ. Jesus had said, before His ascension, that His followers should remain in Jerusalem until they were "endued with power from on high" (Luke 24:49). They waited in Jerusalem with fasting and prayer for the outpouring of God's Holy Spirit. Ten days after Christ's ascension, which was fifty days after the Crucifixion, the eleven apostles and 120 disciples received the power of the Holy Spirit (Acts 2:16–18). These early followers of Christ kept the Ten Commandments by the power of the Holy Spirit, and they performed miracles. Within two generations, they had taken the gospel message throughout the Middle East. Whoever they prayed for also received the Holy Spirit and performed miracles. That is how 3,000 and 5,000 people, on two occasions, converted to Christ and joined His church before AD 100 (Acts 2:41; 4:4). It was while the disciples were staying in the city of Antioch that they were first called "Christians" (Acts 11:26). Lamentably, the power of the Holy Spirit in the former rain gradually died away after two generations. This was due in part to the persecution and death of believers from AD 31 until the end of the century. The apostle John, who was one of the true disciples of Jesus Christ, wrote the twenty-two chapters of the book of Revelation while he was exiled on the Isle of Patmos. He sent this book back to Asia Minor in AD 97. That was the last work of the Holy Spirit in composing the Scriptures, and, with it, He closed the canon of the New Testament.

Smyrna Church Period (AD 100–313), Revelation 2:8–11

In the first century, the church ran into conflict with idol worship under the worship of Diana in Ephesus. But shortly after this, idol worship crept into the church (Rev. 2:8–11). After Bishops Titus and Onesimus, the Christian leaders who endured persecution from Rome—including the death penalty—sought to escape these unmerciful cruelties. As the influence of the worship of Diana the goddess of

Rome was introduced into the Christian faith, so also did the worship of Mary, the mother of Jesus Christ, as a female goddess, and sun worship, through the feigned superiority of Sunday over the seventh-day Sabbath, slowly edge their way into the church. So did Baptism by sprinkling rather than baptism by immersion, especially for children, also slowly gain popularity in the churches, as did Holy Communion without foot washing. This new Christian church, with its idol worship and its festivals based on Roman paganism—which included Christmas and Easter—was very appealing to millions of Roman soldiers, officers, and non-military men and women. Later, this new Christian church would be identified as the Roman Catholic Church. Moreover, Satan's miracles brought in many more millions of people all over the Roman Empire.

Persecution of the Christians began between AD 117 and AD 138 when Roman Emperor Hadrian mercilessly slew millions of the followers of Christ. This persecution was followed by the persecutions of Marcus Aurelius, from AD 161 to 180, of Trajan Decius, from AD 249 to 251, of Valerian, from AD 253 to 260, and of Diocletian, from AD 284 to 305. During the ten prophetic days (which were ten literal years) of the prophecy of Revelation 2:10, the descendants of the apostolic church were killed. Millions of people lost legs, hands, and eyes. It was the climactic scene of Diocletian's persecution, and the axes grew dull and the executioners grew weary of killing Christians. False Christians known as Gnostics reinterpreted the Bible, building the foundation for the Roman Catholic Church.

Pergamos Church Period (AD 313–538), Revelation 2:12–17

This period is known for its continued persecution and its further steps to transfer the day of rest from the seventh-day Sabbath to the first-day "Lord's day." In AD 321, Emperor Constantine was ostensibly converted to Christianity (although he would not be baptized until the year he died). He became a staunch supporter of the new Christianity with its idol worship. Through his influence, almost all the masses of the empire turned to the new idol-worshipping Christian Church. He declared the Sunday a national day of rest, and the church capitalized on his declaration by punishing those who continued to rest on the Sabbath. Thus, the majority of the descendants of the apostolic church ended up observing Sunday as the Sabbath, though, because of Acts

4:11, 12 and Acts 16:31, they did not embrace prayer through Mary and the veneration of the saints, such as Joseph and the twelve apostles. While clinging to the faith of Jesus Christ from AD 100 to 1844, they did begin to observe, in their respective churches, Christmas and Easter, communion services without foot washing, baptism by sprinkling for adults and children rather than baptism by immersion. Yet, they never accepted prayer through Mary, for they recognized it to be idol worship. Many millions of believers received the baptism of blood, being martyred for Christ's sake during the years between AD 313 and 538. During this time, the false doctrines of Jezebel, the Nicolaitans, and the Balaamites deepened and apostasy increased, and church leaders gave close attention to definitions of Christology. The Council of Nicaea, in AD 325, defined Jesus as truly God; the Council of Constantinople, in AD 331, defined Jesus as also truly man; the Council of Ephesus, in AD 431, defined Jesus as both God and man combined in one person; and the Council of Chalcedon, in AD 451, defined Jesus as having distinct divine and human natures.

The Thyatira Church Period, the Dark Ages (AD 538–1563), Revelation 2:18–29

During the church period of Pergamos, persecution, prior to the period, had ended as the eastern portion of the Roman Empire fell into the hands of Odoacer of the tribe of the Heruli in AD 476. Nonetheless, the Roman bishops sustained the dominance of the church of idol worship among the ten kingdoms of Europe after this time. During this period, Clovis, the king of France, became a member of idol-worshipping Christianity and was baptized on Christmas day, AD 496. Anastasius II was ordained pope of Rome on November 24 of that same year. He became the first pope of the idol-worshipping Catholic (or worldwide) church, headed by Rome. Hence, it was named the "Roman Catholic Church." Because he was king of the Franks, Clovis' baptism, as an act of submission to the clergy, and his pact with the Roman Church established the Romans as the supreme spiritual Christian authority in the West and allowed Clovis to consolidate the church's power behind his own conquering designs. It also signaled the beginning of the present Roman Catholic Church as it granted Clovis the church designation of "Novus Constantinus" (the New Constantine), reigning over the "Holy Roman Empire." The promotion of the

Roman Catholic Church was in fulfillment of the biblical prophecy of Daniel 7:24, 25 and Daniel 12:11.

Anastasius II died in Rome in AD 498. Four days after this event, Symmachus was elected bishop of Rome in the Basilica of Constantine, becoming the second pope under the Holy Roman Empire. Within ten years of the period, by his ecclesiastical power, he brought the churches all over the world under his control, cementing the present Roman Catholic principles of doctrine.

Who is the antichrist? The word "antichrist" is composed of two parts, "anti-," which means "against" or "in the place of," and "Christ," the meaning of which is self-evident. Those who stand against Christ's principles are called "anti-Christ." Since the Roman Catholic popes followed tradition instead of God's Word, they are the true antichrist in this world. Revelation 13:18 explains that the number of the antichrist is 666, which corresponds, in the Latin language, to the numerical value of the title "VICARIOUS FILII DEI," which was at one time inscribed in the triple crown of the Roman Catholic popes, thereby fulfilling this antichrist prophecy.

So, antichrist means "instead of Christ" or "against Christ." Christ is the only one who has ever walked the earth as God; there is no other human who is also God. If any other human being in this world claims the prerogatives of God, he or she is antichrist.

This is why the title, VICARIUS FILLI DEI, whose numerical value is 666, is so significant. It means "substitute for the Son of God" in this world. This is a blasphemous name, and, outrageous as it may seem, it was attached to the Roman Catholic popes. (See http://biblelight.net/666.htm.)

Table 9.1. Numeric Value of VICARIUS FILII DEI

V=	5		F=	0		D=	500	
I=	1		I=	1		E=	0	
C=	100		L=	50		I=	1	501
A=	0		I=	1				
R=	0		I=	1	53			
I=	1							
U=	5							
S=	0	112						666

The Seven Trumpets

The book of Revelation uses the symbol of seven trumpets, which correspond to the time period of the feet of iron mixed with clay that represented the ten kingdoms of Europe in the image in Daniel 2. The representation in Daniel ends when a big stone strikes the feet of the image and destroys the whole statue. The stone represents Jesus Christ. He brings human history to a close as He establishes His kingdom. An outline of the events of world history is recorded in these two prophecies. The events portrayed by the seven trumpets began in AD 390 and lasted until AD 476. The ten kingdoms of the Roman Empire will be listed below.

The First Trumpet

In fulfillment of the sounding of the first trumpet, the northern parts of the Roman Empire fell (Rev. 8:7). These included:

1. **The Goths and the Alemanni (AD 390).** These German-speaking tribes joined together to make war against the Roman Empire, and they secured the territory that is now known as Germany.

2. **The Franks in Gaul (AD 380–410).** The French-speaking Franks made war with the Roman Empire, winning their territory and naming it "France." Their nation was formed in AD 420.

3. **The Anglo-Saxons (AD 380–AD 415).** As with the previously mentioned tribes of the northern parts of Rome, the Anglo-Saxons, another powerful barbarian tribe, which spoke English, revolted against the Roman Empire and separated their island from the Roman Empire, naming it "Britain" and forming a third country. The establishment of these three powerful European countries fulfilled the prophecy of the first trumpet. It is from these three powerful tribes that the great nations of Germany, France, and Great Britain evolved.

The Second Trumpet

The symbol of the second trumpet predicted the fall of the southern part of the Roman Empire (Rev. 8:8, 9).

4. **The Vandals (AD 410–430).** Within this ten-year period, the northern part of Africa, with its capital city in Egypt, came under the control of the Vandals. The Vandals were a dark-skinned Hammite tribe of sea-faring pirates. They used their expertise in shipbuilding to construct fleets of warships that controlled the Mediterranean Sea and the other oceans around Africa, and they used their prowess at sea to overcome the Roman navy and take control of Egypt.

5. **The Lombards (AD 437–476).**

    The Latin-speaking Lombards and Suevi joined the Vandals in taking the peninsula of Italy from Rome.

The Third Trumpet

The sounding of the third trumpet predicted the conquest of the western part of the Roman Empire (Rev. 8:10; 11:6).

6. **The Huns (AD 437– 476).** The smaller tribe of the Huns was known in the western parts of the Roman Empire for their ferocious horse-riding warriors under the leadership of Attila. The Huns plundered Rome and carved out the territory of Hungary that now comprises parts of Hungary, Ukraine, Moldova, Russia, Romania, Slovakia, the Czech Republic, Poland, Germany, Belarus, Serbia, Austria, Lithuania, Croatia, and Bulgaria.

7. **The Burgundians (AD 455–476).** The Carthaginians and Burgundians were notorious, Portuguese-speaking sailor-warriors in the Western Roman Empire. Their naval fleets revolted against Rome and secured the territories of Portugal.

8. **The Visigoths (AD 460–476).** Within the same time period, the Spanish-speaking Visigoths also declared war on Rome and separated their territories from the Roman Empire as the country of Spain. Thus, eight countries in all separated by the time of the third trumpet prophecy, fulfilling what God had predicted.

The Fourth Trumpet

Through the symbolism of the fourth trumpet, Jesus Christ declared that the Roman Empire would be divided into the ten nations of Europe, fulfilling Daniel 2:44 exactly.

9. **9. The Ostrogoths (AD 470).** Theodoric was the head of the Ostrogoths. The Ostrogoths came from north of the Black Sea and declared war on Rome, conquering the northern part of Italy.

10. **10. The Heruli (AD 476).** One final barbarian tribe, which attacked the eastern part of the Roman Empire in what is now modern Hungary, was called the Heruli. They allied with the mighty warrior Odoacer and conquered the territory that is now Turkey, Rumania, Bulgaria and the northern part of Greece. With the Heruli, the mighty empire of Rome, established by Julius Caesar, came to an end in world history. The prophecy of the ten horns was fulfilled. From AD 390 to 476, the ten tribes became ten kingdoms, dividing up the Roman Empire into the kingdoms of Germany, France, Britain, Italy, Hungary, Portugal, Spain, and the three kingdoms that would be uprooted—the Ostrogoths, the Heruli, and the Vandals.

Dear friend, prophecy foretold the true history of modern Europe. No one else knew in advance what the history of modern Europe's ten kingdoms would be. Today they have a very high opinion of themselves because they are first and second-world countries. The tribes descended from Shem and Japheth, and their ancestors worshipped idols and followed Lucifer rather than Jesus Christ. Those who worship Jesus Christ have the Scriptures, which reveal the true account of civilization as taught by the living God of heaven, and they benefit from the knowledge of kingdom history that was recorded by God. Which is to say that Israel was entrusted with the historical record of the world's first period of civilization, lasting from 4159 to 1491 BC, which was recorded by Moses the first prophet of the living God of Heaven. After him came thirty-six other prophets, who continued recording the true history of the world up to AD 100 in the Holy Bible by the power of the living God, Jesus Christ. Aside from the sacred history of humankind in the Holy Bible, there is no other reliable history in any of the other eighteen religious books in the world.

The Fifth Trumpet

Can God remain silent knowing such persecutions are taking place? How did God guide His people in the Dark Ages?

Throughout the Dark Ages, as God's people were shedding their blood, God kept a record of the wrongs against them and executed the prophecy of iniquity to punish those who had persecuted them. Because of Abraham and Sarah's lack of faith, Ishmael was born to Sarah's handmaid, Hagar, in 2125 BC, and he became the father of the Islamic nations, which today number in the millions around the world. God used these Islamic nations to punish the Jews, the pagan Romans, and others.

Punishment of the Jews

In 2104 BC, God pronounced a blessing on Hagar's son Ishmael as Hagar and Ishmael were going toward Egypt through the desert of Saudi Arabia (Gen. 21:13, 17–20). An angel showed them an oasis with a fountain of water from which to quench their thirst. That fountain is now called the "Well of Zamzam," and it is located within the shrine of the Masjid al-Haram in Mecca, Saudi Arabia, which is considered by the Islamic people around the globe to be the holiest place on earth. The living God of heaven chose to give Hagar's son Ishmael a special blessing and then later used him and his descendants under Islam to punish the Jewish people for their violation of God's Ten Commandments. In fulfillment of the prophecy of blessing, the prophet of Islam, Muhammad Nabi, received, from AD 609–632, their noble Quran, thereby creating a new religion without idol worship, which was called "Islam" (meaning "surrender"), in direct opposition to the Jewish religion and to the idol worship of the Roman Catholic Church, which was formulated as a political power in AD 508 under Clovis of France.

Punishment of Pagan and Papal Rome

AD 600 was the year of the commencement of the *jihad*, which literally means "striving," or "struggling." However, most understand it to mean "holy war"—and that against the enemies of Islam. It was through *jihad* that Muslims established their Islamic religion in the lands of the Arabian Desert and in the Promised Land of Canaan, covering Jordan, Syria, Oman, Qatar, Iran, Sudan, Tunisia, Algeria,

Morocco, Gambia, Guinea, Mali, and Guinea-Bissau. Mohammed and his supporters conquered these countries on camelback and the celebrated Arabian horse. The Islamic forces conquered several other countries in the following order: Saudi Arabia in AD 632, Egypt in AD 640, Libya in AD 641, Iran (a second time) in AD 700, then Nigeria, Spain, and Tanzania, and North Yemen in AD 800. Mauritania, Turkey, India, and Pakistan in AD 900, and Bangladesh, Malawi, and Afghanistan in AD 1250. Through their merchants, Islam made inroads into Thailand in the 1200s, into the Philippines in the 1300s, the southern parts of Russia and Mongolia in AD 1600, Malawi and Somali in AD 1798. The religion of Islam spread like wildfire, also entering Malaysia and the United Arab Emirates.

Islamists Destroyed the Idol Gods of Pagan and Papal Rome

It is ironic that, after AD 1300, the Islamic descendants of Ishmael destroyed the idol gods of those who had previously persecuted the descendants of the apostolic church. They did this by killing the descendants of the persecutors—the Roman Catholic bishops and priests. God cannot abide His people having other gods. He is "a jealous God, visiting the iniquity of the fathers upon the children unto the third and fourth generations" (Exod. 20:5). No one can escape punishment in this world or the final destruction of hell.

The fifth trumpet prophecy of iniquity was against the Roman popes and their followers from 538 to 1798 (Rev. 9:1–21). Jesus Christ, who is the God of heaven, gave John the Revelator a prophecy about the punishment of the popes who ruled over the church and who would persecute and martyr millions of the descendants of the apostolic church during the Dark Ages. This was under the prophecies of the fifth and sixth trumpets. Both prophecies include the prophetic time element that they should be tormented "five months" and that their torment would be like the sting of a scorpion (Rev. 9:5, 10). In biblical prophecy, when one day equals one year, five months equals 150 years (5 x 30 days = 150 days). Thus, the "five months" of this prophecy are a period of 150 years. In fulfillment of Revelation 9:5, the Mohammed Ottomans of Turkey declared war on July 27, 1299, against Constantinople. Conquering the city, they made war with the Roman Catholic Church for 150 years. As predicted by biblical prophecy, God punished the Roman Catholic hierarchy and members through the Ottoman Empire, turning the same persecution on those who persecuted. In terrible poetic justice, the Jews, Romans, and Catholics, who killed the apostolic Christians, were persecuted by Islamic people, as they killed more than three million Jews and Roman Catholics.

The Sixth Trumpet

The fulfillment of the sounding of the sixth trumpet began in AD 1399. Following immediately on the heels of the fifth trumpet, the sixth trumpet sounded immediately after the prophesied 150 years of war. The sixth trumpet covered a period that was longer than the previous trumpet, that is, it predicted a war lasting 391 years, fifteen days. The angels that would kill a third of mankind during this period would do so for "an hour, and a day, and a month, and a year" (Rev. 9:15, KJV). One hour equals fifteen days; one day equals twenty-four hours; one month equals thirty days; one year equals 360 days. Together these equal 391 years and fifteen days of war. It is possible to interpret the release of the four angels, who are bound at the great Euphrates, as loosing the countries bounded by the Euphrates River (Rev. 9:14)—namely Syria, Iraq, Turkey, and Iran (Persia). These forces took control of the Jews, the idol-worshipping Roman pagans and Roman Catholics, and the fire-god worshipers of Persia in the four nations mentioned above. The religious wars stretched from AD 1399 for 150 years and then an additional 391 years and fifteen days. These were waged by the descendents of the Ottoman Sultan Mohammed of Turkey. From their base, they launched attacks on horse and camelback, using firearms and cannons to conquer Syria, Iraq, Turkey, and Persia.

Incentives to Convert to Islam

Other Islamic rulers were Nader Shah, Timur (most know him as "Tamerlane," a nickname given him for his game leg), Selim I, Muhammad Ghori, and Mahmud of Ghazni. These rulers turned Jewish synagogues, pagan temples, temples of the Persian fire-god, and idol-worshipping Roman Catholic churches into mosques. They also vigorously and systematically established Islam, torturing, persecuting, and threatening, while also providing land, money, and protection from their enemies for those who were willing to peacefully and gradually convert from their previous religion into Islam. Revelation

9:15 says that a third of mankind was killed. This was fulfilled in the conversion to Islam of what are now modern Iraq, Iran, Jordan Syria, Lebanon, Egypt, and Saudi Arabia, and northern Africa.

The "Baptism of Blood" in God's Church

Daniel 7:24, 25, points to the baptism of blood in the persecution of God's faithful. We have previously studied how Jesus Christ and the Holy Spirit divided God's church into two parts, depending on whether they were before or after the crucifixion, and how they divided the Holy Scriptures, according to the old and new covenants, into the Old Testament and the New Testament. Yet, both testaments have the same constitution—the Holy Ten Commandments. Thus, without the Holy Ten Commandments, there would be no Holy Bible or Holy God. Because the people living during the period of the 1260 years (Dan. 7:25; 12:7; Rev. 11:2, 3; 12:6, 14; 13:5) and during the 1290 years (Dan. 12:11) did not have the privilege of following the Bible and God's holy law, they were granted the privilege of going through the "baptism of blood."

Waldenses

Many groups of people, such as the Waldenses, the Albigenses, and the Huguenots, secretly shared God's Word, explaining the Bible to interested people. The original manuscripts of the Bible were written in Hebrew, Aramaic, and Greek. The Old Testament Scriptures were translated into the Greek language because many of the Jews were Hellenized and, therefore, spoke Greek as their primary language. The New Testament was written in Greek (with the exception, perhaps, of the Gospel of Matthew, which may have first been written in Hebrew). Because Rome spoke Latin, the predominant translation of the Bible through the Middle Ages was the Latin Vulgate, though few of the common people understood Latin. It was this Latin version that John Wycliffe, the "morning star of the Reformation," used to translate the Bible into the English language, which some have described as the first "King James Version" since phrasing from the King James Version of 1611 trace back to it. After Wycliffe, the Bible was translated into many languages. William Tyndale also translated the Bible into English, though he did so from the original Hebrew and Greek.

Martin Luther, AD 1517

Martin Luther, a Roman Catholic cleric, protested against indulgences and the abuses of the Pope and, therefore, came out of the Roman Catholic Church. He also translated the Bible into German. Many princes and kings of various countries joined with Martin Luther in establishing Protestant churches throughout Europe. The pope unsuccessfully attempted to have Martin Luther killed. (One hundred years before Luther, Huss and Jerome, and other clergy of the Sardis period were martyred.) Drawing their name from Martin Luther, Lutheran churches were established all over Europe. From the Protestant movement, many other denominations were established in Europe from 1517 to 1798 under the persecution of the popes. This included the Anglicans and Episcopalians, the Presbyterians, the Puritans, the Methodists and Wesleyans, the Mennonites, the Baptists, the Quakers, the Brethren, and many other Christian affiliations. The true churches that fled to the wilderness of America because of persecution are represented in Revelation by the symbol of a woman clothed with the sun (Rev. 12:1, 6).

In 1620, in keeping with the biblical prophecy of Revelation 12:6, under the persecution of the Church of England, the Puritan Christians left on their voyage to the new lands of North America in the ship Mayflower with 102 people on board. These pilgrims and the fortune seekers who accompanied them reached America and fulfilled the prophecy of the woman who "fled into the wilderness." Many others followed them, leaving Europe to come to North America. During the Thyatira period of the church, these Puritan Christians, who were spiritual descendants of the apostolic church, came to North America to start God's true church and to play a role in the establishment of the United States. The true church flourished because, according to the prophecy, she had "two wings of a great eagle, that she might fly into the wilderness to her place" (Rev. 12:14).

One hundred and fifty years after this group of Puritan Christians reached North America, their descendants and other immigrants to the new land joined together in 1776 to form a new nation called the United States of America. With George Washington, their first president, they enunciated the new American Constitution under the emblem of the two-winged eagle, which corresponds to the biblical symbol of the two wings of an eagle (Rev. 12:14). Now every American citizen passport carries the emblem of two wings of a great eagle. This prophecy was fulfilled in 1776.

The French Revolution and the Baser Elements of French Society

As we have already seen under the fifth and sixth trumpets, the two great Islamic wars extended up to AD 1840. Simultaneous with these Islamic wars is the prophecy of Revelation 11 concerning the French Revolution with its citizen revolt against the pope, the Roman Catholic clergy, and the aristocracy in France. Many met their demise under the infamous French guillotine. During the Revolution, the clergy allowed women freedom, and prostitution was accepted in France. The people were immoral, and drinking, stealing, killing, and prostitution were rampant. These practices undermined law and order and the structure of society, causing poverty, hunger, and homelessness. The common people suffered terribly, and, with the earlier departure of the more stable and productive Huguenots, the rougher elements of society revolted.

The Sardis Church Period (ad 1563 to 1798), Revelation 3:1–6

When Thyatira became Babylon, God's remnant in the Thyatira church started Sardis, the fifth church. These were the followers of Martin Luther and the Lutherans, the Methodists, the Mennonites, and the Quakers. These four churches were the leaders, or "angel," of the church of Sardis. It was during this period that the American Revolutionary War was fought. The American Civil War was fought in the next century.

The American Civil War

The American Civil War was fought from 1861 to 1865. Its result is part of the fulfillment of the prophecy of Revelation 12:15, 16, it says, "spewed water out of his mouth like a flood after the woman ... But the earth helped the woman, and the earth opened its mouth and swallowed up the flood which the dragon had spewed out of his mouth." The people of America fought the Civil War and ultimately abolished slavery as an institution in all the United States through the fifteenth amendment to the U. S. Constitution. (President Abraham Lincoln's Emancipation Proclamation was a wartime measure that had only addressed slave states that were part of the Confederacy.)

In this prophecy is an important message from Jesus concerning His faithful people who fled to the wilderness and were sheltered under the great wings of the eagle of the United States, protecting God's church that it might be established all over the world.

The Everlasting Gospel and the First Angel's Message

"Then I saw another angel flying in the midst of heaven, having the everlasting gospel to preach to those who dwell on the earth—to every nation, tribe, tongue, and people—saying with a loud voice, 'Fear God and give glory to Him, for the hour of His judgment has come; and worship Him who made heaven and earth, the sea and springs of water'" (Rev. 14:6, 7).

That "the hour of His judgment has come" is another message of great consequence. It was given to the angel, or leader, of the church of Sardis to proclaim to all the world. The four-part head of the Sardis church was entrusted with beginning the spread to all the world of the everlasting gospel of Jesus Christ's birth, death on the cross, and resurrection. However, the church of Sardis failed to proclaim the second part of this very important message regarding "the hour of His judgment," not knowing the full meaning of the 2300-day prophecy, which came to its fulfillment in AD 1844 for those who are going to heaven at the Second Advent of Jesus Christ.

The Angel of the Church of Sardis and the First Angel's Message

Four major Christian groups—the Lutherans, Methodists, Mennonites, and Quakers—were the collective head of the church in the United States from AD 1798 to 1833. During this period, the biblical prophecy of the former rain and the latter rain (Joel 2:23, 28–31; James 5:7, 8) began to be fulfilled and were accompanied by signs in the sun, moon, and stars, among other phenomena given in Matthew 24:6, 7, 29.

Earthquakes

According to the prophecy, there will be earthquakes, wars, and rumors of wars around the world. Below is a list of some of the deadliest earthquakes.

Table 9.2. Major Earthquakes

January 23, 1566,	Shaanxi, China, with a death toll of 830,000
November 1667	Shemakha, Azerbaijan, with a death toll of 80,000
January 11, 1693	Catania, Sicily, with a death toll of 60,000
December 31, 1703	Tokyo, Japan, with a death toll of 10,000
October 11, 1737	Calcutta, India, with a death toll of 300,000
November 1, 1755	Lisbon, Portugal, with a death toll of 100,000

Other Celestial Signs

May 19, 1780 - beginning at 10 am, the sun was darkened. That same night the moon became as blood, fulfilling the prophecies of Joel 2:31; Matthew 24:29; and Rev. 6:12.

November 13, 1833 - the "stars of heaven", or meteors, fell like immature figs falling from a tree (Mark 13:25) over all North America. On November 25 of the same year, there was a similar shower of stars on the continent of Europe.

Table 9.3. Major Wars During This Period

1299–1449	Islamic wars in the Middle East, including Saudi Arabia and the Sahara Desert in the world's longest war, lasting 392 years and costing more than 15 billion lives
1914 to 1918	World War I broke out and lasted four years, costing 5 million lives
1941 to 1945	World War II, costing more than 7 million lives
1949 to 1957	The Arab-Israeli War
1950	The Korean Conflict
1962	Indo-Chinese War
1975	The Vietnam War
1967	The Arab-Israeli War
1965 to 1972	Wars between India and Pakistan, and between Pakistan and Bangladesh, costing countless lives.

The Philadelphia Church Period (AD 1798 to 1844), Revelation 3:7–13

In the Philadelphia church period (1798–1844), the angel of the church represents William Miller and the 3000 pastors who preached the advent message.

The Philadelphia church period (Rev. 3:7–13) and the second angel's message is as follows: "And another angel followed, saying, 'Babylon is fallen, is fallen, that great city, because she has made all nations drink of the wine of the wrath of her fornication' " (Rev. 14:8).

Nine days of probation every year were given to the people of Israel prior to the Day of Atonement. The Israelites were to offer a sacrifice for their pardonable sins. Those who failed to sacrifice for their pardonable sins were to be excommunicated and stoned to death, and those who committed unpardonable sins were also to be stoned to death. As God gave Israel a period of probation, so did He give ten years of probation (a year for a day) to the church of Philadelphia. William Miller and the other 3,000 pastors should have preached the heavenly judgment under the first angel's message of the Sardis church. However, because they did not, the second angel's message was delivered to the Philadelphia church.

Ten Days Represent Ten Years

God gave ten years to preach the heavenly judgment, though it did not mean that Christ should come in 1844. Not having a full understanding of the message, even William Miller preached the mistaken message that the judgment of the first angel was the judgment of fire upon the earth as he thought Jesus would return.

William Miller

Revelation 10 prophesies about William Miller, the "roaring lion," and his 3,000 fellow pastors who also preached the return of Christ. These were the angels to the church of Philadelphia. At first, they calculated that the end of the 2300 days and the return of Christ would be in 1843, then in the spring of 1844, and finally in the fall of 1844.

It was natural for these preachers to link the event predicted with the Second Coming, for, after Miller began preaching about the nearness of Christ's return in 1831, the spectacular display of falling meteorites, on November 13, 1833, pointed William Miller to the biblical signs of the second coming of Jesus Christ in the sun, moon, and stars. And this was the last of the three signs predicted in Revelation 6:12, 13, which had occurred in their lifetime. With the other Adventist pastors, Miller mistakenly believed that Jesus Christ was going to return in the spring and then the fall of 1844.

The Great Disappointment

Yet, Jesus Christ did not come in 1843 or in the spring or the fall of 1844. Their great hope that they would see Jesus in the clouds turned into the greatest disappointment ever since the dashed hopes of the disciples when Jesus was crucified. Some of the more than 50,000 people in the United States and Europe, who were waiting for Jesus in 1844, gave up their Christian faith and became agnostics. At the same time, Charles Darwin, whose father wanted him to be a Christian minister, formulated the theory of evolution in 1844, and now there are more than 7 million evolutionists around the globe, the majority of which claim that there is no God but that everything came through naturalistic causes over billions of years. The prophecy of Revelation 14 goes on:

"Then a third angel followed them, saying with a loud voice, 'If anyone worships the beast and his image, and receives his mark on his forehead or on his hand ...'" (Rev. 14:9). The three angels' message was proclaimed after the message of the corruption of the Christian church under the angel of the church of Thyatira and the fatal wound under France in 1798. Yet, God's first judgment for humankind started in 1844. God has ordained that there be two judgments for humankind. Both judgments take place in heaven and not on the earth.

God's Heavenly Judgment

Regarding the judgment, Peter declared: "... judgment must begin at the house of God" (1 Peter 4:17, KJV). The "house of God" means those who profess to be God's followers, and the statement indicates that judgment begins *before* Christ comes to earth. According to Daniel 8:14, the sanctuary was to be cleansed, or purified. The time factor of the 2300 years, which started in 457 BC and ended in 1844, tells us that this cannot mean the sanctuary on earth. Therefore, we must conclude that it is the sanctuary in heaven, a sanctuary that Hebrews describes as requiring purification at its inauguration (Heb. 9:23). Thus, the first phase of judgment began in heaven in 1844 and is still going on. The second judgment—which is the judgment of the rebellious—will be held during the millennium (Rev. 20:6; cf. Dan. 7:22).

Those who go to heaven after the first judgment will receive eternal salvation. The Scriptures declare that they will judge others in heaven. Paul wrote, "Do you not know that we shall judge angels?" (1 Cor. 6:3). After going to heaven, we are going to judge sinners and the third of the angels who went against God. Also, the saved will judge millions of sinners during the second judgment during the millennium.

The seventh and final church period—the church period of Laodicea—extends from 1844 to the second coming of Jesus Christ.

The Laodicean Church Period (AD 1844 to the End), Revelation 3:14–22

The Seventh-day Adventist Church, while advanced in biblical reliance over other Christian churches—including the Lutherans, the Methodists and Wesleyans, the Mennonites, the Quakers, the Baptists, the Presbyterians, the Brethren, and the Anglicans—nonetheless recognize that they are the Laodicean church of Revelation. There is something missing from the other denominations.

The Third Angel and Its Message

Revelation 14:9–12 is the third angel's message to the last of the seven churches, that is, to Laodicea. According to Revelation 3:14, the angel of Laodicea is the minister to that church period just as there was also an "angel" to each previous church period, including that of Ephesus. The church of Ephesus was the first Christian church—the period belonging to the twelve apostles. In like manner, the church of Laodicea is the last Christian church, the one made up of believers who "keep the commandments of God and the faith of Jesus" (Rev. 14:12). These two characteristics apply quite specifically to a group of believers in Jesus who keep *all* of God's commandments, including the one that most Christians overlook—the one that calls for worshipping Him "who made heaven and earth, the sea and springs of water" (Rev. 14:7).

The Laodicean church is the last church in this world. After the great disappointment took place on October 22, 1844, the Millerites, or Adventists, pleaded with God for further truth to go forward. At the same time, no one realized the extraordinary work of the Holy

Spirit in the outpouring of the "latter rain" from 1833 forward in many places in the United States.

The Laodicean Church

The first Sabbath-keeping Adventist church was in New Hampshire. A small group of Millerite Adventists gathered one Sunday for a communion service in a church building at Washington, New Hampshire in early 1844. That morning, Adventist pastor Frederick Wheeler exhorted his congregation to keep the commandments of God. A Seventh Day Baptist by the name of Rachel Oakes, who was visiting that day, called the pastor aside to point out that he was not keeping all of God's Ten Commandments himself. He asked, "Whatever do you mean?" And she responded that he was not keeping the *fourth* commandment because the biblical Sabbath is on Saturday and not on Sunday. Pastor Wheeler studied the Bible on the subject, with all sincerity, and discovered that God did not authorize a change in the seventh-day Sabbath. The truth spread to other Adventists, and they adopted the Sabbath, becoming seventh-day-keeping Adventists. (The Adventists would find other forgotten truths in their study of the Scriptures, and those truths would become the pillars of the Seventh-day Adventist message.)

Among the first Adventists to adopt the Sabbath was a man named William Farnsworth. When Pastor Wheeler preached on the seventh-day Sabbath, he quickly took his stand for it and declared that, from the next Sabbath onward, he was going to keep the biblical Sabbath on Saturday. When he asked the congregation who would be willing to join him, twelve others took their stand for God's holy seventh-day Sabbath. From the next Sabbath onward, they worshipped together on the seventh day in the Washington, New Hampshire church, of which Frederick Wheeler was the pastor.

Pioneers of the Laodicean Church of Seventh-day Adventists

A friend of the Washington church, Free-will Baptist minister T. M. Preble, who edited a small Millerite newspaper called *The Hope of Israel*, discovered the Sabbath, possibly from Frederick Wheeler, and published, in March 1845, a 28-page pamphlet entitled, "Showing That the Seventh Day Should be Observed as the Sabbath." One hundred fifty miles from New Hampshire, a well-known retired-sea-captain-turned-Adventist-preacher by the name of Joseph Bates read Preble's tract and was favorably impressed. Immediately, he wanted to meet with the small group at Washington, New Hampshire for study. Walking and riding horseback to Washington, New Hampshire, he met with Wheeler to study the subject from the Bible. Convinced that the seventh day is the Sabbath, Bates returned home rejoicing and wrote a 48-page pamphlet entitled, "The Seventh-day Sabbath a Perpetual Sign." In the summer of 1846, Bates met two young Adventists who would play an influential role in the movement—James Springer White and Miss Ellen Gould Harmon. The couple read Bates' pamphlet on the Sabbath and, accepting the Sabbath, became strong proponents of the Sabbath along with Bates.

Joseph Bates

Health-minded student of the Scriptures from Massachusetts, Joseph Bates, became a committed Christian when his beloved wife Prudence gave him a Bible to read while traveling the oceans as a sea captain. Later, he bought into part ownership of the ship. When he retired, he sold his share of the ship for what was considered a small fortune at the time, but, committed to helping others learn the advent message, he spent his all his money spreading the Adventist message through the printing of tracts and preaching the message as far south as Virginia. It was T. M. Preble's tract on the Sabbath that convinced Bates that the fourth commandment was not nailed to the cross, that it was still binding on all people who believe in the Creator God, and that the biblical Sabbath was on Saturday and not on Sunday as he had grown up believing. His role in promoting the Sabbath gave him a special place among the founders of the Seventh-day Adventist Church, leading out in study at the Sabbath conferences in the late 1840s. He was the oldest of the Adventist founders, which included James White who played a primary role in the organization of the church until his death in 1881.

James White

Twenty-two-year old former schoolteacher James White became a minister in the Christian Connexion Church before he began preaching the Second Advent in 1843. He was one of the 3,000 pastors who experienced the great disappointment in the fall of 1844. After the disappointment, he traveled about New England, visiting the advent believers and encouraging them to hold firm in their faith in the imminent return of Christ. James White first heard Miss Ellen Gould Harmon relate a vision on one occasion in 1845 when she was visiting eastern Maine with William Jordan and his sister Sarah. He recognized that what she had seen was from God and not a satanic delusion. He accompanied her and her sister as they traveled to many places conducting public meetings. August 30, 1846, James and Ellen were married. Shortly thereafter, they received the Sabbath message from Elder Joseph Bates. Together with Bates and Hiram Edson, they were the core leaders of the sabbatarian Adventists. James White wrote on various Bible topics after joining Elder Joseph Bates.

Ellen G. White

Ellen Gould Harmon (White) was born at Gorham, Maine on November 26, 1827. Her parents were Robert and Eunice Harmon. Robert Harmon was a hat maker, and he and Eunice were members of the Methodist church. When Ellen was nine years old, she suffered a disfiguring accident. A jealous schoolmate threw a stone at her, striking her on the nose and leaving it permanently disfigured. Due to the blood loss and other complications of the injury, she was seriously ill for two years, sickly for many years thereafter, and unable to complete formal schooling beyond the third grade. In 1842, when Ellen was fifteen years old, William Miller gave lectures in Portland, Maine. She and her parents accepted the advent message. After the disappointment, unlike many others in the Advent movement, she did not give up her faith in the soon coming of Jesus, and she continued to search for truth from God. Ellen had a deep prayer life and trusted in God. In December of 1844, while she was praying with five other ladies at a friend's house, she received her first vision from God to encourage the advent people.

As has been mentioned, it was not until 1846 that Ellen White came to accept the seventh-day Sabbath. At first, she believed that Elder Bates put too much emphasis on the fourth commandment over the other commandments. Nonetheless, after studying the biblical evidence, she and James began keeping the Sabbath according to Bates' idea of the limits of a day—beginning the Sabbath at 6 p.m. Then, after the Adventists gave closer study in June of 1854, they concluded, on the basis of Scripture, that the Sabbath begins at sunset, whenever that is at a given place and time of year.

From 1844 to 1915, Ellen White received an estimated 2,000 visions and dreams. Additionally, having completed only three years of formal education, she wrote more than 27 books, with nearly 17,500 pages of manuscript. Ellen White was a devoted wife and mother of four boys (two of which grew to adulthood), and, over the years, she cared for other children and had a mother's concern for many more. From the beginning of the Seventh-day Adventist Church, God used Mrs. White to foster the sharing of the Adventist message with the world. As James would later put it: "Without means, with very few who sympathized with us in our views, without a paper, and without books, we entered upon our work." They had no houses of worship; most of their meetings were held in private houses; they had few members. At first, only those who were interested in the Adventist message attended their meetings, though, in time, people were attracted out of curiosity to hear a woman who had had visions.

Hard Manual Labor for James White

To survive while encouraging the advent believers and carrying forward the publishing ministry, James White often took jobs involving hard, manual labor. In 1846, there were fewer than fifty Sabbath-keepers in Maine and only another 50 Sabbath keepers for the rest of New England. From their marriage in 1846 until 1848, James and Ellen worked hard to stretch their meager income to be able to spread the Adventist message.

Ellen and James traveled frequently about to the scattered groups of Adventists who had not given up their faith after the Great Disappointment. Most of their travel was by wagons, sleigh, economy class on the train, and the lower deck when traveling by steamer. In the trains, they regularly had to endure tobacco smoke-filled accommodations, which made the fragile wife and mother faint, and vulgar conversation. To sleep at night, Mrs. White had to lie on the hard floor between boxes and sacks of grain. During the winter, while traveling by sleigh, they huddled under shawls, overcoats, and buffalo blankets to keep warm. Oppressed by the heat in the summer, they would go onto the upper deck to catch the cool night air after their first child Henry was born.

One of James White's jobs to support his family was hauling stone for a railroad company as they were cutting through a mountain. Teaching, which he had done before 1843, did not provide that much money. Aside from being hard work, hauling stones on the railroad barely earned enough money for a family of three to live, much less supplying money for travel to visit the believers. The railroad went near the village of Brunswick, Maine, where he had often previously lectured. Were it not for the Stockbridge Howland family, with whom they lived, they could not have survived. Having difficulty collecting his pay, James left the work of hauling stone and began cutting cordwood in a nearby forest. They received many letters from brethren in different states inviting them to visit. Yet, they had no means for travel. Their reply was that they should wait for the right opportunity. James and Ellen did not wish to be dependent on others, so they were careful to live within their means. They were resolved to suffer want rather than be in debt.

Poverty of James and Ellen White

Things became so desperate for the Whites that Ellen had to decide whether to buy milk or to buy an apron to cover the arms of her baby. She had allowed herself and her child one pint of milk per day. Elder James White gave her nine cents to buy milk for three days before leaving for work. It was wintertime, and, because her little Henry did not have proper clothing, he was suffering from the cold. That morning she did not know whether to buy milk for herself and the baby or to get the baby an apron. At last, she decided to forego the milk and to purchase the warm clothes to cover little Henry's bear arms.

Brother Otis Nichols and his wife of Dorchester, Massachusetts, enthusiastically lent whatever aid they could muster to help the Whites promote God's work. Brother Albert Belden, of Rocky Hill, Connecticut, hosted the first conference of sabbatarian Adventists in an unfinished large room in his home. At a particular time of need, Belden sent the Whites an invitation to live with his family, considering it a privilege to minister to them. Brother and Sister Howland of Maine took care of little Henry until he was five years old. They cared for him in their home as if he were their own and brought him up with proper discipline, which was a tremendous help to the Whites in their ministry of proclaiming God's truth to the world. Brother E. L. H. Chamberlain also helped the Whites from 1846 to 1850 in the work of the Lord and did many things in establishing the work in Maine and New York.

Elder James White went to work mowing fields with a scythe and earned enough money to go to the next conference in Volney, New York. Elder and Mrs. White left their little Henry with Brother and Sister Howland and went to the conference. The Howlands kept little Henry for five years, freeing the Whites for travel in spreading the Adventist message. The Howlands were a very great blessing to the Whites.

From Hay-mowing to Publishing: Middletown, Connecticut, July 1849

When James and Ellen were living in Rocky Hill, Connecticut, at the Belden home, their second child, James Edison, was born—July 28, 1849. Though funds were nearly nonexistent, at this same time, James desired to publish a new little paper dealing largely with the Sabbath truth. Since the brethren with means were choosing to keep their money, James determined that he would earn the necessary funds by mowing fields of grass with a scythe. Thus, at the very time the White's second child was born, James was publishing the first number of the semi-monthly periodical, *The Present Truth*, in Middletown, Connecticut, about eight miles from Rocky Hill. He limped the eight miles from their home carrying the copy, limped the eight miles back with the proofs, and finally borrowed a buggy to bring a thousand copies of the final publication back home. Through the *Present Truth* (published from July 1849 to November 1850), many people embraced the Sabbath truth. He published a second journal called the *Advent Review* from August to September 1850. In November of 1850, he combined the two publications, naming it *The Second Advent Review and Sabbath Herald*. The new paper was issued at Paris, Maine. Some of the brethren surmised, from the horse and carriage that he had been given money to purchase, that he was making money from the paper. Under their criticism and the heavy load of the work itself, and without proper nutrition, James sank under the burden and became so weak that he could not get to the press office without stumbling.

First State Conference

The first "General Conference" of Sabbath-keeping Adventists was held in the state of Connecticut on April 20, 1848. Elder and Mrs. White decided to attend the first meeting. Having received ten dollars for James's cordwood cutting, Ellen used five dollars to purchase much-needed articles of clothing, and they used the remainder for travel expenses to Dorchester, Massachusetts. Ellen patched her husband's overcoat—even piecing the patches—making it difficult to tell what was the original cloth. The White's only trunk contained nearly everything they possessed on this earth, but both of them had peace of mind and a clear conscience regarding their earthly comfort. In Dorchester, Brother Nichols called them to his house and gave them another five dollars to travel to Middletown, Connecticut. When they arrived at Rocky Hill, they only had fifty cents left over.

The Conference was held in a large unfinished chamber in Brother Belden's house. Fifty people were in attendance. Not all fully embraced the Sabbath truth, yet the Conference was still a success. From there, the brethren invited the Whites to go to New York State. As has been stated, they did not have means for travel.

It was not until 1861 that the Seventh-day Adventist Church would be first registered in Battle Creek as a church organization, with a total of twenty-five churches in the United States. At that time, another five state conferences were organized. Fredrick Wheeler was the first Sabbath-keeping Adventist pastor. He worked with James and Ellen White. Rachel Oakes, a Seventh Day Baptist, had pointed out to Wheeler that the fourth commandment is still valid, making Saturday and not Sunday the day for the biblical Sabbath. Stephen N. Haskell was a strong proponent of the seventh-day Sabbath, wrote several books, and supported James White's ministry until White's death.

Uriah Smith. The Whites treated Uriah Smith as a son. From his early association with James White, he was involved in various aspects of publishing. In 1862, James White attended classes conducted by Uriah Smith (*Review and Herald*, June 3, 1862). He was so impressed by Uriah Smith's research that he published the results of the investigation in the pages of the *Review and Herald*. In 1882, Uriah Smith published his book, *Thoughts on Daniel and the Revelation*, which he had researched from 1861 to 1881. James White read proof sheets for the book "and expressed much pleasure and satisfaction because they were so concisely and clearly written" (A. C. Bordeau, quoted by J. S. Washburn, letter to Meade MacGuire, Feb. 18, 1923).

Annie Smith. Annie, who was the sister of Uriah Smith, became part of the White household as she assisted in the publication ministry. She composed several poems about the advent experience, three of which were set to music and appear in the most recent Seventh-day Adventist Church hymnal.

John Nevins Andrews. Mr. Andrews worked with Uriah Smith. "He enjoyed 'severe study' much more than physical activity; in later years he could read the Bible in seven languages and claimed the ability to reproduce the New Testament from memory" (*Seventh-day Adventist Encyclopedia*). He was the first foreign missionary for the Seventh-day Adventist Church.

John Harvey Kellogg. Mr. Kellogg was a pioneer in the health work in the Seventh-day Adventist Church. As a young man, he stayed with James and Ellen White, who sponsored him to study and receive a degree in medicine from Yale University. Later, he became embroiled in church politics to gain controlling interest in the Adventist institutions in Battle Creek. In time, he promoted his own ideas about the nature of God, which led him into apostasy.

Hiram Edson. The day after the Great Disappointment, Edson received a clear vision of the heavenly sanctuary while passing through a cornfield, opening to the Adventists an understanding of the investigative judgment to precede Christ's return.

Among the pioneers of our church who were involved in studying and proclaiming the truths of Scripture are Frederick Wheeler, T. M. Preble, Joseph Bates, James White, Ellen G. White, Otis Nichols, Albert Belden, Stockbridge Howland, E. L. H. Chamberlain, Uriah Smith, Annie Smith, John Nevins Andrews, John Harvey Kellogg, Hiram Edson, and Steven N. Haskell.

The first General Conference at Battle Creek, Michigan. In 1863, the General Conference was organized with 3,500 members, 25 churches, and six individual state conferences. (It was also in 1863 that God gave Ellen White a vision concerning health reform.) The General Conference of Seventh-day Adventists is the Laodicean church, the seventh and last church period in church history.

The Seventh-day Adventist Church started preaching the gospel according to Jesus command, "This gospel of the kingdom shall be preached in all the world for a witness unto all nations; and then shall the end come" (Matt. 24:14). Jesus also commanded His disciples, after His crucifixion and resurrection, "Go therefore and make disciples of all the nations, baptizing them in the name of the Father and the Son and of the Holy Spirit" (Matt. 28:19). The gospel includes the birth, ministry, death, ascension, and second coming of Jesus Christ.

The Seventh-day Adventist Church and the Everlasting Gospel

The Bible speaks of pardonable and unpardonable sins and holy prayer through Jesus' name, which commenced with Jesus' death on the cross, ending blood sacrifices. Instead of having to go to the temple in Jerusalem, we can receive God's free gift of the forgiveness of sins anywhere in the world. Even sins considered unpardonable—except the sin against the Holy Spirit—can be forgiven through the holy blood of Jesus Christ, which is received by faith and symbolized by holy baptism (Mark 16:16). We call this the gospel.

The gospel message of Matthew 24:14 was unwittingly aided in 1811 by Pope Gregory. In that year, he introduced the Gregorian calendar as a witness of the gospel. You may wonder how this promotes the gospel. What happened was that Pope Gregory made the whole world accept a calendar based on the birth of Jesus Christ. Knowingly or unknowingly, the whole world is following the Christian calendar today and acknowledging that Jesus is God by using His birth to divide history. The calendar consists of a 365-day, twelve-month year. Seven months have 31 days: January, March, May, July, August, October, and December; four months have thirty days: April, June, September, and November; one month—the month of February—has twenty-eight days in regular years and twenty-nine days in leap years. Whether Christian, Jew, Hindu, Muslim, or a member of any of eighteen other currently existing religious groups, all have accepted this calendar. It is an accredited "witness of Jesus Christ" that He was born in 4 BC and died in AD 31, and that He went to dwell in heaven until the end of world history. One hundred eighty-five UN nations of this world correspond with one another through letters and make agreements on official stationery, using the same dates—for example, 1950, 1980, 2017—all witnessing to the reality of Jesus' birth. Other mass media, such as newspapers, radio, TV, computers, journals, and magazines, communicate the greatest witness of the gospel through the acceptance of the Gregorian calendar.

The Everlasting Gospel

The everlasting gospel and the message of judgment, beginning in 1844, are the first parts of the three angels' messages, which the last church is proclaiming to the world today under the last world civilization.

Table 9.4. Modern Inventions and the Partial Fulfillment of Daniel 12:4

No.	INVENTION	NAME	COUNTRY	YEAR
1	printing press	Johannes Gutenberg	Germany	1439
2	watch	Peter Henlein	Germany	1524
3	computer	Charles Babbage	U.S.A.	1822
4	camera	Joseph Nicéphore Niépce	France	1826
5	ship	Titanic	Ireland	1912
6	lightning rod	Benjamin Franklin	U.S.A.	1749
7	sewing machine	Barthélemy Thinmonnier	France	1829
8	revolver	Samuel Colt	U.S.A.	1835
9	telephone	Alexander Graham Bell	U.S.A.	1876
10	train	Robert Stephenson	England	1829
11	aircraft	William Samuel Henson	England	1843
12	fountain pen (improvement of)	Lewis Edson Waterman	U.S.A.	1883
13	typewriter	Christopher Latham Sholes	U.S.A.	1867
14	telegraph	Samuel F. B. Morse	U.S.A.	1844
15	tire	John Boyd Dunlop	Scotland	1883

Table 9.4. Modern Inventions and the Partial Fulfillment of Daniel 12:4

No.	INVENTION	NAME	COUNTRY	YEAR
16	first gas-driven automobile	Karl Benz	Germany	1885
17	motion picture camera	Thomas A. Edison	U.S.A.	1897
18	radio	Guglielmo Marconi	Italy	1901
19	airplane	Orville and Wilbur Wright	U.S.A.	1903
20	atomic bomb	Manhattan Project	U.S.A.	1945
21	Saturn V rocket	Wernher von Braun	U.S.A.	1967
22	moon landing	Neil Armstrong	U.S.A.	1969

Chapter 10
Validating the Creation Story from World Population and Morality

The present population had its beginning in the year 2503 BC with the children of the sons of Noah—Shem, Ham and Japheth—and their three wives. Thus, from 2503 BC to the present, nearly 21 billion people have been born in this world. We can reason about the history of humankind by population estimates. If life existed 200,000 years ago, then the number of people on this earth who would have been born and died would now be three hundred billion. However, the present population is approximately seven billion. Unless there was a major extinction event or events, the claim made by scientists that human beings evolved on the planet 200,000 years ago is false. Population evidence points more favorably to the biblical six-day Creation and its chronological history.

The following is an analysis of world population by religion according to recent census figures:

Chapter 10 Validating the Creation Story

Table 10.1. Population of the World According to Religion

	RELIGIONS	POPULATION	COUNTRIES
1	Christians	2,069,883,000	120
2	Roman Catholics	1,092,853,000	190
3	Protestants	364,530,000	203
4	Orthodox	217,030,000	
5	Anglicans	79,988,000	
6	Muslims	1,254,222,000	
7	Hindus	837,262,000	22
8	Buddhists	372,974,000	25
9	Chinese folk religionists	398,106,300	8
10	New-religionists	105,106,100	
11	Sikhs	24,295,200	7
12	Jews	14,551,000	46
13	Spiritists	12,732,600	
14	Baha'is	7,503,000	
15	Confucians	6,425,300	8
16	Jains	4,413,700	1
17	Shintoists	2,680,300	2
18	Zoroastrians	2,733,900	3
19	Other religionists	1,118,000	
20	Non-religious	784,269,000	
21	Atheists	148,660,000	6
	Total Population of the World	7,791,321,800	(6,672,536,400)

Manorama Yearbook, vol. 42, p. 467, Manorama Publishing House, India, 2007

Each year, world population grows by 131.4 million births and an overall growth in world population of 76 million. Hence, at present, there are approximately 7.5 billion people living in this world. How many billion people have been born and have died in this world from 2503 BC to the present? From 2503 BC until the present, there have been 21 billion people who have been born in this world.

The present population of the world is seven and a half billion, as based upon an estimate from the 2.5 million children born every year in the world. However, there has been a steep decline in the death rate from 1950 onward, due to modern medical science and the advancement of technology, and life expectancy has doubled.

According to modern evolutionary theory, human life has existed for 200,000 years. If this assertion is true, then what should today's population be? Scientists claim that man has existed on the planet for 200,000 years. If this were true, then there would be exponentially more than the approximately 7 and a half billion people. Thus, the claim must be incorrect. The current population aligns far better with the biblical six-day Creation and the chronological history recorded in the Bible.

How many countries are in the world today? There are 197 nations in the world; 193 are members of the United Nations, two are observers—the Vatican and Palestine—and Taiwan is recognized by 21 UN members and one UN observer and Kosovo is recognized by 111 UN states and Taiwan.

Table 10.2. Countries of the World		
1. Afghanistan	12. The Bahamas	23. Botswana
2. Albania	13. Bahrain	24. Brazil
3. Algeria	14. Bangladesh	25. Brunei
4. Andorra	15. Barbados	26. Bulgaria
5. Angola	16. Belarus	27. Burkina Faso
6. Antigua and Barbuda	17. Belgium	28. Burundi
7. Argentina	18. Belize	29. Cabo Verde
8. Armenia	19. Benin	30. Cambodia
9. Australia	20. Bhutan	31. Cameroon
10. Austria	21. Bolivia	32. Canada
11. Azerbaijan	22. Bosnia and Herzegovina	33. Central African Republic
34. Chad	63. Germany	91. Laos

Table 10.2. Countries of the World

35. Chile	64. Ghana	92. Latvia
36. China	65. Greece	93. Lebanon
37. Colombia	66. Grenada	94. Lesotho
38. Comoros	67. Guatemala	95. Liberia
39. The Democratic Republic of the Congo	68. Guinea	96. Libya
40. Costa Rica	69. Guinea-Bissau	97. Liechtenstein
41. Cote d'Ivoire	70. Guyana	98. Lithuania
42. Croatia	71. Haiti	99. Luxembourg
43. Cuba	72. Honduras	101. Madagascar
44. Cyprus	73. Hungary	102. Malawi
45. Czech Republic	74. Iceland	103. Malaysia
46. Denmark	75. India	104. Maldives
47. Djibouti	76. Indonesia	105. Mali
48. Dominica	77. Iran	106. Malta
49. The Dominican Republic	78. Iraq	107. Marshall Islands
51. Egypt	79. Ireland	108. Mauritania
52. El Salvador	80. Israel	109. Mauritius
53. Equatorial Guinea	81. Italy	110. Mexico
54. Eritrea	82. Jamaica	111. Micronesia
55. Estonia	83. Japan	112. Moldova
56. Ethiopia	84. Jordan	113. Monaco
57. Fiji	85. Kazakhstan	114. Mongolia
58. Finland	86. Kenya	115. Montenegro
59. France	87. Kiribati	116. Morocco
60. Gabon	88. Kosovo	117. Mozambique
61. Gambia	89. Kuwait	118. Myanmar (Burma)
62. Georgia	90. Kyrgyzstan	119. Namibia
120. Nauru	145. Saint Lucia	160. South Africa

Table 10.2. Countries of the World

121. Nepal	146. Saint Vincent and the Grenadines	161. South Korea
122. Netherlands	147. Samoa	162. South Sudan
123. New Zealand	148. San Marino	163. Spain
124. Nicaragua	150. Saudi Arabia	164. Sri Lanka
125. Niger	151. Senegal	165. Sudan
126. Nigeria	140. Qatar	166. Suriname
127. North Korea	141. Romania	167. Swaziland
128. Norway	142. Russia	168. Sweden
129. Oman	143. Rwanda	169. Switzerland
130. Pakistan	144. Saint Kitts and Nevis	170. Syria
131. Palau	145. Saint Lucia	171. Taiwan
132. Palestine	146. Saint Vincent and the Grenadines	172. Tajikistan
133. Panama	147. Samoa	173. Tanzania
134. Papua New Guinea	148. San Marino	174. Thailand
135. Paraguay	150. Saudi Arabia	175. Timor-Leste
136. Peru	151. Senegal	176. Togo
137. Philippines	152. Serbia	177. Tonga
138. Poland	153. Seychelles	178. Trinidad and Tobago
139. Portugal	154. Sierra Leone	179. Tunisia
140. Qatar	155. Singapore	180. Turkey
141. Romania	156. Slovakia	181. Turkmenistan
142. Russia	157. Slovenia	184. Ukraine
143. Rwanda	158. Solomon Islands	185. United Arab Emirates
144. Saint Kitts and Nevis	159. Somalia	186. United Kingdom
187. United States of America	191. Vatican City	195. Yemen

Table 10.2. Countries of the World

188. Uruguay	192. Russia	196. Zambia
189. Uzbekistan	193. Venezuela	197. Zimbabwe
190. Vanuatu	194. Vietnam	

Adam's Six Senses

Adam and Eve used language to communicate with each other, though Adam's first conversation was with Jesus Christ, his Creator, before Jesus Christ created Eve. Adam and Eve's ability to speak was a sixth sense, distinguishing human beings from other intelligent creatures made on the sixth day of the Creation. Jesus Christ solemnized their wedding, instituting the Ten Commandments as the seventh sense, which should be strictly followed. On the seventh day, God set an example of rest for Adam and Eve that they, in turn, could demonstrate their trust in God and obedience to Lucifer and the fallen angels by resting and worshipping the living God of heaven on the Sabbath. It was the second person of the triune God, Jesus Christ, who created the man and the woman.

Forming Adam from the miry clay, God created him with limitations that the heavenly angels do not have. God had created human beings in His image and likeness. He was created higher than the angels, for he was made to understand good and evil. God left Adam and Eve to decide whether they would live or die. Even today we have the same decision—whether we will live forever or whether we will be completely destroyed. The Bible revealed this choice through the creation of the first man Adam. As soon as Adam sinned, the process of dying began for the human race.

The last chart is of the various organized Christian churches in the world.

Table 9.3. Thirty Major Groups of Christian Denominations

1.	Catholicism
2.	Eastern Orthodoxy
3.	Oriental Orthodoxy
4.	Church of the East

Table 9.3. Thirty Major Groups of Christian Denominations

5.	Anglicanism
6.	Proto-Protestant groups
7.	Lutheranism
8.	Anabaptism – Amish, Mennonites, Shakers
9.	The Reformed Tradition (Calvinist) – Continental Reformed churches, Presbyterianism, Congregationalism
10.	Methodism and the Holiness Movement
11.	Baptists – Holiness Baptists
12.	Spiritual Baptist Movement – Apostolic Churches, Pentecostalism, Charismatics, Neo-Charismatic Churches, and African Initiated Churches
13.	African Initiated churches
14.	Quakers (Society of Friends)
15.	The Stone-Campbell Restoration Movement – Disciples of Christ, Christian Churches, Churches of Christ
16.	Plymouth Brethren and Free Evangelical churches
17.	Early Sabbath-keeping Movements (predating Millerism) – The Christ's Assembly and Seventh Day Baptists
18.	Ecumenical Churches and Denominations – Uniting/United Churches Movement, Nondenominational Evangelical Church Movement, Multisite Church Movement
19.	Pentecostalism – Pentecostal Holiness Movement, Other Charismatic Movements, Neo-Charismatic Movement
20.	Millerites – Advent Christians, Seventh-day Adventists, British-Israelism, Church of God, Sabbath-keeping Movements (separated from Adventism), Sacred Name Groups
21.	Oneness Pentecostalism
22.	The Church of Jesus Christ of Latter-Day Saints and other Mormon groups
23.	Unitarianism and Universalism

Table 9.3. Thirty Major Groups of Christian Denominations	
24.	Bible Students groups
25.	Swedenborgianism
26.	Christian Science
27.	Messianic Judaism, Jewish Christians, Esoteric Christianity
28.	African Methodist Episcopal
29.	African Methodist Episcopal Zion
30.	National Baptize Convention (African Methodist Episcopal)

Chapter 11
God's Last Church Starts in the Wilderness of America

How did the United States of America, symbolized by the "wilderness" (Rev. 12:6, 14) and by the buffalo (Rev. 13), help the last church of Laodicea to grow and flourish?

John wrote: "Then I saw another beast coming up out of the earth, and he had two horns like a lamb and spoke like a dragon. And he exercises all the authority of the first beast in his presence, and causes the earth and those who dwell in it to worship the first beast, whose deadly wound was healed. He performs great signs, so that he even makes fire come down from heaven on the earth in the sight of men" (Rev. 13:11–13).

God showed John a beast with two horns like those of a lamb. This two-horned beast was in addition to the mighty beast, at the beginning of the chapter, which was to arise out of the sea. The two-horned beast is the mightiest kingdom to arise in the last days of earth's history. These beasts represent two great nations of the earth. The first beast had seven heads and ten horns, the kingdoms of the Roman Empire. It came into existence through Julius Caesar and his successors and the pagan Roman Empire as it was divided into the ten kingdoms of Europe. That it is described as being like a leopard shows its connection to the kingdom of Alexander the Great; that it is described as having the feet of a bear shows its connection to the kingdom of Medo-Persia; that it is represented as having the mouth of a lion shows its connection to the first and greatest world empire, that of the Babylonians.

Political History of the United States of America

The second part of Revelation 13:3 indicates that the deadly wound received by the first beast does not kill the beast. Rather the wound is healed. That means the Roman Catholic papacy was to be restored, the defeated empire was to get back a very small territory, the Vatican. The second beast (Rev. 13:11), the two-horned beast, or buffalo, is the symbol of the mightiest nation in modern history—the United States of America. The picture is of the history of the earth in the last days. Jesus Christ, the heavenly, living God gave eight visions with eight prophecies regarding the United States of America, the second beast-nation in Revelation 13, a mighty nation that is predicted to support the first beast-nation, the Roman Empire, in its war against the biblical God of heaven.

Jesus Christ reserved the continent of North America for the descendants of the apostolic church and the Protestants who would be persecuted for Jesus' sake.

From 4159 BC to AD 1620, a period of 5,799 years, God had this sub-continent in safekeeping. In 1492, Columbus discovered North America, and, in 1620, the first voyage of the Mayflower launched waves of immigration, as the descendants of the apostolic church came to America. Some 156 years later, in 1776, a mighty nation was born in fulfillment of biblical prophecy.

The United States of America, which arose in the western hemisphere of this globe as a promised land for the descendants of the apostolic church, was established on the basis of two fundamental principles: a state without a king and a church without a pope. These principles were symbolized by the beast's two lamblike horns and were showcased in the United States Constitution, signed in 1787. The aid to religious liberty was also symbolized by the two wings of a great eagle in the depiction of Revelation 12:14. Likely unaware of the symbolism, George Washington and the other American leaders unanimously accepted the two-winged eagle as the emblem of the United States of America. Now every United States passport has this seal and emblem from biblical prophecy.

The prophecy, in Revelation 13:11, of the "beast coming out of the earth," which points to the United States of America arising from the wilderness, accords with Revelation 12:14 where the woman is given wings to fly into the wilderness, where she is nourished and protected from the serpent.

God's last church must arise within the territory of the second beast-nation, that is, within the territory of the United States of America. As the seventh prophecy for God's church declares: "... she is nourished for a time and times and half a time" (Rev. 12:14), that is, the 1260 years were to come to completion in the United States of America. The descendants of the apostles, God's children who suffered in the dark days of persecution under the church periods of Sardis, Philadelphia, and Laodicea, would be protected by the power represented by this second beast, the American bison. This prophecy was fulfilled to the letter. Jesus Christ gave John the vision of the American bison. Though John the Revelator described what he saw, he did not understand it. The beast he saw represented a powerful and prosperous people. Much of America is still very pious, and the nation has powerful weapons that can be used for justice and peace. That is why John the Revelator pictured this mighty nation as an American bison, a beast whose habitat has only been on the North American continent and nowhere else.

At the foundation of the American Constitution are two fundamental principles: a state without a king and a church without a pope. These two great principles provide for peace, equal rights, equal justice, equal religious liberty, and freedom of speech for the entire nation. God knew, in AD 97, that this second nation represented by a beast would arise upon the North American continent. He knew this also before the six days of Creation. In the first creation, God created all the resources needed—all the gold, silver, copper, brass, iron, coal, radium, platinum, uranium, titanium, petroleum and water. These He created in abundance for the benefit of His last-day church, connected spiritually to the church of the apostles. Following the 1260 years of terrible persecution, there would be a place of rest and peace until shortly before the second coming of Jesus Christ.

After the 1260-year period that began in AD 538, the prophet Daniel prophesied that, in the last days, human knowledge would increase (Dan. 12:4). The United States of America has played a major role in fulfilling this prophecy. People who migrated to America have made great advances in knowledge in these last days. During the 18th and 19th centuries, many new inventions were made: automobiles, trains, airplanes, ships, rockets, spacecraft like the Challenger, and many other devices. Humans traveled successfully into space and Americans landed on the moon. Human beings (many of whom were in America) invented electricity, the telegraph, the telephone, TV, radio, wireless, the sewing machine, the printing press, the watch, the camera, the cinema, photography, the typewriter, the video camera, the computer, the laser printer, and the laser beam.

In the field of medicine, humans have invented the EKG, the x-ray, the CT scan, and the MRI. In the field of defense, humans invented and refined the rifle, the handgun, the artillery cannon, the tank, the submarine, the torpedo, rocket radar, the supersonic jet plane, the ICBM, the atomic bomb, the hydrogen bomb, the cobalt bomb, and the nuclear warhead. The United States of America, pictured by the second beast in Revelation, has enough nuclear weaponry to destroy the earth sixteen times over.

In the field of education, human beings have now published books and periodicals covering an ever-increasing range of scientific inquiry. In the field of medicine, human beings can now perform open-heart surgery, brain surgery, and neurological surgery, and have perfected methods of artificial fertilization to produce "test tube babies."

In the field of religion, humans have printed Bibles by the billions of copies in more than 1,200 languages for billions of people all over the world, and the home base for much of this work has been in the United States. Americans are spending billions of dollars to propagate God's message to the entire world. Daniel 12:4 says that men will run to and fro, seeking the knowledge of God. This prophecy has been fulfilled.

In the field of architecture, humans have built millions of miles of roads and railroads; they have constructed dockyards to produce ships and submarines; they have built multistoried skyscrapers and great bridges across broad rivers and other bodies of water. They have developed health retreats, hospitals, colleges, schools, universities, and power plants, including those powered by nuclear fission.

As the years have passed, Bible prophecy concerning signs and wonders in the heavens have also been fulfilled. The signs and wonders do not apply solely to the second beast of the United States of

America, though, of course, the signs that led up to the Great Disappointment on October 22, 1844, had a major role in the Advent movement in America.

Next, we will consider the fulfillment of the National Sunday Law.

Fulfillment of the Sunday Law

Revelation 13:12 is a prophetic depiction of the support by second beast (or the United States of America) of the first beast, which had seven heads and ten horns. The horns are the ten European kingdoms; the ten crowns are the ten nations under the Roman Catholic Church and the pope. In keeping with this prophecy, from 1776 to 1987, the United States did not officially recognize Vatican City, or the Holy See, as a nation. For 210 years, because of its Protestant principle of a church without a pope, the United States Constitution prohibited the linking of the United States with the Holy See through an official ambassador. However, President Ronald Reagan changed all that by sending William Wilson as the United States' ambassador to Vatican City and, hence, to the papacy. Thus, the prophecy was fulfilled.

There were many Sunday laws in the United States from 1847 to 1897. Long before Reagan's appointment, in fulfillment of this prophecy, the original thirteen American colonies, which were largely Protestant, enacted laws to guard the sanctity of Sunday as a holy day. At that time, virtually all Protestant church members observed Sunday as their holy day—"the Christian Sabbath." Protestant clergy influenced the state legislatures to pass Sunday laws from 1847 to 1897. As a result of these Sunday laws, those who opened their places of business or offices on Sunday were punished. No one could buy or sell except those who aligned with the first beast of Revelation 13—the papacy— by receiving what the Catholic Church has historically identified as the "mark" of its authority among all the churches—its changing of the Sabbath commandment by the sanctification of the observance of the first-day Sunday instead of the seventh-day Sabbath. Protestants and Catholics alike were paying homage to the Pope, for it was through the influence of the pope that Constantine's original Sunday law made Sunday a sabbath. To this day, one-third of Protestant church members continue to view Sunday as a Sabbath. This, of course, does not include Seventh-day Adventists or other seventh-day sabbatarian Christians. Though the prophecy has been fulfilled, the effects of the prophecy may continue universally.

The first beast of Revelation 13 could not issue its mark of Sunday observance without the aid of the second beast, the buffalo, which is to make an image to the first beast, causing people everywhere to pay homage to the first beast. The United States of America was to lend its support to the Roman Catholic Church giving life to the "image" of Catholicism, which is the enforcement of the church's dogmatic principles regarding Sunday legislation. Upholding Sunday as a sacred day, all the states of America will join together in passing a national Sunday law, prohibiting anyone, under penalty of law, from opening up shop on Sunday.

In a partial sense, this was fulfilled throughout the United States for a period of fifty years from 1847 to 1897, even after the end of slavery. Even before 1847, the thirteen colonies that formed the United States of America passed Sunday blue laws prohibiting anyone from opening their stores, shops, or markets on Sunday. Those who violated the Sunday law were punished by their respective states and churches. The Sunday law movement continued in many states from 1847 to 1897, and no one in those states was free to buy and sell on Sundays, for, if they did, they would receive a very severe punishment. As time passed, new states joined the union and chose not to support the Sunday law.

Validation for this history can be found in Uriah Smith's *Daniel and The Revelation*, pp. 619–622 (1897 edition).

Was the National Sunday Law Fulfilled?

Now, in these last days, many countries in Europe observe Sunday as their national weekly holy day. More than forty-eight commonwealth countries have Sunday as their weekly rest day. Nearly one-third of Christians observe Sunday mass and church worship, which is an indication of how many Christians still observe the real seventh-day Sabbath. Besides Europe, the international Sunday law is found throughout the world. India's 1.7 billion people have Sunday as their national weekly holiday by default because of the large number of Sunday observers in the country where seventh-day Sabbath keepers are in the minority. The Sunday law is already affecting them. There are over 1,253 million inhabitants in the fifty Muslim-majority nations of the world. With the exception of Turkey, the people have Friday as their weekly national holy day. In Muslim-majority nations, Sabbath-observing Seventh-day Adventists would naturally expect a "Friday law" instead of a "Sunday law." China, with its 1.371 billion inhabitants, and Russia, with its 144.1 million inhabitants, have Sunday as their weekly rest day. So, billions of people knowingly or unknowingly hold Sunday to be their weekly day of rest, and some 7.5 billion people knowingly or unknowingly have an international Sunday law. The default weekly holy day is Sunday. This means, in a limited fashion, that the Sunday law has already come. However, there is no death penalty attached to it as we find in the passage (Rev. 13:15). Thus, the prophecy is in the process of fulfillment around the world for the majority of nations and people of the earth.

The United States of America and the "Big Boss" Prophecy of Revelation 13:13.

We find a further fulfillment of Revelation 13:13 by the United States in the statement "that he even makes fire come down from heaven on the earth in the sight of men" (Rev. 13:13). With a stockpile of nuclear weapons such as atomic, hydrogen, cobalt, and helium bombs, the United States keeps peace around the world. As the world's mightiest military superpower, the United States has played the role of the "Big Boss" among the 185 countries in the United Nations as they did when they reduced the power of Japan by dropping the atomic bomb to end World War II.

Fire Came Down from Heaven

During the conflict in the Pacific theater during World War II, the mighty island nation of Japan joined forces with Hitler's Nazi Germany and Mussolini's Fascist Italy in fighting the rest of the world. It seemed that no one could stop Japan's aggression against other countries. The allied forces, under the leadership of General Dwight D. Eisenhower, were almost defeated, and General Douglas MacArthur, commander of the eastern forces, had almost completely given up hope that Japan could be defeated. In the meantime, the United States president gave full power to the secretary of the allied forces, General Eisenhower, to win the war. The United States had entered the war after Japan bombed Pearl Harbor, Hawaii. President Harry S. Truman ordered the dropping of two small atomic bombs over the cities of Hiroshima and Nagasaki, destroying them. Within minutes, the deployment of these two horrifically destructive bombs, which brought down fire from heaven, broke the backbone of Japanese resistance and brought Japan to the table of complete surrender to the allied forces, ending four years of terrible war after victory in Europe had already been achieved.

Nearing the end of the twentieth century, the mighty armies of Saddam Hussein marched into Kuwait to capture its oil. It was only a step away from Saudi Arabia and its wealth, where the most holy shrines of Mecca and Medina are found. It would have brought the Islamic religion under Saddam Hussein's control, and all the other Islamic nations of the world would have had to bow to him. Having done so, he could have united all Islamic forces against Israel to capture Jerusalem, the holy city of Christians and Jews, making him the savior of the Islamic religion.

To Saddam Hussein's chagrin, King Fahd bin Abdul Aziz of Saudi Arabia contacted President George Bush to help him meet the aggression of the Iraqi forces. President Bush and America's allies began a defensive air campaign against the aggressor. The forces of Saddam Hussein were stopped within ten kilometers of the wealthy oil fields of Saudi Arabia. If King Fahd had not asked for American help or had he delayed two or three hours more, the world's biggest oil field would have been captured or destroyed under Saddam Hussein's master plan. Six month's time was given to Saddam Hussein and his military regime of 300,000 soldiers. Entering Kuwaiti soil, the Iraqi forces killed thousands of Kuwaiti citizens and burned more than seven hundred lucrative oil fields. On January 17, 1991, the allied forces started the largest air campaign against Iraq's 500 Soviet-built MiG-29, MiG-25, and MiG-23 fighter-bombers, and the French-made Mirage F1 fighters. The American and allied response in "Desert Storm" was made up of over 1,800 US jet fighter planes. After a continuous 42 days and nights of the campaign with 6,000 operations and more than 100,000 tons of bombs raining down upon the enemy, making holes like a wire mesh across the soil of Iraq, forcing the complete withdrawal of Saddam Hussein's military regiments from Kuwaiti soil, and freeing the nation of Kuwait from Saddam Hussein.

Worship the Image of the Beast

To conclude our study, we must consider that the last prophecy regarding the buffalo in Revelation 13 foretells how the United States will worship the first beast, the system headed by the pope of Rome.

Deference for the papacy on the part of the United States will lead other nations to also worship the first symbolic beast in Revelation 13. In 1987, then President Ronald Reagan's accorded the Vatican official status as a nation sending a state ambassador to the Vatican, thereby fulfilling the last part of the prophecy.

The War Ending Slavery in the United States of America

Revelation 12:14 provides the time frame and location in which God's faithful would find respite from persecution. The time frame was between 538 and 1798; the location was North America, the "wilderness" that provided a place of refuge for those seeking religious liberty. Yet, there was an obstacle to the promise of "liberty for all"—it was the institution of slavery, which the second beast of Revelation 13 had to solve for itself. To fulfill the promise of this prophecy, the American Civil War was fought for over four years until of the ending of slavery became its central focus, and not just saving the Union. When President Abraham Lincoln abolished slavery in the rebellious states, he turned the tide in the war, and, shortly thereafter, the Confederate forces surrendered. Then he skillfully succeeded in ending slavery forever through an amendment to the Constitution, adding two more amendments to guarantee everyone in the nation the same "unalienable rights endowed by the Creator"—the rights to "life, liberty, and the pursuit of happiness."

Conditions for the Latter Rain

May 20, 1863, Seventh-day Adventists held their first General Conference, selecting John Byington to be the first General Conference President of Seventh-day Adventists, with a church membership of about 3,500 believers in the United States. These converts came through the hard labors of Elder James White, Sister Ellen White, and those who joined the church in its then brief history from 1845 to 1863. Under the power of the Holy Spirit, the period of the latter rain began.

Not even Elder James White or Ellen White, at first, understood the period of the latter rain. In the power of the latter rain, they did not perform any miracles of healing, because they did not keep the Ten Commandments. However, God the Holy Spirit gave sister Ellen

White direct visions. In her early ministry, He revealed secret sins to her. When she delivered the prophetic testimony, the subject of the vision was often caught off guard in facing the truth that God revealed to Mrs. White. Frequently, the person surrendered to God for the glory of His cause. Traveling day and night from Maine to the Dakotas and from Michigan to California, Elder James White and Ellen G. White added to the number of Sabbath keepers in the 25 churches that formed from 1844 to 1863 under the six local conferences within the General Conference.

The Sacrificial Work of Elder James White and Sister Ellen G. White

In 1865, Elder White had a stroke of paralysis. It was a very heavy blow to Sister White and their children and to God's work. After fifteen months, he recovered, though he later had two more strokes. Nonetheless, God gave him nearly total recovery with time. Elder White was elected three times to the presidency of the General Conference, from 1865–1867, 1869–1871 and 1880. August 6, 1881, he passed away without a struggle, a great warrior for God's cause, laying down to rest.

God Compacts the Plan of Salvation for Humankind

From 1491 BC to the day that Christ died on the cross in AD 31, Jesus Christ and the Holy Spirit did not forgive open sins against the Ten Commandments. This was the first path of salvation. The prophecy of the great multitude predicted that salvation would come simply by accepting the name and the blood of Jesus Christ. Jesus Christ and the Holy Spirit knew that Lucifer and the angels that followed him would attempt to keep people from going to heaven through their violation of the holy Ten Commandments, and, to the original eighty open sins, there are now twenty-five more. Lucifer allowed few people to enter the gates of heaven from Adam until the cross. The number in the great multitude, who will be saved at the second coming of Jesus is limited. That is why Jesus Christ and the Holy Spirit of God compacted the plan of salvation for humanity.

The First Path of Salvation Until the Cross

From Adam until the time of Christ, God expected His people to keep the Ten Commandments, offer blood sacrifices, and fast and pray. The name of Jesus Christ was unknown until His first coming. Yet, it is through the name of Jesus that all people are saved under the Old and New Testament. All are saved by faith in the Messiah who was to come or who has come. All are saved when they lovingly follow God's commands. Lucifer believed there to be only one way for humanity to be saved. He wanted to tempt everyone to compromise their faith in God as he had tempted King Solomon, the great king who built the golden temple but also went on to build an altar for other gods.

The Second Path of Salvation

In His wisdom, Christ prophesied a second path of salvation (Jer. 16:16), knowing that the Catholic Church would claim to change the times and laws of the Ten Commandments (Dan. 7:24, 25). The second path of salvation is: "Believe on the Lord Jesus Christ, and you will be saved" (Act 16:31; 4:11, 12) through prayer in Jesus' name (John 16:24, 26) and the "baptism of blood" under the persecution by the Jews and then by pagan and papal Rome, which lasted from the crucifixion until the end of the Dark Ages in 1798. Until 1844, Jesus Christ overlooked the violation of the Sabbath commandment as the people were rediscovering forgotten Bible truth. Thus, Satan did not know the secret of God and started to kill the descendants of the apostolic church from AD 34, the year that Stephen was martyred. The persecution of the apostles' descendants would last "until the fullness of the Gentiles" should come in (Rom. 11:25). By this means, the great multitude would be sealed for the second coming of Jesus Christ.

The Third Path of Salvation

After finishing the number of the great multitude in 1844, Jesus Christ gave the third path of salvation found in Revelation—"keep the commandments of God and the faith of Jesus" (Rev. 14:12). This is applicable to the last church period of LAODICEA within the Seventh-day Adventist Church.

It has always been God's desire that His church comprehend and keep His law. As Jesus said, "If you love Me, keep My commandments" (John 14:15). It is still God's desire that His people keep His law in these last days. Since God has opened the Bible to His church, the church is accountable to keep His law faithfully. John wrote: "Blessed *are* those who do His commandments, that they may have the right to the tree of life, and may enter through the gates into the city" (Rev. 22:14). (In this book, I have explained the requirements of the Ten Commandments.)

The Last-day Work of Sister Ellen G. White

Ellen White died in 1915. Since her death, no one in the Seventh-day Adventist Church has been given the spiritual gift of prophecy. Thus we see that the second appearing of the Holy Spirit, or the latter rain, must have begun some time between Miller's preaching of the Advent in 1831 and Ellen White's death in 1915. God gave many precious truths through her visions and writings, which edified, exhorted, and comforted the church (1 Cor. 14:3) and encouraged the church to study the Scriptures to formulate its doctrines. Though Ellen White may not have understood the full significance of all that she wrote, God faithfully guided the church through the counsels God gave her, leading the church to develop different ministries as it fulfilled its mission to spread the gospel to the world.

The Last Prophetess to This World

For nearly 70 years—from 1844 to 1915—Ellen White served the Lord by voice and pen, writing some 50,000 pages of counsels to the Seventh-day Adventist Church. Under God's guidance through those counsels, 136,000 believers joined the church, 3,876 churches were established in thirty-three Union Conferences in North and South America, Europe, Africa, Asia, and the islands, with 9,476 workers and ordained ministers, and 40 publishing houses printing in ninety-five languages (http://documents.adventistarchives.org/Statistics/ASR/ASR1915.pdf). She died in 1915, the last prophetess in the world.

Some important truths promoted through the visions of E. G. White are:

- Believers in Christ who recognize that their bodies belong to the Holy Spirit should not use tea, coffee, or other stimulants (*Spiritual Gifts*, vol. 4a, p. 128).
- God's people should not read fictional love stories (*Testimonies*

for the Church, vol. 7, 1902, p. 165).
- Medical missionary work is the right hand of the gospel message (*Testimonies for the Church*, vol. 7, p. 59).
- The biblical Sabbath is on the seventh day of the week ("A Word to the Little Flock," p. 18).
- The members of the church, meeting in General Conference session, have authority in the church (*Testimonies for the Church*, vol. 8, 1904, pp. 236, 237.

The Seventh-day Adventist Church and Noncombatancy

Another important counsel God gave Seventh-day Adventists through Ellen G. White was that they should not fight in any wars. To engage in war generally means a direct violation of the sixth and fourth commandments. After the American Civil War commenced and James White and others exhausted $400 per person to keep young men out of the war, Elder James White wrote somewhat controversially in the *Advent Review and Sabbath Herald* that church members could take part in the Civil War to protect their fatherland. However, the Holy Spirit guided them not to take part in the civil war, where the sixth and fourth commandments of God would be in continual violation. Because of a vision God gave Ellen G. White, the General Conference entreated the United States government and received noncombatancy status and escaped violation of the sixth and fourth commandments of God. Today the Seventh-day Adventist Church participates in the war as noncombatants.

Is There Any Holy Place on This Earth?

After 607 BC, there was no holy place, no holy city, and no holy country on the face of this earth.

Jeremiah prophesied: "But if you will not heed Me to hallow the Sabbath day, such as not carrying a burden when entering the gates of Jerusalem on the Sabbath day, then I will kindle a fire in its gates, and it shall devour the palaces of Jerusalem, and it shall not be quenched" (Jer. 17:27). In the year 607 BC, Nebuchadnezzar, the Babylonian emperor, invaded Jerusalem and captured the city, kindling a fire in the world-renowned golden temple. Just before the king of Babylon invaded Jerusalem, Jesus Christ instructed His prophet Jeremiah to remove to Mount Nebo the holy ark, which contained the covenant of the Ten Commandments and other holy articles and which had two golden cherubim atop it. That was where, in 1451 BC, the prophet Moses stood and saw the Promised Land of Canaan and was laid to rest in death. The Most Holy Place articles were hidden and sealed. Jeremiah, the prophet of the Lord, did as God instructed him and sealed all the holy articles in a cave. Because of the hardness of the people's hearts, God allowed Nebuchadnezzar to invade Jerusalem, and He withdrew His power and presence from Judah. Since God's people rejected His holiness, there was no longer a holy Jerusalem on the face of the earth. Yet, Haggai prophesied that the second temple would be more glorious (Hag. 2:9), because the holy Jesus Christ would come to the temple, even though the rebuilt temple would be humbler than the one constructed by Solomon, which would be polluted by ungodly people. In the words of Jesus, they would make it a "den of thieves" (Matt. 21:13; Mark 11:17; Luke 19:46). The same week Jesus uttered those words, He wept over Jerusalem (Matt. 23:37). Later, He promised to send down a New Jerusalem from heaven (Rev. 3:12; 21:2). So with the holy law of God hidden away, the temple would no longer be a holy place from 607 BC onward.

Ellen White described what took place: "With mourning and sadness they secreted the ark in a cave, where it was to be hidden from the people of Israel and Judah because of their sins, and was to be no more restored to them. That sacred ark is yet hidden. It has never been disturbed since it was secreted. For many years Jeremiah had stood before the people as a faithful witness for God; and now, as the fated city was about to pass into the hands of the heathen, he considered his work done and attempted to leave, but was prevented by a son of one of the false prophets, who reported that Jeremiah was about to join the Babylonians, to whom he had repeatedly urged the men of Judah to submit" (*Prophets and Kings*, pp. 453, 454).

Fasting Prayer

Fasting prayer is an abomination unto the Lord.

"Not everyone who says to Me, 'Lord, Lord,' shall enter the kingdom of heaven, but he who does the will of My Father in heaven. Many will say to Me in that day, 'Lord, Lord, have we not prophesied in Your name, cast out demons in Your name, and done many wonders in Your name?' And then I will declare to them, 'I never knew you; depart from Me, you who practice lawlessness!'" (Matt. 7:21–23).

The present Protestant and Catholic world proclaims a day of fasting and all night prayers so that God will give His people all their wants and needs. However, Jesus rebukes those who do not practice God's law, for the law is the foundation of God's government. Much of popular Christianity claims that the law was nailed to the cross. Yet, if the law were nailed to the cross, how would people know what sin is? By the law is the knowledge of sin (Rom. 3:20; 7:7; 1 John 3:4). If people do not know what sin is, what value would they put in grace, in the blood of the Savior that was shed for the sins of the world, and in the church and its fellowship? What peace would they have and what assurance of eternal life through Christ?.

When someone who denies God's law performs miracles, it is not difficult to figure out where the power comes from. There are only two sources of miracle-working power on the face of the earth. One source is God (Mark 16:17); the other source is the power of evil (2 Thess. 2:9; Rev. 13:13). The apostles did miracles while obeying God's Word and His law. If someone is not willing to accept God's Word and His commandments, there is always the cyanide capsules test to prove where the miracles originate. That means that even if you take cyanide capsules, you should not die. However, we are not to put God to a test (Deut. 6:16; Matt. 4:7; and Luke 4:12). Unless people respect that humans still need God's moral law, whatever they do will not be from God. Such people fulfill Paul's description: "Whose god is their belly" (Phil. 3:19). Those who are in darkness should come to the light, which is what Jesus Christ calls them to do. Otherwise, they are worshipping Lucifer-turned-Satan as their god, along with the third of the angels who followed him.

The Seventh-day Adventist Church and the Latter Rain

As it has done throughout its history, the present Seventh-day Adventist Church is looking forward to having the latter rain poured out in these last days. Through the prophet Joel, God revealed that He will pour out His Spirit as He provides signs in the sun, moon, and stars. These signs began a long time ago, and the Lord was faithful in calling many people to explain the Bible through the spirit of prophecy. Why do we still expect the latter rain? What additional truths do we need to follow when we do not follow the truth that has already been revealed? James talked about the former and the latter rain. which means that he compared the working of the Holy Spirit to two events. The illustration connects with what those living in the former time expected—that the former rain would start the crops growing, and it connects with what those living in the latter time will expect—that there will be sufficient rain to produce a full harvest of crops. Those living during the former rain do not harvest the crops that come with the latter rain. There is a gap in between the latter rain and the harvest. Those who have just put in their crops cannot expect to have a successful harvest. When you understand that the latter rain period is tied to the gift of prophecy and that the prophet died in 1915, then you will conclude that the latter rain is over, as Ellen G. White is no longer alive to have visions and to pronounce prophecies. Nonetheless, the Lord is merciful in allowing the Seventh-day Adventist Church time to absorb the truths to be followed and to proclaim those truths to the world. We can see that what Ellen White predicted, via her visions, is happening or has happened in the world. What she wrote about the church and about health reform, is for us to teach and follow today. What further teaching is required in order for us to expect the latter rain? How well do we understand the Scriptures in a practical way?

The expectation of the Seventh-day Adventist Church for the latter rain is that, when the latter rain is poured out, the church will go forth proclaiming biblical truth in the power of the Holy Spirit. Then everybody will reach new people to be saved individually though connected to different factions of Seventh-day Adventists. Then the Sunday laws and national Sunday laws will follow. At the end of the latter rain, probation will be closed and the last plagues will fall as Jesus Christ returns to earth and takes each group to heaven. At present, there are at least three groups of Seventh-day Adventists with different ways of preparing candidates for membership. Each is waiting for the latter rain, praying for the latter rain.

I would assert that, if we do not believe that the latter rain was finished at the death of Sister Ellen G. White in 1915, then Sister White got her visions from Satan and her nearly 17,500 pages manuscript are from him.

Someone might well counter that her death did not end the work of the Holy Spirit, which will continue until the return of Christ. Ellen White herself wrote:

It is true that in the time of the end, when God's work in the earth is closing, the earnest efforts put forth by consecrated believers under the guidance of the Holy Spirit are to be accompanied by special tokens of divine favor. Under the figure of the early and the latter rain, that falls in Eastern lands at seedtime and harvest, the Hebrew prophets foretold the bestowal of spiritual grace in extraordinary measure upon God's church. The outpouring of the Spirit in the days of the apostles was the beginning of the early, or former, rain, and glorious was the result. To the end of time the presence of the Spirit is to abide with the true church. (*The Acts of the Apostles*, pp. 54, 55)

I would assert that the true Seventh-day Adventist church member should believe that the latter rain ended in 1915 and that the esteemed Sister Ellen G. White was the last prophetess of Jesus Christ inspired by the Holy Spirit. I would also assert that, if those who are still waiting for the latter rain, do not believe the latter rain ended in 1915, then they consider Sister White to be a "devilish prophetess," and that would mean that she was not a true prophetess for the last days. Dear fellow Seventh-day Adventist believer, where do you stand on this matter?

According to the Bible and the Spirit of prophecy, the former rain was poured out before AD 100 and the latter rain was to be poured out to prepare for the Second Coming. In this book, I have asserted that the purpose of the second coming of the Holy Spirit was to produce sacred writings and, therefore, that He was lifted from earth at Ellen White's death in 1915 when her writing and visions ceased. Nonetheless, I would also affirm that the Holy Spirit is still present on earth to guide God's people in following the truth that has been revealed to us.

Jesus said: "Many will say ... have we not prophesied in Your name, cast out demons in Your name, and done many wonders in Your name? And then I will declare to them, 'I never knew you; depart from Me, you who practice lawlessness!' " (Matt. 7:22, 23). He also said: "For false christs and false prophets will rise and show great signs and wonders to deceive, if possible, even the elect" (Matt. 24:24). Paul wrote: "Now the Spirit expressly says that in latter times some will depart from the faith, giving heed to deceiving spirits and doctrines of demons" (1 Tim. 4:1). Many who claim to follow Christ are using His name while performing miracles in the power of Lucifer. They are deceiving themselves and others. Christians and people who belong to other religious groups perform many signs and miracles, including healing the sick. So, what is the difference between true Christians and other miracle workers?

What God Wants His People to Know in These Last Days

God is preparing His church to be "a glorious church, not having spot or wrinkle or any such thing, but that she should be holy and without blemish" (Eph. 5:27). This means that the members and leaders of the church organization should keep God's holy Ten Commandments and have the faith of Jesus Christ (Rev. 14:12). Every Adventist believer needs to understand the principles underlying the Ten Commandments.

The following are the key points of this book. Though Ellen White did not make these points directly, I have inferred them from Scripture and her writings. I urge that they be understood and taught to believers.

1. The biblical God—the Father, Son, and Holy Spirit—are equal in all respects; they synchronize their minds with one another and made humankind in their image so the Spirit could synchronize with the human mind.

2. Philippians 2:5–7 tells what took place before Jesus was born of the Virgin Mary as described in the Gospels of Matthew and Luke (Matt. 1:23; Luke 1:27).

3. "The entrance of sin into heaven cannot be explained. If it were explainable, it would show that there was some reason for sin. But as there was not the least excuse for it, its origin will ever remain shrouded in mystery" (*Review and Herald*, March 9, 1886).

4. I have asserted that there was a "FIRST PLAN OF SALVATION" for the fallen angels before Adam and Eve fell 6,000 years ago.

5. The descending form of a "dove," which represented Jesus' anointing as Messiah at His baptism (Acts 10:38) is not what the Holy Spirit actually looks like.

6. We should not pray to modern pictures of Jesus Christ, for it is an abomination unto the Lord. Whether one does so

ignorantly or knowingly, it makes no difference (Matt. 24:15; Dan. 12:11).

7. The brain controls how we live and move and breathe in this world.
8. Thinking takes place in the brain, though thoughts affect the emotions and, hence, the heart (Prov. 23:7).
9. There is a major spiritual conflict occurring on earth between the holy angels of God and the third of the angelic host who followed Lucifer.
10. The six-day Creation of this earth involved Jesus Christ (John 1:3; Heb. 1:2) and the Holy Spirit (Gen. 1:2).
11. God created the sun, moon, and stars before the six-day Creation but "set" them in the heavens during the six-day Creation (Gen. 1:17).
12. Regarding the periods of the early and the latter rain, Ellen White lived within the latter rain period.
13. I have listed 1,975 verses in the Bible that contain discrepancies, colloquial usages, and hidden meanings.
14. The church becomes Babylon when it imbibes teachings that do not originate in the Scriptures, which were inspired by the Holy Spirit.
15. We must understand the truth about the 144,000.
16. Marriage is a holy institution and its disregard is a violation of the Ten Commandments.

Ten Groups in the Seventh-day Adventist Church

Today we can identify ten groups among those who claim the name "Seventh-day Adventist." Besides the organized church, these include:

1. The Seventh-day Adventist Reform Movement, with its General Conference headquarters in Roanoke, Virginia, United States of America, which originated in Germany over the decision of the official church in Germany to allow its members to serve in the army, carry arms, and fight on the Sabbath.

2. Davidian Seventh-day Adventists or "Shepherd's Rod," which was named after the first publication of founder Victor T. Houteff.
3. Desmond Ford, whose principal disagreement with the church is his view of the gospel, which is incompatible with judgment for believers in Christ.
4. Michael Clute, who is divergent over his belief that God does not kill or destroy.
5. Ron Spear, Hope International, and *Our Firm Foundation*, which was a response to evangelical dialogues that the group believed threatened historic Adventism.
6. Colin Standish of Heartland Institute, who supports the Seventh-day Adventist Church but has concerns similar to those of Ron Spear.
7. Larry Wilson of Wake-up America, which does not have members but offers tracts, books, and tapes on end-time prophecy.
8. LaVerne E. Tucker (deceased) and the Quiet Hour, which is an independent but supporting ministry of the Seventh-day Adventist Church.
9. Bill Dull of Living Springs Institute, Putnam Valley, New York, which is an independent but supporting ministry of the Seventh-day Adventist Church.

What key teachings do these groups hold in common that differ from what I have taught in this book?

1. They do not recognize the biblical triune God of heaven's bodily and mental likeness to Adam. Neither do they recognize how the triune God communicates through the mind and are equal in all respects.
2. They accept the virgin birth of Jesus Christ.
3. They do not believe that the latter rain started in 1833 and ended in 1915, inspiring William Miller, E. G. White, James White, Joseph Bates, Hiram Edson, Uriah Smith, J. N. Andrews, and many others with direct visions from God.
4. They do not support baseless divorces and remarriage (*Adventist Home*, p. 344).

5. They promote modern pictures of Jesus Christ in their publications.
6. They directly and indirectly support the celebration of Christmas on December 25, sending of Christmas greetings, singing Christmas carols in their churches, baptizing and serving holy communion on the Sabbath day, welcoming VIPs on Sabbath, videotaping and taking photos on the Sabbath in the churches, having child dedication in the churches, conducting funeral services, and celebrating birthdays in Sabbath school.

More Explanation from the Spirit of Prophecy

From 1844 onward, God overlooked the violation of the holy Sabbath in the fourth of the holy Ten Commandments. Yet, very slowly the triune God raised the standard of obedience to His holy Ten Commandments and validated the principles of organization for the Laodicean church to include (1) a system of church government with democratically elected delegates, (2) disfellowshipping opens sinners, (3) promoting health principles in diet and living, (4) abstaining from health and character-destroying chemicals such as intoxicating liquor, tea, coffee, tobacco, opium, LSD, cocaine, heroin, and other dangerous drugs (5) avoiding pornography, blue films, and live sex shows, (6) shunning horse racing, card playing, and the lottery, (8) not misusing politics for one's own gain, (9) not manufacturing arms and ammunition nor using it illegally, (10) not smuggling nor evading taxes.

Jesus Christ Died on the Cross.

Why was it necessary for Jesus Christ to die on the cross? What is the benefit for mankind of Jesus Christ's crucifixion? What did Jesus' death on the cross mean? After the cross, there were no special children of God. Through Jesus, all people are accepted of God wherever they live. The people do not need to use a passport to travel from their respective countries; they do not need a visa to travel to the nation of Israel, nor do they need to offer sacrifices in the temple in Jerusalem to get forgiveness for their sins.

What is faith? To whom does the word "faith" point us? What is the connection between faith and human beings?

The word "faith" in the Bible is not as broad a term as "grace" (which means any one of God's gifts), "saint" (which means a person whose mind and life are devoted to God), or "spiritual" (which means that which links to the Spirit of God). The English word "faith" has a very simple and specific meaning. It means to "believe" or "trust." Both synonyms equally convey the meaning of "faith." Biblically we have to ask another question: To whom must we direct our faith and to what end? And what faith must we have to possess eternal salvation? Paul and Silas said, "Believe on the Lord Jesus Christ, and you will be saved" (Acts 16:31). John on Patmos coupled the keeping of "the commandments of God" with "the faith of Jesus" (Rev. 14:12). What does the "faith of Jesus" mean? Part of what it means is that we must believe that Jesus Christ is not just a carpenter's son or just the Son of God, but that He is the second person of the triune God.

What is the meaning of "grace"? Can we be saved by grace without the law of the Ten Commandments?

Almost all Christians preach that we are saved by grace. The apostle Paul explains in his fourteen New Testament books that the mosaic and ceremonial laws have fulfilled their purpose. He uses words like "grace," "mercy," "spiritual," and "saints." According to Paul, the ceremonial laws reached their fulfillment and were therefore abolished at the cross. Yet, he does not say this about the holy Ten Commandments (see Rom. 13:9; 1 Cor. 7:19). The apostle Paul's concept of grace went into effect the day that Jesus died. We do not need to go to the temple in Jerusalem to receive forgiveness of pardonable sins. We do not need to offer a sacrifice. Jesus has shown us the way to get forgiveness wherever we are. Jesus Christ will give forgiveness for your pardonable sins immediately on the same spot without going to Jerusalem or buying a lamb for a sacrificial offering. This is the central truth Paul was seeking to communicate in his fourteen epistles in the New Testament.

Will the blood of Jesus Christ cleanse us from all our sins (1 John 1:7)? Today's Protestant ministers are preaching: "The blood of Jesus Christ will cleanse us from all of our sins." So saying, they imply that we do not need to keep the Ten Commandments, for they believe that the commandments were nailed to the cross. If a man has two wives and children from each, will the blood of Jesus Christ cleanse his sin of adultery? If a man rapes many girls, kills them, and very cleverly disposes of their bodies and is never charged with the crime by the authorities, will the blood of Jesus cleanse his sins? There is no answer to these questions. If a Protestant pastor answers, "Yes," that will trigger another question. Does this mean that anyone can go to heaven—idol worshipers, fornicators, etc.? Only if they are actually cleansed from their sins. In the case of the sins mentioned above, a man who has two wives and children from each or even a woman who has two husbands and children from each will receive the forgiveness of Christ's blood *if* the person repents and follows God's Word.

The same requirement is expected of any Seventh-day Adventist who wants to go to heaven by the blood of Jesus Christ. No one who knows the holy Ten Commandments of God can continue to violate them and still expect to go to heaven.

Will God forgive our unknown sins through the blood of Jesus Christ? Yes, on the day of our holy baptism He will, but if we repeat those sins and forget God, we can only expect eternal death. What we are describing is the concept of "probation." Probation means a period of time that has been allotted for a person or group of people to achieve or maintain certain objectives. This concept applies to us in the following way: God is the One who grants eternal life. We humans have a certain amount of allotted time to receive eternal salvation from Him. If we waste that time, our opportunity to receive eternal salvation will be forever past. This concept is further developed under the topic of the 144,000. In 1844, the final judgment began for the people who lived from the time of Adam until the cross. Since God selects the 144,000 from the remnant church of the Seventh-day Adventists, only faithful Seventh-day Adventists can be considered for the 144,000. Their selection is after the close of the probation of the great multitude. Even if a person who is a baptized member of the Seventh-day Adventist Church stands firm in the Lord, salvation only comes through the grace of God. Therefore, upon what basis do we go to heaven? We must believe, be baptized, and follow the holy Ten Commandments. Faithful obedience is what prepares the 1,44,000. By the grace of God, we may be members of the great multitude, which is the best that can happen to those who are not part of the 144,000.

Chapter 12

The 144,000, a Special Group of People

Who are the 144,000? Which church do they come from?

Many are confused about the message of the hundred and forty-four thousand people of God in Revelation. There are many understandings of this subject in the Christian world. Many churches that have a teaching on this subject would like to believe that they will be part of the 144,000—especially Pentecostal groups. They claim that they are the ones who will be numbered among the hundred and forty-four thousand, and some take the white garments and not being married literally. What does the Bible say about this subject?

The 144,000 in Scripture

The seventh and fourteenth chapters of the book of Revelation are the only places in Scripture that mention the 144,000. The seventh chapter tells how a certain number from each of the twelve tribes will add up to 144,000.

> And I heard the number of those who were sealed. One hundred *and* forty-four thousand of all the tribes of the children of

Israel *were* sealed: of the tribe of Judah twelve thousand *were* sealed; of the tribe of Reuben twelve thousand *were* sealed; of the tribe of Gad twelve thousand *were* sealed; of the tribe of Asher twelve thousand *were* sealed; of the tribe of Naphtali twelve thousand *were* sealed; of the tribe of Manasseh twelve thousand *were* sealed; of the tribe of Simeon twelve thousand *were* sealed; of the tribe of Levi twelve thousand *were* sealed; of the tribe of Issachar twelve thousand *were* sealed; of the tribe of Zebulun twelve thousand *were* sealed; of the tribe of Joseph twelve thousand *were* sealed; of the tribe of Benjamin twelve thousand *were* sealed. (Rev. 7:4–8)

We need to interpret this passage according to prophetic principles.

Explanation from *Daniel and Revelation* Written by Uriah Smith

Adventist author Uriah Smith explained how the twelve thousand from each tribe can be applied to our day.

The Number to Be Sealed.—The number sealed is here stated to be one hundred forty-four thousand. From the fact that twelve thousand are sealed from each of the twelve tribes, many suppose that this work must have been accomplished as far back at least as the beginning of the Christian Era, when these tribes were literally in existence. They do not see how it can apply to our own time, when every trace of distinction between these tribes has been so long and so completely obliterated. We refer such persons to the opening language of the Epistle of James: "James, a servant of God and of the Lord Jesus Christ, to the *twelve tribes* which are scattered abroad, greeting. *My brethren*, count it all joy when ye fall into divers temptations." Those whom James here addresses are Christians, for they are his brethren. Some were converts from paganism and others were Jews, yet they are all included in the twelve tribes. How can this be? Paul explains in Romans 11:17–24. In the striking figure of grafting which the apostle there introduces, the tame olive tree represents Israel.

Some of the branches, the natural descendants of Abraham, were broken off because of unbelief in Christ. Through faith in Christ the wild olive scions, the Gentiles, are grafted into the tame olive stock, and thus the twelve tribes are perpetuated. Here we find an explanation of the language of the same apostle: "They are not all Israel which are of Israel," and "he is not a Jew, which is one outwardly, ... but he is a Jew, which is one inwardly." Romans 9:6–8; 2:28, 29. So we find on the gates of the New Jerusalem—which is a New Testament, or Christian, city—the names of the twelve tribes of the children of Israel. On the foundations of this city are inscribed the names of the twelve apostles of the Lamb. (Revelation 21:12–14).

If the twelve tribes belonged exclusively to the Jewish era, the more natural order would have been to have their names on the foundations, and those of the twelve apostles on the gates; but no, the names of the twelve tribes are on the gates. As through these gates, so inscribed, all the redeemed hosts will go in and out, so all the redeemed will be reckoned as belonging to these twelve tribes, whether on earth they were Jews or Gentiles.

Of course we look in vain for any marks of distinction between the tribes here on earth; and since Christ has appeared in the flesh, the preservation of the genealogy of the tribes is not necessary. But in heaven, where the names of the church of the firstborn are being enrolled, we may be sure there is order, and that each name is enrolled in its own tribe.

So the names are symbolic and the number is literal, for John declared: "After these things I looked, and behold, a great multitude which no one could number, of all nations, tribes, peoples, and tongues, standing before the throne and before the Lamb, clothed with white robes, with palm branches in their hands, and crying out with a loud voice, saying, 'Salvation *belongs* to our God who sits on the throne, and to the Lamb!'" (Rev. 7:9–10).

Two Groups of People to Meet Jesus Christ

1. The 144,000 firstfruits
2. The great multitude: from Adam until the second coming of Jesus Christ.

Revelation 14:1–5 says, "Then I looked, and behold, a Lamb standing on Mount Zion, and with Him one hundred *and* forty-four thousand, having His Father's name written on their foreheads. And I heard a voice from heaven, like the voice of many waters, and like the voice of loud thunder. And I heard the sound of harpists playing their harps. They sang as it were a new song before the throne, before the four living creatures, and the elders; and no one could learn that song except the hundred *and* forty-four thousand who were redeemed from the earth. These are the ones who were not defiled with women, for they are virgins. These are the ones who follow the Lamb wherever He goes. These were redeemed from *among* men, *being* firstfruits to God and to the Lamb. And in their mouth was found no deceit, for they are without fault before the throne of God."

Here John describes the character of the 144,000. Those who want to go to heaven as part of the 144,000 must have these qualities as enumerated by God as revealed in Revelation 14:4, 5. Such qualities are:

1. They should not defile themselves with women.
2. They are virgins.
3. They have no deceit in their mouth.
4. They must be without fault.

These are the four qualities that describe those who will go to heaven from among those living in the last days.

They Should Not Defile Themselves with Women.

What does a woman represent in prophecy? Jeremiah 6:2 says, "I have likened the daughter of Zion to a lovely and delicate woman." A pure woman represents the pure church; a corrupted woman represents the corrupted or confused church, which is called Babylon. The message regarding the 144,000 is for the last-day church, and they should leave Babylon in answer to God's call (Rev. 18:4). The last true church is those who respond to the Laodicean message while accepting the biblical message of the Seventh-day Adventist Church.

One could say that, to be a part of the 144,000, a person must be born into the Seventh-day Adventist Church, though not merely by physical birth but by being "born again" into "the love of the truth" (2 Thess. 2:10). The 144,000 do not violate the true Sabbath of the fourth commandment. One could say that those who were born in a family holding membership in a Sunday-observing church but who came into a Sabbath-keeping church can only be saved as part of the great multitude since they were once a part of a church that was defiled by human tradition, rather than being born and brought up in the Seventh-day Adventist Church and not being "defiled with woman." Revelation 14:12 calls attention to those "who keep the commandments of God and the faith of Jesus Christ" as essential identifying marks of the true church. In other words, we can logically say that, among the many Christian denominations, only the Seventh-day Adventist Church emphasizes keeping *all* the commandments of God and having the faith of Jesus Christ. So, the message regarding the 144,000 is only for those who accept the Seventh-day Adventist message, which is God's last-day message from Scripture.

They Are Virgins

Paul wrote: "For I am jealous for you with godly jealousy. For I have betrothed you to one husband, that I may present *you as* a chaste virgin to Christ" (2 Cor. 11:2). The prophetic meaning of "virgin" is a "pure church" that has "pure doctrine." It should not be taken literally as a female who has not had sexual relations. The pure church is represented by a virgin girl or a woman because all people and all God's spiritual children come into existence through a long line of mothers that began with Eve. So, prophetically a woman represents a church, and a pure woman represents a pure church. God is holy and His law is holy. Those who follow the Ten Commandments with their 105 stipulations are the virgin church. The 144,000 are those who faithfully obey God's law from their spiritual birth.

They Have No Deceit in Their Mouth

From birth, the 144,000 will never violate any of the holy Ten Commandments. Their faithfulness is like that of the seven thousand who never bent the knee to Baal during the time of Elijah. 2. They are the wisest who have ever lived in the history of this world—wiser than King Solomon. 3. They have a complete grasp of the Holy Bible, and they have answers for the questions that arise regarding the triune God of heaven.

They Are Without Fault

From their birth, the 144,000 live without fault. Zephaniah 3:13 says, "The remnant of Israel shall do no unrighteousness and speak no lies, nor shall a deceitful tongue be found in their mouth; For they shall feed *their* flocks and lie down, and no one shall make *them* afraid." The message of the blessed 144,000 is not an ordinary message. It is ordained by the second person of the triune God of heaven for the remnant church of Seventh-day Adventists and not for any other Christian denomination, for the 144,000 are to come from the Seventh-day Adventist Church.

How the 144,000 Sealing Message Relates to the Second Coming of Christ

Until the 144,000 are sealed by Jesus Christ, He will not come to this world. Until the last of the 144,000 are numbered and sealed, the heavenly judgment, which began in 1844, will be extended by the triune God of heaven and the Second Coming will be delayed. This is because the 144,000 are to be firstfruits to the Lord under the blessed prophecy of Daniel 12:12.

The Meaning of the Blessed Prophecy of Daniel 12:12

The prophecy regarding the 144,000 is a blessed prophecy that links to Daniel 12:12, which says, "Blessed *is* he who waits, and comes to the one thousand three hundred and thirty-five days." The 1335 days given to Daniel the prophet in this prophecy are tied to time. This blessed prophecy of 1335 days covers 1335 years, beginning in AD 508 with the setting up of the abomination and ending in AD1843, the time of the height of interest in the prophecies of Daniel. The following year, 1844, the fervor of the Philadelphian period gave way to the lukewarmness of the Laodicean period. Daniel 12:12 speaks of a blessing. Those who joined the Laodicean church were to become the most blessed people in the whole world.

The people in the final church period are blessed above the other six church time periods—from AD 31 to 1844—and the time before the church periods— from 4159 BC until AD 31. People from the time of Adam to the time of William Miller can go to heaven as part of the great multitude, but none is so special as the 144,000 who live to see Jesus come.

Do the 144,000 receive any blessed privileges above those given to Enoch, Elijah and Moses? Adam can go to heaven, and Enoch, Moses, and Elijah are already in the celestial realms. Yet, none of them has the blessed privilege of going to heaven like this special group. Enoch, Moses, and Elijah already went to heaven, and the redeemed will be joining them there. Currently, the three men already in heaven cannot be with Jesus Christ always. The 144,000 are going to govern the 1,500 million people of God who are going to heaven at the Second Coming. For a thousand years, 144,000 people will govern over Adam, Enoch, Moses, and Elijah in heaven. Then, as the redeemed descend to earth at the close of the millennium, the 144,000 will also reign over the 1,500 million people of God on the earth made new.

Why are these people so special? Though Moses wrote six books in the Bible, he had no idea what Daniel and John were going to write. Though Daniel and John the Revelator wrote down their prophecies, they could not fully explain them. Even the great reformers, such as Martin Luther, John Wesley, and the others, who led out in the Reformation, brought many truths to the world without being able to fully explain the Scriptures. Yet, the 144,000 will have full knowledge of God's Word since the prophecy of Daniel will have been fulfilled in their days. Daniel's prophecy says that, in the time of the end, "knowledge shall increase" (Dan. 12:4). Jesus also declared: "For there is nothing covered that will not be revealed, nor hidden that will not be known" (Luke 12:2). Truths kept in secrecy have been revealed. So, the 144,000 will have a full understanding of God's holy law, of the prophecies, for they have had the advantage of all the writings composed under the latter rain through the spirit of prophecy. They have had extensive details about Jesus Christ, showing Him to be the King of kings and the Lord of lords, as He ceases being the sin-bearing Son of Man. Throughout eternity, they will teach the saved in heaven, starting with Adam, and they will bring praises and glory to the Lord Jesus Christ.

Explanation of the 144,000 Remnant from *The Great Controversy*

Upon the crystal sea before the throne, that sea of glass as it were mingled with fire,—so resplendent is it with the glory of God,—are gathered the company that has gotten "the victory over the beast, over his image and over his mark and over the number of his name." With the Lamb upon Mount Zion, "having the harps of God," they stand, the hundred and forty and four thousand that were redeemed from among men; and there is heard, as the sound of many waters, and as the sound of a great thunder, "the voice of harpers harping with their harps." And they sing "a new song" before the throne, a song which no man can learn save the hundred and forty and four thousand. It is the song of Moses and the Lamb—a song of deliverance. None but the hundred and forty-four thousand can learn that song; for it is the song of their experience—an experience such as no other company have ever had. "These are they which follow the Lamb whithersoever He goeth." These, having been translated from the earth, from among the living, are counted as "the first fruits unto God and to the Lamb." Revelation 15:2, 3; 14:1–5. "These are they which came out of great tribulation;" they have passed through the time of trouble such as never was since there was a nation; they have endured the anguish of the time of Jacob's trouble; they have stood without an intercessor through the final outpouring of God's judgments. But they have been delivered, for they have "washed their robes and made them white in the blood of the Lamb." "In their mouth was found no deceit, for they are without fault" before God. "Therefore they are before the throne of God, and serve Him day and night in His temple. And He who sits on the throne will dwell among them." They have seen the earth wasted with famine and pestilence, the sun having power to scorch men with great heat, and they themselves have endured suffering, hunger, and thirst. But "they shall hunger no more, neither thirst any more; neither shall the sun light on them, nor any heat. For the Lamb which is in the midst of the throne shall feed them, and shall lead them unto living fountains of waters: and God shall wipe away all tears from their eyes." Revelation 7:14–17. (*The Great Controversy*, pp. 648, 649).

Here are some other statements from Ellen White about the 144,000:

> Soon we heard the voice of God like many waters, which gave us the day and hour of Jesus' coming. The living saints, 144,000 in number, knew and understood the voice, while the wicked thought it was thunder and an earthquake. (*Early Writings*, p. 15)

I saw that the four angels would hold the four winds until Jesus' work was done in the sanctuary, and then will come the seven last plagues. (*Early Writings*, p. 36)

This was the time of Jacob's trouble. Then all the saints cried out with anguish of spirit, and were delivered by the voice of God. The 144,000 triumphed. (*Early Writings*, p. 37)

While Satan has been urging his accusations, holy angels, unseen, have been passing to and fro, placing upon the faithful ones the seal of the living God. These are they that stand upon Mount Zion with the Lamb, having the Father's name written in their foreheads. They sing the new song before the throne, that song which no man can learn save the hundred and forty and four thousand which were redeemed from the earth. "These are they which follow the Lamb whithersoever He goeth. These were redeemed from among men, being the first fruits unto God and to the Lamb. And in their mouth was found no guile: for they are without fault before the throne of God." Revelation 14:4, 5. (*Prophets and Kings*, p. 591)

And as we were about to enter the holy temple, Jesus raised His lovely voice and said, "Only the 144,000 enter this place," and we shouted "Alleluia!" (*Early Writings*, p. 19)

"I saw there the tables of stone in which the names of the 144,000 were engraved in letters of gold. After we had beheld the glory of the temple, we went out, and Jesus left us and went to the city. Soon we heard His lovely voice again, saying, 'Come, my people, you have come out of great tribulation, and done My will; suffered for me; come in to supper, for I will gird Myself, and serve you.' [Luke 12:37.] We shouted, 'Alleluia! glory!' and entered into the city. And I saw a table of pure silver; it was many miles in length, yet our eyes could extend over it. I saw the fruit of the tree of life, the manna, almonds, figs, pomegranates, grapes, and many other kinds of fruit." (*Early Writings*, p. 19)

One of the marked features in the representation of the 144,000 is that in their mouth was found no guile. The Lord has said, "Blessed is the man ... in whose spirit there is no guile" [Psalm 32:2]. They profess to be children of God, and are represented following the Lamb whithersoever He goeth. They are prefigured before us as standing on Mount Zion, girt for holy service, clothed in white linen, which is the righteousness of the saints. (Ms. 7a, 1896 in *Manuscript Releases*, vol. 14, p. 93)

The 144,000 are the remnant—or remainder—of those who have left behind all the teachings of Babylon that they might become the pure and holy people of God.

The Meaning of the "Remnant Church"

Paul wrote in Romans, "Though the number of children of Israel be as the sand of the sea, the remnant will be saved" (Rom. 9:27). John wrote in Revelation, "The dragon was wroth with the woman and went to war with the remnant of her seed" (Rev. 12:17, KJV). God gave these two important verses because, in a "remnant," very few members of a very large group of people remain. In the case of the remnant in Revelation, they will be a very unique and faithful group of God's true people. From the "church" in the Garden of Eden to the Flood, only eight people remained alive. These eight were the remnant church of God following the Flood. Likewise, immediately after the crucifixion, there were only 120 faithful Jews left in Jerusalem out of the millions of the city's inhabitants. Of the twelve apostles, only John the beloved remained at the cross of Jesus. Except for a few of the women, the other disciples ran away; one even fled naked to save his life. John was certainly one of the faithful of God during this early church period. Jesus Christ established His church with those 120 faithful Jews, taking the church into the first church period of Ephesus from AD 31 to 100. Soon after AD 100, the Ephesus church was corrupted and became Babylon, as the majority of Christians violated God's Ten Commandments. Christ rejected the majority, who were unpardonable sinners, from the church, and He started with another remnant in the second church period of Smyrna from AD 100 to 313. The same thing happened again when He started the third church period of Pergamos from AD 313 to 538, and again when He started the fourth church period of Thyatira from AD 538 to 1798, and still again with the fifth church period of Sardis from AD 1798 to 1833. When He started the sixth church period of Philadelphia, once again He began with a small remnant from the previous church period of Sardis, which included William Miller and the 3,000 pastors who preached the Advent message. Last of all, following the great disappointment, when the number of Advent believers numbered around 50,000, Jesus Christ took another small remnant of believers, including Joseph Bates, James White, Ellen Harmon and about a dozen other people, into the seventh church period of Laodicea. It was from this remnant that He started the Seventh-day Adventists, who were organized in 1863 at Battle Creek. From 1844 to the present, God has been looking for a commandment-keeping people.

In 1891, Sister Ellen G. White wrote: "The church has long been contented with little of the blessing of God; they have not felt the need of reaching up to the exalted privileges purchased for them at infinite cost. Their spiritual strength has been feeble, their experience of a dwarfed and crippled character, and they are disqualified for the work the Lord would have them to do. They are not able to present the great and glorious truths of God's Holy Word that would convict and convert souls through the agency of the Holy Spirit. The power of God awaits their demand and reception" (*Testimonies to Ministers and Gospel Workers*, p. 175). In 1893, she applied Jesus' statement about Capernaum, in Luke 10:15, to Seventh-day Adventists, "And thou, Capernaum [Seventh-day Adventists, who have had great light], which art exalted to heaven [in point of privilege], shall be brought down to hell" (*Review and Herald*, Aug. 1, 1893, bracketed in the original). In 1903, she wrote: "In the balances of the sanctuary the Seventh-day Adventist church is to be weighed. She will be judged by the privileges and advantages that she has had. If her spiritual experience does not correspond to the advantages that Christ, at infinite cost, has bestowed on her, if the blessings conferred have not qualified her to do the work entrusted to her, on her will be pronounced the sentence: 'Found wanting.' By the light bestowed, the opportunities given, will she be judged" (*Testimonies for the Church*, vol. 8, p. 247). In 1904, she declared: "Many who once were earnest Adventists are conforming to the world—to its practices, its customs, its selfishness. Instead of leading the world to render obedience to God's law, the church is uniting more and more closely with the world in transgression. Daily the church is becoming converted to the world" (*Testimonies for the Church*, vol. 8, p. 118).

According to the writings of Ellen White, the church declined, following its organization, and allowed itself to be corrupted by the world. Nonetheless, God saw fit to give her the vision concerning the 144,000. The 144,000 are not corrupted by any Babylonian doctrine, and they have a full grasp of the identification of the saints in Revelation 14:12. The confused churches, known as "Babylon," reject the remnant message of Revelation 14:12. The book of Revelation has two messages regarding Babylon, within the time frame of the seven churches of prophecy. These are in Revelation 14:8 and in Revelation 18:2. The first of these calls attention to the confusion, or the uncertain trumpet, that was sounded in Sardis, the fifth church period, regarding doctrine in the four Protestant groups. During the sixth church period, the Philadelphia church became Babylon because of confused doctrine regarding Jesus' Second Coming in 1844. The last church of Laodicea began under the leadership of sabbatarian Adventists Joseph Bates and James White, and Ellen G. White. Originally, many Adventists were concerned about organizing as a church because they associated organization with the second message about Babylon, found in Revelation 18:1, 2. They feared that they would become like Babylon and would suffer Babylon's end. This is why they delayed the first steps of organization until 1861.

Though the church had adopted traditions from the fallen churches, these people understood the meaning of the Ten Commandments for their lives. Yet, they did not understand or preach the prophecy regarding the 144,000, neither did they preach that the 144,000 should be born Adventists and know the truth. Nor did they encourage everyone to enter the 144,000 to get ready for the kingdom of God. This is likely because Ellen White herself wrote in 1901: "It is not His will that they shall get into controversy over questions which will not help them spiritually, such as who is to compose the hundred and forty-four thousand. This those who are the elect of God will in a short time know without question. ... Spend not your time in seeking to know that which will be no spiritual help. 'What shall I do to inherit eternal life?' This is the all-important question, and it has been clearly answered. 'What is written in the law? How readest thou?' " (*Selected Messages*, book 1, pp. 174, 175). The church continues to avoid this subject.

Chapter 13

Armageddon and the Seven Last Plagues

> Then the sixth angel poured out his bowl on the great river Euphrates, and its water was dried up, so that the way of the kings from the east might be prepared. ... And they gathered them together to the place called in Hebrew, Armageddon.
>
> —Revelation 16:12, 16

John described the time when God's wrath will be poured out in the seven last plagues: "The nations were angry, and Your wrath has come, and the time of the dead, that they should be judged, and that You should reward Your servants the prophets and the saints, and those who fear Your name, small and great, and should destroy those who destroy the earth" (Rev. 11:18). An outcome of the sixth plague is the battle of Armageddon.

When Will the Battle of Armageddon Be Fought?

The battle of Armageddon and the drying up of the Euphrates River are yet to take place. Among the many rivers in this world, both big and small, the river Euphrates carries the name of the ancient river that flowed around the Garden of Eden along with the three other rivers. However, during the time of the Flood, in 2503 BC, the Pison and Gihon rivers were destroyed. But rivers that approximate the original Hiddekel (now called the Tigris) and the Euphrates still flow around the old area of the Garden of Eden.

After the Flood, Noah's ark settled in the mountains of Ararat. Noah's children lived in the plains and valleys of the river Euphrates and settled and multiplied over the next few centuries in the land of Shinar, later called "Mesopotamia"—the land between two rivers. When Babylon was finally conquered by Medo-Persia, it became part of the Medo-Persian Empire. Later its territories became the two Islamic nations of Iran and Iraq. The second generation of mankind began in this region, and the language of proto-Hebrew was spoken by Noah's descendants when, in 2320 BC, the God of heaven scattered the existing 59 tribes at once, recording nearly 2009 languages in their brains simultaneously. Thus, from Shinar, they spread over the world in groups, according to their common language, over the next ten to fifteen centuries. Linguistically, there are 127 divisions of Asia, Africa, and Europe. The Medo-Persian Empire was also formed before 531 BC (Esther 1:1).

Many important historical events took place in the region of the Euphrates. The world's final war is also linked to the River Euphrates. In the region of the river Euphrates from 2502 to 2136 BC, the biblical God of heaven taught the people during the second period of human civilization. In 2270 BC, humans built the world's very first tower of Babel, which was from 300 to 350 feet tall, and God destroyed it with lightning, the remains of which are said to exist to this day. In 2136 BC, God called Abraham, the nineteenth generation from Adam, from the region of the river Euphrates in Ur of the Chaldees and told him to go to Canaan, which would be the Promised Land for his progeny. In 607 BC, God called king Nebuchadnezzar of the Chaldeans by name to punish the royal descendant of King Solomon. He gave the lands of Israel and of Judah, with the sacred temple in Jerusalem, into Nebuchadnezzar's safe keeping to be later returned to the Jews. King Nebuchadnezzar was responsible

Chapter 13 Armageddon and the Seven Last Plagues

for building the second wonder of the ancient world—the hanging gardens of the royal palace on the bank of the River Euphrates in Babylon, the capital city of the world. This was the world empire in Daniel's prophecies in chapter 2 and 7—the Babylonian Empire. The biblical God of heaven gave two prophecies locating the world's last events in the region of the River Euphrates.

The first prophecy is found in Revelation 9:5–21 in the symbolic prophecy of the fifth trumpet, which was to last five months, or 150 years (Rev. 9:5, 10). The prophecy was fulfilled in the Islamic war against the pagan Roman Empire and the popes. The second part of the prophecy was to last 391 years and 15 days with a war that is described as a second "woe" (Rev. 9:15, 12) During this time, pagans, and Roman Catholic Christians converted to Islam in fulfillment of this prophecy, and Babylon became Baghdad, and Constantinople became Istanbul.

The second prophecy set in the region of the River Euphrates deals with the drying up of the water. The river of water in the biblical prophecy symbolizes the people of that nation who would be destroyed by way of war, famine, earthquake, and other natural calamities, such as cyclones. However, the prophecy immediately explains that war devastated these lands.

How much do you know about modern defense technologies for nuclear war or the so-called "star wars"? Have you thought any time about them? We are living in a crucial time. At any time, the world's final battle may break out in the Middle East. The United States of America has more than 16,000 nuclear warheads and 2,500 intercontinental ballistic missiles. Each missile travels at more than 12,000 miles per second. With these 16,000 warheads, the United States can destroy our earth more than sixteen times over using just one space shuttle like the Challenger.

Nine Navy fleets have 100 to 200 warships per fleet, and each fleet has from six to ten submarines with a crew of 3,000 to 50,000 men. Each fleet also has many aircraft carriers with nuclear missiles and an ICBM advanced technology launching pad, with Patriot missiles. They have many kinds of bombs, including "Tomahawk" missiles, mustard bombs, oil gas bombs, "bunker buster" penetrating missiles, nuclear bombs, hydrogen bombs, cobalt bombs, and laser guided missiles. They have many types of aircraft, like the Indian HF-24 fighter bomber, the F-15 Eagle, the Soviet BI-1 rocket-powered fighter, the

Lockheed F-177 Nighthawk stealth bomber, and the Boeing KC-135 Stratotanker refueling aircraft. Each air force has thousands of high-tech aircraft, which they used in the first Gulf War. Finally, the United States has laser beam weapons to intersect and destroy ICBMs at the speed of 186,000 miles per second.

At the same time, Russia has 26,000 nuclear warheads. These could destroy the whole earth twenty-six times over. Not only that, but they also have nearly 6,000 ICBM launching pads aimed all around the world at strategic locations including the capital cities of other nations. The launch controls of these 26,000 nuclear warheads are conveniently kept accessible to the President of Russia wherever he goes—even while traveling abroad. Russia also has an equal number of fighter jet planes, naval fleets, space shuttles, and other advanced defense technologies.

In addition, there are more than 475 nuclear power stations around the world. If all the nuclear power plants were destroyed, the whole world would be turned into a graveyard without nuclear war. We should all be aware of these advancements in technology and their power to destroy. According to the daily news on Islamic radio and TV, the thirty-six Islamic countries are just waiting for their chance to attack Israel. Because of the religious war of *jihad*, which will not get quenched at all, war will be burning in every one of 90 million Islamic religious people's minds. At the same time, none of these thirty-six Islamic countries have nuclear power. Nonetheless, in fulfillment of biblical prophecy, the USSR was slowly broken into pieces, and fifteen separate nations came into existence since 1992. Among the fifteen new nations, five nations of Islamic majority will, one day or another, declare themselves to be independent Islamic nations. If they declare themselves independent Islamic nations, then they will have access to at least 5,000 nuclear warheads from the break-up of the Soviet Union. Each former Soviet country has its own autonomy and is not subject to the other Russian nations. Prior to the breakup of the Soviet Union, 26,000 nuclear warheads were spread out over the country. If an Islamic nation has an opportunity to get 500 nuclear warheads, the five new Islamic states under Russia will turn their nuclear power against Israel. Thus, the final destruction cannot be far away. This is Bible prophecy. The battle of Armageddon could be fulfilled in this world at any time.

The war arsenal of the United States and Russia

Let us consider the usage and the power of the bombs available to the world's superpowers:

1. **The modern nuclear detonator.** During the device's operation, the atmosphere, affected by electrolysis, is defused from all electronic software and from radio, TV, radar, and computers.

2. **Penetrating bombs.** Creating very deep ditches like an earthquake, they are used to destroy bridges, roads, railroads, etc.

3. Neutron bombs. The imperceptible radiation and shock to the earth that only takes a second kills hundreds of thousands of people.

4. Tomahawk cruise missiles. These are like cluster bombs, for they cover a larger area and completely destroy those on it.

5. Oil gas bombs from high altitude. These explode, igniting poisonous gas and absorbing oxygen all at once, depriving the blood of oxygen and killing multiple millions of people.

6. Small 500-ton atomic bombs. These were dropped from B-29 bombers over Hiroshima and Nagasaki, Japan, in 1945. They nearly obliterated an entire six square miles of buildings, roads and bridges, trees, vegetation, animals, and people. They did more than kill the people, they turned them to ashes. At the height of the nuclear reaction, they reached 1,800º Celsius, or 5,000º Fahrenheit. Such heat turned all the roofs of the houses into plumes of bright red flames, like those of a steel plant when iron is melted. The people in the houses were turned into ashes, in whatever position they were found—sitting, standing, or walking. And that was only the amount of heat produced by a small 500-ton atomic bomb. The melting point of iron is less than 600º Fahrenheit. At 1,800º Celsius, steel, iron, and any other metal turn to ashes and the whole region becomes a graveyard. The radiation of the blasts in Japan affected nearly 60 miles of buildings, trees and vegetation. Those who ate the radiated vegetables, grains, and animal flesh were also affected. Children were born disfigured. Cancers afflicted many people all over their bodies for many years.

7. But, remember, what we have described was the work of *small* **atomic bombs.** Current hydrogen bombs can produce ten times greater destruction than one of the earlier atomic bombs. A cobalt bomb can produce forty times more power than an atomic bomb.

8. Additionally, the explosion of any ordinary 500-megaton nuclear power station is equivalent to 5,000 to 10,000 cobalt bombs. Just imagine! The United Nations estimates that the effects of the Chernobyl nuclear power plant disaster in Russia in 1986 are still with us today. So, dear reader, we are not exaggerating the results of the destruction that nuclear bombs could cause. All Christians should understand from history the kind of destruction that could result from the nuclear arsenals of the United States and Russia and all the other nuclear powers in the world. The battle of Armageddon will fulfill prophecy and the River Euphrates will be dried up, according to Revelation 16:12.

When will the seven last plagues begin? What will world conditions be during that time? What is the purpose of the seven last plagues? Who will be affected by them?

The Seven Last Plagues

Jesus Christ of the triune God of heaven gave John the Revelator a vision of the seven last plagues in Revelation 15 and 16. He did not describe them in scientific terms but through prophetic symbols. Neither did Moses describe the six days of Creation in Genesis 1 in scientific terms but, rather, in the normal language of that time. The first four days of the Creation had to do with the atmosphere and the water molecules that occupied the space above our earth. One aspect of the character of our biblical triune God of heaven is that He is a jealous God, "visiting the iniquity of the fathers upon the children to the third and fourth *generations* of those who hate" Him (Exod. 20:5). In Revelation 11:18, we read: "And should destroy those who destroy the earth." God puts these seven last plagues upon the stiff-necked "beast" and its followers. Just as He put the ten plagues upon the stiff-necked Pharaoh and the Egyptians who kept Israel, the people of God, in slavery. Jesus Christ, the second member of the triune God of heaven, taught the Egyptian pharaoh and his people a very great lesson through the ten plagues that showed God's superiority to the pharaoh's gods so he would let the children of God go. Just as He did with the Egyptian pharaoh, so will the God of heaven, in these last days, stand up against the beast, which represents the Roman Catholic papacy that persecuted the apostles' spiritual descendants during the 1260 long years of the Dark Ages when millions of people were killed for believing in Jesus Christ. The same living God of heaven imposed these seven last plagues to punish their descendants of the third and fourth generation.

Jesus Christ had given the duration of these last seven plagues through His prophet John: "Therefore her plagues will come in one day—death and mourning and famine. And she will be utterly burned with fire, for strong *is* the Lord God who judges her" (Rev. 18:8). According to this prophecy, these seven last plagues will affect the entire world, and they will last one complete year of 360 days. (A day equals one year in Bible prophecy.) Isaiah predicted: "Moreover the light of the moon will be as the light of the sun, and the light of the sun will be sevenfold, as the light of seven days, in the day that the LORD binds up the bruise of His people and heals the stroke of their wound" (Isa. 30:26).

Before the Seven Last Plagues: God's People Will Leave the Cities

God's children will leave the big cities to live in smaller towns and will then leave the smaller towns, for their own safety, before the start of the third world war, or Armageddon, to live in remote villages where there will be no nuclear attacks. To survive this dire circumstance will require storing food and water for from one to two years of time. All of God's children need to be prepared for these last days, for there is no alternative arrangement for survival. We should not live near nuclear power stations, which can expose us to dangerous radiation. During the war, the 475 nuclear power stations in the world may be attacked at any time by the ICBM rockets of an opposing nation like the United States or Russia. It behooves us to understand the dangers and to enter a place of safety during the seven last plagues. Those who are wise will understand the peril of the times. The foolish will be oblivious and will reap the consequences. During this period, all electrical power will be cut off; sources of fuel will be exhausted; the high ways will be destroyed, and there will be no roads in and out of the cities; food and water will be polluted by radiation; food sources—either of flesh food, eggs, milk, or even vegetables—will be unsafe as they will be affected by radiation and will cause cancers all over the body.

For this reason, we must prepare underground shelters to give us safety from the radiation, and we must begin eating a pure vegetarian diet without flesh foods, eggs, or milk, and we must use pure fresh water. During this period, we will be able to use solar electrical appliances because the sun's heat will be seven times hotter—700º F of heat can be converted into electrical power that can be used to run refrigerators, to preserve our food, and air conditioners, to cool the room temperature. These are options for the children of God during the seven last plagues, which we should carefully consider and pre-plan to survive the seven last plagues.

Sequence of the Seven Last Plagues

I would assert that the sequence of the seven last plagues is not given in chronological order, for I believe the sixth plague, regarding the drying up of the Euphrates, must come before the other plagues because I believe that it is caused by a nuclear explosion. "Then the sixth angel poured out his bowl on the great river Euphrates, and its water was dried up, so that the way of the kings from the east might be prepared" (Rev. 16:12).

The Second Plague: Cancers All Over Human Bodies

As we mentioned about the third world war, when the button is pressed to start the war, the people on the earth will be immediately bombarded with very intense and dangerous radiation, such as affected Chernobyl when the nuclear power station melted down. When the radiation spreads, everyone will get ugly growths and will die in great anguish. Babies will be born with disfigured bodies and will face nuclear. Areas affected by nuclear attacks will not even produce ordinary grass. The second plague predicts cancers or grievous sores. "So the first went and poured out his bowl upon the earth, and a foul and loathsome sore came upon the men who had the mark of the beast and those who worshipped his image" (Rev. 16:2). The radiation of the nuclear attack will produce cancer, the fruit of human inventions intended for defense but employed by God to destroy those who destroy the earth. These are the result of the first plague that came from nuclear weapons and the second grievous plague of cancer which affects the body of men, women, and children. Without the first plague, the second plague will not occur.

The Bible says the plague only falls upon those who have the mark of the beast and those who worshipped his image. "So the first went and poured out his bowl upon the earth, and a foul and loathsome sore came upon the men who had the mark of the beast and those who worshiped his image" (Rev. 16:2). Here God is identifying two groups of people who receive His punishment.

Who Has the Mark of the Beast?

The biblical meaning of the mark of the beast is the claim of the authority to transfer the holiness of the Sabbath to Sunday and those who acknowledge that authority by keeping Sunday holy. Besides the first group who have the mark of the beast is a second group who worship the beasts "image." The consequence of directly worshiping the beast and following its teachings is a "cancer" that they cannot escape, for it is the inevitable wrath of God.

All those who do not follow God and His ways will be affected by the plagues. All those who knowingly reject God and follow their own ways will be punished "tenfold" by the rest of the plagues that they will endure for 360 days.

The Third Plague: All Life in the Sea Will Die

"Then the second angel poured out his bowl on the sea, and it became blood as of a dead *man;* and every living creature in the sea died" (Rev. 16:3). The third plague concerning the death of sea life suggests that this is the first plague in which the radiation of nuclear weapons in a third world war will kill the animals in the oceans. Then, when their bodies decay, the smell will be terrible and the water will be changed into blood, causing an epidemic that spreads to the living creatures all over the world.

The Fourth Plague: Water Became Blood

"Then the third angel poured out his bowl on the rivers and springs of water, and they became blood" (Rev. 16:4). Under the fourth plague, the rivers and fountains of the earth became blood. This suggests the effect of nuclear radiation or the direct power of God, as under the ten plagues of Egypt when the Nile River was turned to blood. When all sources of water are turned to blood, many people will die.

The Fifth Plague: Terrible Heat

"Then the fourth angel poured out his bowl on the sun, and power was given to him to scorch men with fire" (Rev. 16:8). This fifth plague of God will be the natural follow-up to the first plague with the nuclear fallout of the third world war. During the war, the United States and Russia, the two superpowers, will use their nuclear and conventional bombs, causing nuclear radiation around the globe, tainting the atmosphere and destroying the vegetation that produced oxygen for the atmosphere. This will result in the death of humans and animals on this earth. So, naturally, with less oxygen, the proportion of hydrogen will be greater in the atmosphere, and more heat will be produced. The tiny size of the water molecule as a ratio of 1:7 is common when the temperature is between 105º and 112º F. Ten times hotter would increase the temperature from 105º to 735º F. At such temperatures, there will be skin affections in men, women, and children, producing sores all over their bodies. Then there will be irritation, itching, leaking of fluids from their bulging skin and terrible pain and agony. No drinking water, because all the water has become blood under the previous plague, will be torment for every human and animal under the fifth plague. Through this terrible heat, foretold by Isaiah, "the light of the sun will be sevenfold" (Isa. 30:26), and those under the plague will experience the wrath of God. No one can escape the vengeance of the triune God.

The Sixth Plague: Darkness

"Then the fifth angel poured out his bowl on the throne of the beast, and his kingdom became full of darkness; and they gnawed their tongues because of the pain" (Rev. 16:10). According to Revelation, the sixth plague will only affect the beast and the beast's supporters, though this means that millions of people around the world will suffer under the plague. They have already been affected by the radiation of nuclear fallout, with ugly disfigurement and cancers all over their bodies, with a shortage of drinking water, and death. Yet, those who did not die under the first four plagues suffer the scorching on their bodies of the fifth plague and then the darkness of the sixth.

God's people will not be affected by any of these plagues. They will be protected by their guardian angels. Their food and water will be supplied. The enemies will not destroy their shelters, and the holy angels of God will protect them. The events of the seven last plagues are not so complicated as one might think. Under the plagues, all 233 nations of the world and islands of the sea will be affected as war-torn areas are affected now. So no nation or people will help another. Every one of the seven and a half billion people on this planet will have to provide for his or her own life, health, food, clothing, and shelter.

Almost all the people will die in a single year. Those who survive will bury the dead. If everyone in a village is killed or a city is completely destroyed, then the dead bodies will be left exposed without anyone to care for them. This will take place for one whole year of 360 days, which is allotted for the seven last plagues. Unbelievers and those who reject Christ's teaching will be affected more than other religious groups. I have asserted in this book that, during the sixth plague, the river Euphrates will be dried up by the deployment of a nuclear bomb in Iraq and Iran. Only the people of that region will die from the blast.

A Special Resurrection

According to Bible prophecy, a special resurrection will take place at the end of the sixth plague. Daniel wrote: "And many of those who sleep in the dust of the earth shall awake, some to everlasting life, some to shame *and* everlasting contempt" (Dan. 12:2). In this special resurrection, two groups of people will be resurrected. One of these will be resurrected to everlasting life. These are people who died trusting in the Lord, and they will be resurrected in a glorified state though not with immortal bodies. If they previously lost a leg, in the special resurrection they will come alive with two legs and with any other body part that they lost before dying. This is the first group of people. The second group of people consists of those who witnessed the crucifixion of Jesus Christ like Annas, Caiaphas and the other Jewish leaders who condemned Him, and the Roman soldiers who arrested and tortured Him on the cross. These also will be resurrected in a special resurrection to see Jesus coming in the clouds (Matt. 26:64; Mark 14:62). Yet, their resurrection will be for eternal death. Those who witnessed the crucifixion will also witness the second coming of Jesus Christ.

Together with those who are alive at the end of time, they will witness Christ's glorious return as Savior and Lord, as John foretold: "Behold, He is coming with clouds, and every eye will see Him, even they who pierced Him" (Rev. 1:7). The two aforementioned groups of people will live to witness the seventh and last of the plagues—hailstones.

Closing of Heavenly Judgment—"It is Done"

According to Revelation, "Then the seventh angel poured out his bowl into the air, and a loud voice came out of the temple of heaven, from the throne, saying, 'It is done' " (Rev. 16:17). According to Daniel 8:14, the heavenly judgment began in 1844 in heaven for all who received forgiveness of their sins directly from God by believing in the blood of Jesus Christ. This covers all who have done so from Adam to those living until the end of the sixth plague. God Himself says, "It is done," indicating the closing of judgment for all people with no more judgment from that time on. When the first person of the Godhead utters these words in heaven, a great earthquake will begin in the city of Jerusalem and reverberate all around the world. Then too, the special resurrection, mentioned above, will take place, and select individuals will be resurrected by the voice of God, proclaiming, "It is done." All who are resurrected in this special resurrection will live until the end of the seven last plagues.

The Seventh Plague: Hailstones

"Then the seventh angel poured out his bowl into the air, ... and great hail from heaven fell upon men, *each hailstone* about the weight of a talent" (Rev. 16:17, 21). The plague of hailstones will be the last plague of the triune God of heaven. These hailstones will be the natural product of the reduction of the size of water molecules by the superheating of the effects of the sun. Almost all the oxygen will separate very quickly and the hydrogen gases will produce more cool air, converting within minutes into very large hailstones from the oxygen in the water molecules, and it will fall as a rain of hailstones, killing men, women, children, and animals. Especially will the enemies of Christ, who have been specially resurrected to witness the second coming of Jesus Christ, suffer the plague of hailstones. The children of God who have kept the holy Ten Commandments and have had faith in Jesus Christ will have their food and water provided and the protection of the holy angels against natural disasters and their enemies within other Christian religious organizations who will attempt to kill them. Holy angels will protect them from being harmed by their enemies and the terrible sevenfold heat caused by the radiation of nuclear warfare. God will protect His children. Their efforts will hasten the second coming of Jesus Christ. Scattered all over the world, the 144,000 and the great multitude will welcome Jesus Christ as their King of kings and Lord of lords.

The Earth Rotates at a Very High Speed

As this event takes place, the earth will be rotating rapidly, enabling the people on the earth to see Jesus like an old-fashioned cinema projector shows a film. It is the speed of the film that enables a person to see the actors talking, walking, running, dancing, and fighting. In a similar way will people get to see Christ and the multitude of angels coming in the clouds of heaven. The Bible says: "Behold, He is coming with clouds, and every eye will see Him, even they who pierced Him" (Rev. 1:7).

At the second coming of Jesus Christ, four groups of people will be living on the earth.

1. Millions of ungodly Christians who suffered for a year under the seven last plagues. Almost half dead, these will attempt to kill the children of God by the power of Satan but will not succeed.

2. The rest of the living who are part of the other eighteen religious groups will also experience the plagues. Then, a special group of people, including Pilate, Annas, Caiaphas, the other Jewish leaders, and the Roman soldiers who took part in the crucifixion of Jesus Christ, will come back to life in the special resurrection and experience the plague of hailstones.

3. The third group of people will be the Laodicean church and other church members who willingly rejected the light of the remnant church.

4. The last group will be the 144,000 people who are born in the remnant Seventh-day Adventist Church who have obeyed God's commandments from their birth and who, along with the great multitude from Adam until the end, have eagerly waited to welcome Jesus Christ.

Paul gives a clear picture that, at His second coming, Christ is not going to come down to this earth but will stay above the earth in the clouds and receive the children of God in the air. "Then we who are alive *and* remain shall be caught up together with them in the clouds to meet the Lord in the air" (1 Thess. 4:17). Paul added, in First Corinthians, that God's children will be changed "in a moment, in the twinkling of an eye, at the last trumpet. For the trumpet will sound, and the dead will be raised incorruptible, and we shall be changed. For this corruptible *must* put on incorruption, and this mortal must put on immortality. So when this corruptible has put on incorruption, and this mortal has put on immortality, then shall be brought to pass the saying that is written: 'Death is swallowed up in victory' " (1 Cor. 15:52–54). As Paul indicated, at the final trumpet call, the earth will shake and the graves will open and the dead in Christ will rise from the grave, or wherever they died, with immortal bodies to meet Jesus Christ in the air.

Journey of Seven and a Half Days to Heaven

"When He opened the seventh seal, there was silence in heaven for about half an hour" (Rev. 8:1). On the basis of biblical prophecy, half an hour of silence means seven and a half days of silence in heaven, due to the second advent of Christ. The usual activities of the angels, such as flying to and fro from heaven to the earth and singing in heaven, will be interrupted. The angels will accompany Jesus to sound the trumpet of impending judgment and eternal destruction, and they will glorify the Lord Jesus and the Holy Spirit before Satan and his evil angels for redeeming millions of men, women, and children from this sinful earth to heaven, proving that Jesus Christ and the Holy Spirit are equal to the first person of the triune God of heaven.

To prove this same truth to all the other inhabited planets in the rest of the universe, Jesus Christ takes these children of God to visit the other planets over the course of a seven-and-half-days' journey that ends in heaven. During the seven-and-half-days' journey, all the children of God from the earth will visit and stay on one planet and will observe the holy Sabbath with billions of angels and millions of the sons of God on that particular planet, then they will continue on their journey to heaven. What a surprise privilege for the children of God! After the children of God have left this earth for heaven, the rotation speed of the earth will slow down and return to its original speed.

All human beings, animals and plants will be completely destroyed by the increase in the speed of the rotation of the earth, and no humans will remain alive for Satan and his evil angels to tempt or manipulate. Being deprived of something to do is the greatest punishment that could be given to these fallen angels and to Satan. The earth will be desolate, and the wind will blow the dust of the earth for one thousand years, as John said: "But the rest of the dead did not live again until the thousand years were finished. This *is* the first resurrection" (Rev. 20:5). This scripture tells us that the second coming of Jesus Christ is not the final event on planet earth. Revelation 20:7 says, "Now when the thousand years have expired, Satan will be released from his prison." Once the millennium in heaven is finished, Jesus Christ will come to earth a third time, traveling with the golden city of the New Jerusalem, descending from heaven to earth, which will be made new.

The Millennium in Heaven

Most Protestant Christians believe that the millennium is going to take place on this earth and use Matthew 25:32–46 as their support. They believe that, during the second coming of Jesus Christ, He will come to this earth with His angels to rule against antichrist and that this is when He carries out judgment like a shepherd dividing the sheep from the goats. The sheep that will go to His right hand (the position of favor) are the righteous, and the goats that will go to His left hand are unrepentant sinners. To those He puts on the right hand He says, "Come, you blessed of My Father, inherit the kingdom prepared for you from the foundation of the world." Most Protestant Christians also believe that the unrepentant sinners will go into the everlasting punishment of an eternally burning hell. Yet, they forget that "everlasting fire" in Matthew 25:41 is fire that completely consumes its object, as we discover by comparing Jude 7 with 2 Peter 2:6. "Eternal fire" turned Sodom and Gomorrah into "ashes."

The New Jerusalem

Jesus told His disciples: "In my father's house are many mansions; if *it were* not *so*, I would have told you. I go to prepare a place for you. And if I go and prepare a place for you, I will come again and receive you unto Myself; that where I am, *there* you may be also" (John 14:2, 3).

According to this verse, Jesus Christ has now gone to heaven where He is preparing a place in the beautiful New Jerusalem for the children of God. Some day soon He will come back to earth to take God's children to heaven.

The Architectural Dimensions of the New Jerusalem

God communicated through Jesus Christ and His angel a view of the architectural dimensions of the New Jerusalem that His prophet John was to share with the church (Rev. 21:11–21). Here are the dimensions, and this is not fiction:

$$\begin{aligned} \text{The city's length} &= 375 \text{ miles} \\ \text{The city's breath} &= 375 \text{ miles} \\ \text{The city's height} &= 375 \text{ miles} \end{aligned}$$

The architectural view of the golden city of the New Jerusalem is that it will have a tremendous height—375 miles tall, the equivalent of 144,000 stories, which is appropriate for a city that is to house 144,000 special people.

In this huge 144,000-storied building, more than 15 to 20 billion people can be accommodated. This city of splendors has a compound wall 288 feet tall with a 1,500-mile circumference and three gates of pearls on four sides of the city. The street of the city will be pure gold resembling transparent glass. There will be no bathrooms or sewage drainage systems. Moreover, in the golden city, there is no temple. There is no need of the light of the sun or the moon, for Jesus Christ the Almighty God will be the light of that golden city. In addition, each man, woman, and child will have his or her own bright robe of light to the light the golden city. The twelve gates will be watched over by the holy angel welcoming God's people.

Life During the Millennium

As we transform from a mortal to an immortal body, our regular clothing will disappear and we will be encircled in robes of bright light. Any disfigurement of our faces or difference in color will be corrected, and we will grow to our intended stature of nearly fourteen feet. Our children will also grow up to maturity, aging will stop, and one hundred years of age will be considered youthful. All will be virgins during the one thousand-year period in heaven within the golden city of Jerusalem. The food of the saints will be fruits, and they will drink the pure water of life as did our first parents, Adam and Eve, in the Garden of

Eden. There will be no excretion from the body. Everything eaten will be digested and become part of the living cells of the body. For long years on end, there will be no pain, sickness, sorrow, tears, or death. In heaven, there will be no marriage for one thousand years. Reproduction will have stopped when our bodies have been transformed in immortality. The redeemed will be able to walk or to fly, by the assistance of the holy angels, according to each one's own choice. The holy angels will take the redeemed to the 144,000-story apartment building, which will have been allotted to each person individually in the golden city of God.

The Second Judgment Will Take Place During the Millennium

The first judgment of the biblical triune God of heaven has been going on in heaven since 1844. We do not know when our name will be called out for judgment. Whenever it is, we should want our name to be written in the book of life and the book of remembrance for having received "full forgiveness of sins" from the triune God of heaven. However, if our name is not written in the book of life, our name will not be called out by God, for we will have been already reserved for eternal death. During the millennium and under the supervision of the 144,000, the children of God in heaven will judge millions of sinners, the fallen angels, and Satan who enticed them all into sin. Paul wrote: "Do you not know that we shall judge angels" (1 Cor. 6:3).

Hell and Destruction

The second resurrection, at the end of the millennium, is for unrepentant sinners who will live briefly, along with Satan and his angels, long enough to show that they have not repented. John wrote: "Blessed and holy *is* he that hath part in the first resurrection. Over such the second death has no power. ... Now when the thousand years have expired, Satan will be released from his prison and will go out to deceive the nations which are in the four corners of the earth, Gog and Magog, to gather them together to battle, whose number *is* as the sand of the sea" (Rev. 20:6–8). The triune God of heaven will resurrect all sinners who died in rebellion— from Cain, the brother of Abel, to the very last person born of more than 21 billion people to have lived on the earth. Each will receive his or her eternal reward—destruction and eternal death.

Following the second resurrection, God will purge this earth of all sinners, including Satan and the fallen one-third of the angels. Then He will restore the earth to its original perfection, as we read in Hebrews: "Whose voice then shook the earth; but now He has promised, saying, 'Yet once more I shake not the earth, but also heaven' " (Heb. 12:26). This is a dual prophecy, meaning that it has two fulfillments. It was first fulfilled at the time of the Flood by the shaking and tilting of the earth from 90º to 23½º by the power of the first person of the triune God. This tilting resulted in 40 days and 40 nights of rain, which flooded and destroyed the whole earth. Once again, the same first person of the triune God will shake the earth by His power, bringing the earth back to its original 90º position. During this event, a tremendous physical reaction will take place in the atmosphere. The rapid expansion of hydrogen all around the earth, like that of a nuclear bomb blast, will move the earth again to the gap of 5,000 miles, producing a great vacuum. The pressure of the vacuum will trigger the combining of hydrogen, cobalt, helium, xenon, radon, and phosphorous gases, heating up the sky with the enormous heat of a nuclear furnace at 10,000 to 20,000º Celsius heat that will flash around this globe like lightning.

This nuclear furnace lava, when it is poured out by God upon the planet, will completely consume the billions of rebellious human and angelic beings. No one can escape the final destruction of the lava of the nuclear furnace coming from the sky that is described in Revelation 20:14, 15 as "the lake of fire." The tremendous heat of this nuclear furnace will consume away all sinners according to their sins. And that time, the videotape of their brain will bring back to memory all their sins and wicked deeds, declaring God's justice as they die in pain and agony, according to the resistance of their wills. During this time, those who had the Bible in their hands and who preached to their flock against the truth will receive "ten times the pain and agony" as their innocent flock. Here is how the prophetess portrays the scene.

> Many of the wicked were greatly enraged as they suffered the effects of the plagues. It was a scene of fearful agony. Parents were bitterly reproaching their children, and children their parents, brothers their sisters, and sisters their brothers. Loud,

wailing cries were heard in every direction, "It was you who kept me from receiving the truth which would have saved me from this awful hour." The people turned upon their ministers with bitter hate and reproached them, saying, "You have not warned us. You told us that all the world was to be converted, and cried, Peace, peace, to quiet every fear that was aroused. You have not told us of this hour; and those who warned us of it you declared to be fanatics and evil men, who would ruin us." But I saw that the ministers did not escape the wrath of God. Their suffering was tenfold greater than that of their people. (*Early Writings*, p. 282)

At the same time, Satan and the evil angels review their sins, declaring God's justice before the unfallen holy angels. The lava of the nuclear furnace will utterly destroy them.

The Mount of Olives Turns into Pure Gold

The nuclear fiery furnace from the sky will produce more than 20,000º Celsius of heat. Along with the final destruction of this earth, Jesus Christ will simultaneously do something else. The area of the Mount of Olives will turn into a land of pure gold, a square plane, 375 miles wide by 375 miles long prepared as a deep foundation for the celestial city.

The golden city of the heavenly New Jerusalem will descend from heaven and dock with exact precision by the power of Jesus Christ in the site prepared for it. That these two events coincide may suggest another scientific theory. How is it possible that, with the flashing of lightning and the clapping of thunder, a nuclear furnace above the earth will produce enough lava to melt the earth and, at the same time, form a pure golden foundation for His holy 140,625-square-mile city to land on? It is possible because that is what the Bible predicts. During earth's final destruction, God will prepare the Mount of Olives in Israel to receive the New Jerusalem.

Before the final destruction of sinners—earthly and heavenly—the New Jerusalem will descend from heaven to this earth as John described, "Then I, John, saw the holy city, New Jerusalem, coming down out of heaven from God" (Rev. 21:2). The splendid golden city of the New Jerusalem will slowly descend from heaven to earth. As it descends, the 15 to 20 billion people of God will be within the 144,000-storied city and will land by God's power on the earth. At that time, this earth will be without any green vegetation, and it will appear to the people in the city as a desolate wilderness.

The Earth Made New

The re-creation of the earth will be much like the six days of the Creation. The earth will return to its original position of 90º as before the Flood. Once again, Jesus Christ and the Holy Spirit will be responsible for the creation of a new biosphere on the earth before the witnessing eyes of the 15 to 20 billion children of God within the New Jerusalem. However, the transformation of the earth will not take six days, but, rather, it will occur within the twinkling of an eye. How thrilling it will be to witness this great event! This will be the first time God's human children will have witnessed God's creative acts. No longer will there be an ocean of seven miles depth. No longer will there be jagged high mountains like the Himalayas. No longer will there be any deserts on the earth, nor thorns, thistles, or stony lands. However, there will be beautiful flowing rivers, lofty trees, bowing grass, lush, fertile gardens, and all manner of fruit trees as far as the eye can see. The children of God will not have to protect their feet with footwear, for the ground will be carpeted with soft green grass. There will be no rain nor seasons in the new earth. The inhabitants will cultivate the land and produce fruit-bearing trees, plants, and vines. With all the earth's many life-giving fruits, created by our God, the inhabitants will continue to eat the fruit of life and will live forever and ever. Just like in the six-day Creation, the triune God of heaven will make different kinds of animals and birds, but, this time, all the animals and birds and creatures of the water will be created before the children of God within the New Jerusalem.

Life in the New Earth

After the creation of the new earth, the children of God will come out from the New Jerusalem and scatter across the earth to live, returning to the Holy City only on Sabbaths and new moons (Isa. 66:23). People will scatter and occupy the earth, build houses, and live forever. The biblical prophecy explains about the life that the children of God will live in the new earth. Isaiah wrote, "They shall build houses and inhabit *them;* they shall plant vineyards and eat their fruit" (Isa. 65:21). The new earth will also be occupied by newly created birds, animals, and fish, for Isaiah wrote: " 'The wolf and the lamb shall feed together; the lion shall eat straw like the ox, and dust *shall be* the serpent's food. They shall not hurt nor destroy in all My holy mountain,' says the LORD" (Isa. 65:25).

While living in the earth made new, the children of God will marry and have families with children without the pain of childbirth, as the biblical prophecy declares: "They shall not labour in vain, nor bring forth for trouble; for they *are* the seed of the blessed of the LORD" (Isa. 65:23, KJV). The Revised Standard Version has much the same. However, the King James Version and the Revised Standard Version have not translated this statement correctly. The Tamil translation gives a more accurate rendering of the Hebrew: "They shall not labor in vain, they will give birth without pain, they and their children shall be the blessing of God." The verse says that their children will be blessed of God and live eternally. Their physical bodies will be just like they were in heaven. They will have happy families and live in their own houses where they once lived, though it will be on the new earth. The children of God will live very happily without sickness, sorrow, pain, tears, or death. Forever they will live joyfully, gently, and meekly, with kindness and affection for others. The first person of the Godhead, Jesus Christ, and God the Holy Spirit will be worshipped at all times, but God's children will gather in the New Jerusalem from month to month and from holy Sabbath to holy Sabbath as a way to remember the original six-day Creation. Every preparation day all the multitudes of the earth will journey to the golden city with help from their individual angels. They will stay in the city for the whole Sabbath, each occupying their own respective rooms in the 144,000-storied golden building, and they will joyfully worship the triune God on the Sabbath day and then return to their respective places around the new earth until their next gathering before the Lord. WHAT A JOYFUL EXPERIENCE THAT WILL BE!

Whether you experience what God has planned depends what you decide today. Every journey begins with a single step. In the words of poet Maryam Kazmi:

> One song can spark a moment
> One flower can wake a dream
> One tree can start a forest
> One bird can herald spring
> One smile begins friendship
> One handclasp lifts a soul.
> One star can guide a ship at sea
> One word can frame the goal
> One vote can change a nation
> One sunbeam lights a room
> One candle wipes all darkness
> One laugh will conquer gloom
> One step must start each journey
> One word must start each prayer
> One hope will raise our spirits
> One touch can show you care
> One voice can speak with wisdom
> One heart can know what's true
> One life can make the difference
> You see it's up to YOU!

(Footnotes)

1. A historical source for this book was "the book of Jasher" (see Josh. 10:13).
2. A historical source for 2 Samuel was "the book of Jasher" (see 2 Sam. 1:18).
3. According to the superscriptions of the Psalms, David wrote 73 psalms, Moses wrote 1, Asaph wrote 12, the sons of Korah wrote 11, Heman wrote 1 with the sons of Korah, Solomon wrote 2, and Ethan wrote 1.
4. Historical sources for 1 Kings were "the books of the acts of Solomon" (1 Kings 11:41), "the book of the chronicles of the kings of Judah" (1 Kings 14:29; 15:7, 23; 22:45), and "the book of the chronicles of the kings of Israel" (1 Kings 15:31; 16:5, 14, 20, 27; 22:39).
5. Historical sources for 1 Chronicles were "the book of the kings of Israel and Judah" (1 Chron. 9:1), "the book of Samuel the seer," "the book of Nathan the prophet," and "the book of Gad the seer" (1 Chron. 29:29).
6. Historical sources for 2 Kings were "the book of the chronicles of the kings of Judah" (2 Kings 8:23; 12:19; 14:18; 15:6, 36; 16:19; 20:20; 21:17, 25; 23:28; 24:5) and "the book of the chronicles of the kings of Israel" (2 Kings 1:18; 10:34; 13:8, 12; 14:15, 28; 15:21).
7. Historical sources for 2 Chronicles were "the book of Nathan the prophet," "the prophecy of Ahijah the Shilonite," "the visions of Iddo the seer" (2 Chron. 9:29), "the book of Shemaiah the prophet" and of "Iddo the seer" (2 Chron. 12:15), "the story of the prophet Iddo" (2 Chron. 13:22), "the book of Jehu the son of Hanai" (2 Chron. 20:34), "the book of the chronicles of the kings of Israel" (2 Chron. 20:34; 33:18), "books of the kings of Judah and Israel" (2 Chron. 16:11; 25:26; 27:7; 28:26; 32:32; 35:27; 36:8), and "the story of the book of the kings" (2 Chron. 24:27); and "the vision of Isaiah the prophet" (2 Chron. 26:22; 32:32).

TEACH Services, Inc.
P U B L I S H I N G

We invite you to view the complete
selection of titles we publish at:
www.TEACHServices.com

We encourage you to write us
with your thoughts about this,
or any other book we publish at:
info@TEACHServices.com

TEACH Services' titles may be purchased in
bulk quantities for educational, fund-raising,
business, or promotional use.
bulksales@TEACHServices.com

Finally, if you are interested in seeing
your own book in print, please contact us at:
publishing@TEACHServices.com
We are happy to review your manuscript at no charge.

www.ingramcontent.com/pod-product-compliance
Lightning Source LLC
Chambersburg PA
CBHW071143160426
43196CB00011B/1995